D1614828

.1

PORTUGAL'S
STRUGGLE
FOR LIBERTY

PORTUGAL'S STRUGGLE FOR LIBERTY

by Mário Soares

translated by Mary Gawsworth

London   George Allen & Unwin Ltd
Ruskin House   Museum Street

This translation © George Allen & Unwin Ltd, 1975

ISBN 0 04 946010 2

Printed in Great Britain
in 11 pt Baskerville type
by Clarke, Doble & Brendon Ltd
Plymouth

TO MARIA DE JESUS
wonderful companion in all the long struggle
and in memory of
António Sérgio
Bento de Jesus Caraça
Jaime Cortesão
Manuel Mendes
Maria Isabel Aboim Inglês
Mário de Azevedo Gomes
My beloved friends who showed the way.

Preface to the English Edition

Completed and published in France when I was in exile, events have to some extent caught up with my book already. But to end it I expressed my firm intention—this in April 1972—of returning to my own country 'when the time was right'.

On 25 April 1974 the Portuguese army abruptly overthrew the longest-running dictatorship in the world. Forty-eight hours later I was on the way to Lisbon, and on 1 May we saw the rifles stuck with carnations as everybody fraternised with the soldiers and the entire nation turned out with a delirious welcome for those who, snatched from the prisons or back home from banishment, had spoken out the whole time against tyranny, error and lies.

General António de Spínola, heading the Junta of National Salvation, asked me to share the responsibilities of government. This Junta sprang from the Armed Forces Movement, where the moving spirits were young soldiers whose views on the present situation and future of the country were born of the impact of harsh reality and largely matched my own as set forth in these pages, and those of the Portuguese Socialist Party. I found myself Minister of Foreign Affairs, with the task of terminating that worst of our afflictions, the colonial war.

The war had gone on far too long already; thirteen years by now. It was for opposing it that I had been thrown into prison yet again and subsequently forced into exile. The Portuguese, who forged the first link between the continents in the fifteenth century, might fittingly be expected to lead the process of decolonisation, and indeed had done so in the case of Brazil, after the triumph of our liberal revolution in 1820. But a blind, twentieth-century regime, bent on defending minority rights, had set itself, at the cost of other people's lives, against the essential change and had jeopardised the best chances we had in Africa, as well as our world position. There was not a moment to lose.

All my thinking was based on one fact : the peoples of Guinea, Angola and Mozambique, fighting for their dignity and independence, were as much victims of Fascism as were the Portuguese, to whom self-determination was equally denied. How many African nationalists, including such prominent leaders as Eduardo Mondlane and, perhaps, Amilcar Cabral, had perished at the orders of the criminals who had Humberto Delgado killed? But his butchers are known, and they will be brought to judgement. Now the yoke is eased, Fascism and colonialism are collapsing together. Independence for the colonies and the liberation of Portugal are part of the same thing, and mutual recognition of this fact will be the most satisfactory beginning for the bonds of brotherhood that are to be established between Portugal and her former colonies as they take their place among the free nations.

Guinea Bissao is a free nation at the present time. Recognised by most of the world, her admission to the United Nations was recently sponsored by Portugal herself. As for Mozambique, agreements were signed on 7 September, to be followed by full and effective independence in June 1975. In Angola negotiations will be longer and more arduous because of the many races and movements involved, the high percentage of whites among the population; above all, because of the interest, if not greed, of elements foreign to Portugal and Angola alike. But these negotiations, too, will have the desired result. Reason and justice demand it and it is part of the programme of the Armed Forces Movement, as of the constitutional law of 27 July 1974, recognising the right to independence of all our colonies.

Portugal must set up new relations, not only with her one-time possessions, but with Europe and everyone else as well; and here I include the Socialist countries, the third world and the unaligned nations. But this is not to imply that she has altered in any way. What the free world is seeing with wonder and emotion now is Portugal as she really is, not the toiling, patient, pig-headed, decent-hearted image presented for so long by the ludicrous propaganda-mask. We are *not* resigned, fatalistic, proud of nothing but our past. We are, on the contrary, eager for freedom and justice, intent, after half a century of oppression and obscurantism, on working out our destiny for ourselves.

We are done, now, with the bad old days when the lackeys of Salazarism ran round exalting the achievements of the extreme Right in its every manifestation and angling for its support. We are done with the shameful diplomacy that consisted merely of requests—and at what cost they were made!— to the delegates of other nations not to vote against our indefensible positions in the various international assemblies.

The dictatorship in Portugal was a nightmare for Africa, a handicap to Europe, an embarrassment to our allies and a threat to peace. Historians will eventually reveal the entanglement of Salazar with Mussolini and Hitler, and the part he played after the war in sheltering the vanquished and the vindictive and in hampering the détente. Détente and Fascism did not go together. But at last Portugal herself has brought Fascism to an end, thanks to the decisive action of her armed forces, whose demands were virtually those of the clandestine democratic organisations and who knew they voiced the hopes of the people and the interests of the nation. Now it is for us to forge a true working democracy.

That is an urgent, stirring task, but a very hard one, for we are not going to accept any more façades. The Portuguese people have just given proof of their exceptional maturity, their political sensibility and sharp awareness of contemporary problems. They stand ready for the great democratic choice which, after fifty years of enforced silence, they will soon be called upon to make. In March 1975 they will elect deputies to the Assembly that is to frame the new constitution of the Republic.

Though the Right and the extremists may have gone to ground for the time being it would, however, be a grave mistake to suppose that they are done for. Nothing is heard at the moment from Fascists and para-Fascists, to say nothing of Fascists who studiously ignore each other, but already they are active underground. When as yet we have barely begun to assess the appalling heritage they leave, they are fostering social unrest and attempting to sabotage the economy. They try to scare the emigrants out of sending money home and spread reports that the country is teetering on the verge of Communism and about to abandon her alliances. In actual fact even the provisional government, in agreement with the Armed Forces Movement and the Communist Party itself, is refusing to consider any reform that goes beyond recognised democratic bounds, and is proclaiming loud and clear that we must abide by our natural traditional alliances.

In the time of Salazar and Caetano, Portugal was a refuge for the agents and survivors of international Fascism, a sort of paradise where they could settle all kinds of plots and plans without interference. One can well believe that they do not willingly say good-bye to such facilities. In the world-wide organisations of reaction, the Portuguese dictatorship is sadly missed.

That is why we, unlike the tools of Salazar and Caetano, are demanding, not secret complicity, but free and total support from our allies and the Community of Europe. We want to take part, as of full right, in the construction of a Europe whose face is turned to peace and progress. We appeal for the moral and material support of all our well-wishers, not forgetting those countries with which we are making or renewing friendly contacts. When a democracy dies—and we saw it happen recently in Chile—there is anger and protest from democratic countries and parties, from humanitarian bodies and men of good will everywhere. It is right and proper that this should be so, but it is not what matters most. Rather than wring our hands over crime and shame, we must henceforth prevent them. Fascism in Portugal was an insult to the world's conscience and for that very reason the making of democracy in Portugal and its defence against the unsleeping intrigues of the international Right, while it primarily concerns the Portuguese themselves, concerns also every nation, and every individual, who is in love with liberty.

When it came out in France, with Fascism still enthroned in Portugal, this seemed to me two sorts of book rolled into one —a contribution to history and an uncompleted testimony. More than anything it could, I hoped, serve as a departure-point.

And now that hope comes true. I have brought to the building my handful of stones, and this is one of them. For us as a nation a page of history has turned, almost coinciding, as is happens, with the last page of my original text; which is a further, very happy, reason why the book is out of date. And, given the speed at which things move, this preface, too, may lag behind events unless it is soon in print. This is not the kind of thing that keeps.

To extend my book to cover current events I would have to write another volume. The Struggle for Liberty is over. The army, being a part of the nation as a separate military caste is not, and suffering with the rest from the blood-sodden absurdity of Fascism and colonialism, has restored liberty. Portugal can speak freely now and the world has heard her voice.

But if that page of history has finally turned, my own part is not finished yet. I share the battle still, as I did from my exile in 1972, engaged in the same cause. So deeply, indeed, that I see no likelihood of any respite, any lull in which I might follow this book with a personal contribution to the history of liberated Portugal; the true Portugal that we are seeing now.

Publisher's Note

The text of the original edition has been left unchanged in spite of the momentous events in Portugal in the Spring of 1974. When this book was written, Mário Soares was in exile. Essentially it is an account of Portuguese life and politics under the dictatorship and of the author's part in the struggle for a more democratic form of government. The book was finished more than two years before the fall of Caetano and his associates, but it clearly foresees that event. No attempt has been made to bring it up to date nor to improve the text in the light of recent history. Only a new author's preface has been added.

Preface to the French Edition (1972)

This is a book with a history of its own. It was begun on the small African island of São Tomé to which the Government had deported me in March 1968 for an indefinite term, without trial; and the idea for it came when I heard the radio announcement that Salazar had been operated on for brain haemorrhage. I thought then that the end of a chapter of Portuguese history must surely be in sight. While he lived no true account of the struggles that went on in my country could possibly be published, but now he was seriously ill and liberty might be just around the corner. As though in answer to this hope Marcello Caetano, who succeeded him, sanctioned my return in November. Back in Lisbon, however, with more urgent things to see to and a profession to follow, I had to lay the work aside.

Opportunity to take it up again occurred, alas, much sooner than I ever expected. I had been a dozen times in prison under the old dictator, faced three indictments and finally deportation. Exile had been the one experience missing, and Caetano duly forced it on me in August 1970. In the course of a long trip abroad I had attacked Portuguese colonial policy in an interview at the Overseas Press Club of New York in April, and later taken part in a debate of the Council of Europe at Strasbourg on the violation of human rights in Portugal. This led to an incredibly virulent campaign against me in the papers, on radio and television, to say nothing of slogans and insults chalked on walls, pamphlets and books and anonymous letters, nor the fact that its directors did not hesitate to threaten and intimidate my family. The whole multiple operation culminated in yet another trial and a treason-charge that could have meant a sentence of anything of from eight to twelve years. In the middle of it all my father died suddenly in Lisbon and I came home, without notifying the authorities, at dawn the same day. The day after his funeral I was summoned by the police. The court had warrants out for my arrest, but I was given eight hours to leave the country. Otherwise, I went to prison. For the time being, I took the road to exile.

So the book I had begun at São Tomé has had to be finished abroad. Since it is written primarily for the Portuguese people I tried, in spite of everything, to have it published first at home. Marcello Caetano, like Salazar before him, might reserve his most interesting political titbits for the foreign press and foreign correspondents, but to imitate him meant inviting the sort of obvious conclusions I wanted to avoid. Through various friends I approached likely publishers in Portugal, but for fear of reprisals none of them dared accept it, and when I attempted to publish at my own expense I could not, for the same reason, find a printer. I had to give in. The book cannot, so far, come out in Portugal; Salazar is dead, but Salazarism is with us still.

Living for some months in the little Italian village of Piediluco, where a friend lent me a house, and then in a left-bank hotel in Paris, I have had neither materials for research nor the references with which to fill up gaps and put involuntary errors right. The book is a simple testimony, nothing more, founded on personal experience and my own political commitment. If it is not history in the grand sense of the word it will, I hope, do something to bring a few unfamiliar aspects of Portuguese Fascism into the light of day.

It is an unfinished testimony, for the battle, I know, goes on : I shall continue it, and nothing is more certain than that others will. A testimony, then, that may take its place in the long, hard fight of the Portuguese to regain their liberty; these are things that happened recently, people we should know about, events that no one hears of and which should be related. And, looking to the future, I hope that here is a departure-point.

Contents

Chapter One

Apprenticeship to Politics

I went as a student to the Faculty of Literature of Lisbon University in October 1942, when I was seventeen and the Second World War had become an epic struggle whose end was nowhere yet in sight. But it presented the youth of my generation with clearcut political and moral options : to make any sense at all you had to stand up and be counted, for or against.

I looked upon myself as 'against', actively engaged in the conflict with Fascism. Salazar's regime was for me one and the same with the Nazi version. The totalitarianism, the hatred of democracy and freedom, the disregard for individual human rights—he had adopted it all, slightly watered down for home consumption. He was even trying, though not too successfully, to introduce certain elements of the Nazi mystique, with the worship of uniforms, the vast parades, the hymns and the saluting.

Having been brought up in a Republican and liberal family, I loathed the whole system from the bottom of my heart. My mother was a woman of great good sense, anti-clerical and extremely brave. My father, a furious Republican in spite of his own Catholic background, was for ever engaged in one conspiracy or another. He had been in energetic, revolutionary opposition under the Monarchy and held office under the First Republic of 1910–26.[1] Several times a member of the National

---

[1] The initial revolutionary attempt to proclaim a Republic was made at Oporto on 31 January 1891. On 28 January 1908 there was an attempted rising against the dictatorship of João Franco, President of the Royal Council. This was put down, but the King, Carlos I, was assassinated some days later and Manuel II dismissed the dictator. The Republic was proclaimed on 5 October 1910.

Assembly, a prefect, and Colonial Minister in Domingos Pereira's Government in 1919, he took arms against the dictatorships of Pimenta de Castro in 1915 and of Sidónio Paes three years later; and when the military dictatorship came in on 28 May 1926 he naturally opposed that too.

Up to the outbreak of the Spanish Civil War there was widespread resistance to this regime in Portugal. It was led by the political parties of the Republic, banned now under the new dispensation, by the workers' movements connected with the General Confederation of Workers and influenced by anarcho-syndicalism; by large sections of the army, and the navy with its more pronouncedly Republican traditions; by Freemasons, intellectuals of the Seara Nova ('New Field') group and by university students. The struggle itself assumed a flagrantly revolutionary form. Riots, strikes, revolts, acts of violence and sabotage, bestrew this little-known period of our history. Inexorably the regime responded with prison sentences, torture, deportations without trial, mass dismissals, persecutions of every kind, in a wave of repression affecting thousands of families. Politically, economically and often physically, the military dictatorship knew how to eliminate the most conspicuous figures of the First Republic, those who managed the workers' movements and the liberal-minded intellectuals.

Because of his activities, my father spent practically his whole life between 1926 and 1935 in gaol, in exile or in hiding. I can remember visiting him at the Aljube prison in Lisbon where long afterwards we were to share a cell. I also remember going one icy morning to bid him goodbye in the fortress of Peniche when they were sending him for a second term to the Azores, and the sense of impotence and rage with which my mother and I watched the ship as it sailed away. And there were the meetings at weird times and places when he was in hiding, the long detours and the dodging in and out of taxis to avoid the vigilance of the police : not the kind of thing that one forgets.

When he came back from the Azores in 1934, after a sentence imposed by a military court, my father opened the school which he ran until his death in July 1970. We were very badly off and he did the best he could, with my mother's tireless aid. But his left leg had to be amputated after a serious illness and as he approached sixty he was forced to devote his days to the school and all its problems. Nevertheless, my adolescent years, from 1936 to 1945, went by in relative peace and quiet.

My father's friends often joined us for dinner, men from political families shut out from public life since 1926. Every Sunday afternoon they spent hours at our house discussing current events. This talk of theirs was my first political school and I would listen fascinated.

When civil war broke out in Spain the immediate effect for us was that Fascism became twice as severe at home. With absorbed interest I followed the ups and downs of the contest, even if I did not always fully grasp the implications. Names and faces—of Azaña, Indalecio Prieto, Negrín, la Pasionaria, Largo Caballero—were bathed in a heroic light. And it was now, between the ages of twelve and fifteen, that I became aware of a duality that I found at the same time exalting and depressing. On the one hand was the official, pro-Franco propaganda flooding the newspapers and blaring out from Radio Club Portugal[2] and which my school-fellows, who all more or less believed it, brought into the classroom with them; and on the other was the atmosphere of my own family circle, secret, fervent and devoted to the legitimate Republican cause.

Towards 1936 the Government created its para-military and Fascist youth organisation, the *Mocidade Portuguesa*, or MP. When you were ten you had to join and don the uniform round cap, the green shirt, the boots and khaki trousers. There was also a leather belt with a large metal clasp ornamented with S for Salazar, like an owner's brand, though authority later claimed that this stood in fact for *Servir*. We were doing patriotic service, according to Salazar's interpretation of that word.

[2] This private broadcasting station played an essential part in Franco's propaganda during the Spanish War. Its director, Jorge Botelho Moniz, was head of the *viriatos*, the Salazarist Portuguese militia that fought with Franco.

The Fascist salute was obligatory, at attention, arm out-stretched. There was compulsory drill on Saturdays and the older ones did weapon-drill as well. For the members of Portuguese Youth, as for their elders in the adult Fascist militia known as the Legion, there were war-songs and war-cries. Whoever was taking the parade used to open it by shouting, 'Portuguese, who lives?' Without quite knowing what he meant, we were supposed to yell back, 'Portugal! Portugal! Portugal!' at the tops of our voices. He would then shout again, louder than ever, 'Portuguese, who leads us?' The answer to this one was of course 'Salazar! Salazar! Salazar!' Marcello Caetano, later Prime Minister, commanded the Youth Move-ment from 1940 to 1944, frequently wore its uniform though he was getting on for forty, and gave the salute with all becoming gravity.

Such gravity, though, was far from universal and resistance to the regimentation was expressed in many ways. Plenty of boys, myself among them, managed by one means or another never to put their uniforms on at all and by the time that Caetano was presiding, in his boots, over the parades, I was following other masters.

In 1941–42, my last year at school, I encountered three men who were to have the greatest influence upon me. The first, Alvaro Salema, taught me philosophy. He was an unorthodox Marxist, haloed for us with tremendous prestige owing to a long period of deportation in the Azores. The second, Alvaro Cunhal,[3] was a remarkable man, with a luminous, penetrating glance that bespoke great inner strength. Released from prison and preparing to go underground to reorganise the Communist Party, he gave me lessons in geography. The other was Agostinho da Silva, with whom I studied literature : a sort of lay mystic and the instigator of an important cultural movement.

These three, so different in temperament and ideology, represented, each in his own way, uncompromising hostility to

[3] Today general secretary of the Portuguese Communist Party. He went underground in 1941 and was arrested eight years later. He escaped from Peniche in 1959 and has since lived in exile.

the regime, a hostility whose socialist slant marked them off from people like my father and his friends, whom they used to call the old-style, bourgeois opposition. With one voice they dissuaded me from my intention of entering the law school. A citadel of reaction, they said; what on earth should I do there? They succeeded in steering me to history and philosophy in the Faculty of Literature instead.

The cultural life of Portugal was, in fact, developing outside the universities. The movement of renewal to be known as neo-realism, then beginning to make itself felt in art and letters, was characterised by its response to social and political problems. In some measure its practitioners went back to the 'generation of 1870' who had believed all literature should be 'committed'.[4]

My first encounter with these people, I remember, was at a meeting held in the offices of the newspaper *O Século*. It was Alvaro Cunhal who took me there, for in his quiet way he never lost a chance to make new converts. He knew that committed literature formed a very good introduction to active politics.

Some time after this I went to a concert of Gregorian music, with a lecture by our leading composer, Fernando Lopes Graça—an occasion interrupted by a squad of Fascists for whom our listening to the concert was evident proof of subversive tendencies. It was my first contact with the police. I was caught up in the rush for the door and arrested, only to be set free with the regulation warnings an hour or two later. That day, at any rate, I knew my name was not on the files of the mysterious PVDE, as the political police were then called; it was not to be absent for much longer.[5]

[4] The young progressive intellectuals of Coimbra University, the 'generation of 1870', included Eça de Queiroz, the novelist. Their aim was to apply the methods of science to all the disciplines. Trans.

[5] The security police of Portugal have borne four successive titles. At the beginning of the dictatorship they were an 'investigation force'. Then, until 1945 the Police of Vigilance and State Defence, or PVDE. Until 1969 they became the International State Defence Police, the PIDE, and after the advent of Marcello Caetano were the DGS, or General Security Department. This is by no means their last appearance in this book.

The year before I went up there was a good deal of unrest in the universities due to the raising of students' fees. The cost of education, it should be noted, served to emphasise social differences, for the *liceu*, or secondary school, was a luxury and the university open to a tiny minority only. Now, in 1941, this situation led inevitably to violent confrontations among the students. Class privilege was defended by a small but active group of its possessors, consisting of embryo leaders in the *Mocidade Portuguesa* and the militants—especially the female militants—of the Catholic Student Youth movement, who were wild reactionaries in any case. On the other side stood a determined handful, often Communists, bent on mobilising what we then called 'straight anti-Fascists'. Between the two there lay, of course, the great apathetic and non-vocal mass of those to whom politics meant nothing and who saw little further than the football field. All the same, the Young Communists managed to recruit even the don't-cares in the hour of battle.

I myself first met the student Communists through Guilherme da Costa Carvalho in my last year at the *liceu*. Costa Carvalho came of a well-to-do family but his whole career has been an example of devotion to his ideals and his youth and much of his adult life were passed in prison or in hiding.[6] He read me a homily on what, in his view as a Communist, was wrong with the liberal opposition, and on its political shortcomings. I heard of wonderful tomorrows and the new social dawn his comrades were to usher in.

The preaching of Communist doctrine was no revelation, nor did it delude me. I was armed against it by the influence of my father's circle who, while admiring in the Communists a spirit of sacrifice and practical sense, nevertheless had reservations about their disregard for public liberty and the methods they employed. Could the end justify *every* means? My father and his friends thought not. And yet these people had something which attracted me strongly and which I had found nowhere else—the call to action. Also, theirs was the only

---

[6] He came out of gaol again recently, a very sick man.

organised and active force of opposition in the university.

In 1942 the Soviet Union was bearing the brunt of the Nazi offensive more or less alone. The Battle of Britain was over and the fate of the world hung on what was happening at the gates of Moscow rather than in the African desert. Of this we were all perfectly aware and it made us forgive and forget many things—the Soviet pact with Germany, the Red Army's invasion of Finland and Poland, even the Moscow trials and the welter of internal quarrels at the end of the Spanish Civil War. Euphoria was in the air. We saw the apostles of progress joined in grand alliance; we saw Stalin, through the eyes of Roosevelt, as patriarchal, jolly Uncle Joe; and yonder all before us lay, or so we hoped, democratic anti-Fascist brotherhood.

When term ended I went for part of the summer to the seaside village of Foz do Arelho and there met a group of friends who were staying with the lawyer Humberto Lopes, in a kind of holiday soviet. I was six or eight years younger than the rest, at once their Benjamin and their disciple, ready to step into the line when my turn came. Dedicated to the struggle against Fascism, they brought me still nearer to the Communists. I have never known the call of religion, nor what it is like to belong to any religious fellowship, but I imagine that what I felt as a novice among them was much the same sort of thing.

The Russian campaign was then at its height. We followed troop movements on the map with passionate attention and laughed our heads off when the *Diário de Notícias* said that Hitler was going to win. In the evenings we went to the local school, where the master possessed the only radio in the district, and indulged in the secret national crime of Portugal—listening-in to the BBC.

When those holidays in 1942 were over and I was getting ready to start at the university, I had in my pocket a letter of introduction to Jorge Borges de Macedo, who is today Vice-Rector at Lisbon. He was then the leading spirit there and through him I became decisively involved in the student struggle with Fascism.

The Faculty of Literature, when I joined it, was to be found in the old Convent of Jesus. One passed through the gateway and down some steps to the cloister and lecture-rooms. 'The only college in the world that puts you on the downward path,' said Professor Rodrigues Lapa, whom it dismissed for political reasons.

The first thing that matters in a college, however, is the spirit and quality of the teaching it offers and though the Faculty of Literature at Lisbon had been impressive enough some years before, the rise of Fascism had entailed a sad falling-off in the 1930s. Indeed, this was true of the university as a whole, with its political purges and all the impediments to freedom of instruction that were put in the way of staff and students alike. Chairs were awarded for political loyalty rather than professional qualifications and every applicant for a readership had to take a written oath of allegiance to the established social order and swear that he was neither a Communist nor a member of any secret society—in other words, a Freemason. It lay with the security police to decide whether or not this declaration were true and their word was final. No appeal.

Most of the professors I knew in the department were secondraters, incompetent and uninterested in their jobs. There comes to mind a vegetarian named Delio Santos, who was more devoted to theosophy than theology and always advising us to go to the circus, his great enthusiasm being for charlatans in telepathic acts. And there was Moreira de Sá, a man publicly and demonstrably accused of plagiarism, whom the Dean sought to exonerate by telling us, 'You all think he's stupid, but you are all quite wrong. He just finds speaking and writing rather difficult.' To be brief and take one more name from the roll, we had Joseph Prud'homme personified in Mário de Albuquerque. His fatuities were the delight of foreign students, whose summer courses would be enlivened by his discourse on 'Parrots: Their Discovery and What it has Meant to the Civilisation of Portugal'.

One professor only had the root of the matter in him, Vitorino Magalhães Godinho. Everybody knew it and the students worshipped him. It was he who introduced to Portugal the methods of the historians Marc Bloch, Lucien Febvre and Fernand Braudel. Fascism could not come to terms with such a man, nor he with Fascism and he was sacked in 1943, right in the middle of the university year. However, we managed to hire a private hall, asked him to carry on his lectures there, and had twelve months of profitable instruction.

But the master, mine and my generation's, was beyond all doubt António Sérgio. As far as the Salazarist university was concerned, he did nothing but argue with it. A prolific essayist, past fifty when I met him, he was the unflagging opponent of totalitarianism and its spurious culture, and had earned for his pains a long stretch of exile and several prison sentences. A born teacher, he had worked out a system of co-operative Socialism for Portugal that would leave human rights and liberties untouched. He, more than anyone else, instilled in us the love of culture as a free adventure of the mind and gave us the habit of analysing domestic politics in the light of contemporary events in the rest of Europe.

Many of us differed from António Sérgio at one time or another and he himself encouraged us to do so. Some of his arguments were, indeed, beyond us, especially his theories on everyday political action; but his stature has grown with the passing of years and no one now disputes that he has been the great restorative force of this century in the culture of Portugal. Yet the university never considered him, as it never considered the majority of the intellectuals and scientists of our day, fit to teach. It preferred to bar them, or to throw them out.

Nevertheless, in spite of everything, there did exist among the students a small, active and combatant world : that of our own group. We served our difficult apprenticeship to freedom of thought in those impassioned debates we held in the corridors about anything we happened to be reading or anything that was going on. It was a comparatively secret world, unknown to most of the professors and their pupils, and to it I owe my university education. To the university as a teaching institution I owe nothing.

Undergraduate societies at that time were half asleep. Their officers might not be freely elected but were merely appointed from above, and nobody was interested. They were, in fact, nothing but management committees set up by the heads of faculties, needing the confirmation of authority and so in no way representative. In the 1930s, when the Government really tried to starve the societies to death, there had been some lively student opposition and uncounted victims in our three universities of Lisbon, Oporto and Coimbra. Strikes had led to expulsions and arrests, people had been killed and wounded; but the student movement that had been an autonomous body in the days of the First Republic had come to a standstill by 1942. Yet, despite all official efforts, the *Mocidade Portuguesa* never took root in the universities, and this although the regime allowed no other organisation to recruit young people.

The flame of rebellion was not lit again until 1944. In that year the students at Coimbra, weary of the 'management committees' contrived to hold free elections for committees of their own. Times had changed and Fascism was almost everywhere in retreat. The committee they elected had for chairman their idol Francisco Zenha, who was reading law. But unhappily the victory was not for long. It marked the beginning of new battles that were to culminate in 1957 and 1962 and Zenha, who has remained one of my dearest associates, paid for his presumption with years in gaol.

At Lisbon in 1943 we also tried, and failed, to secure a freely-elected body in the Faculty of Literature. I recall the great efforts we made to get up a common list of candidates with the Catholic Student Youth group, the JUC. The man we were wanting to bring forward was Lindley Cintra, a militant Catholic who, although already liberally inclined, had his reservations about student strife. He was to hold a chair later and from 1962 onwards he emerged as one of the bravest and most resolute figures in the university.

I grew more interested in political problems after my second year, and came to know the Communist group in the faculty

under Jorge de Macedo. This was very much a closed shop.
It had contacts in the departments of medicine, law, technology
and veterinary science, yet attained no lasting influence over
the student majority. Moreover, it had no coherent policy to
propose, nor the necessary means of action. When I joined,
all it did was circulate the publications of the clandestine
Communist press and, later on, those of the National United
Anti-Fascist Movement, or MUNAF, and paint slogans on
the wall: 'Death to the PVDE', for instance, or 'Down with
Tarrafal' (the concentration-camp for political prisoners on
one of the Cape Verde islands off the African coast). It also
studied the theoretical problems of Marxism.

And so it was now that I read, in secret, much of Lenin,
material by Stalin, Dimitrov and Thorez, the *Anti-Dhüring*
of Engels, Bukharin's *ABC of Communism* (a recommended
work, though its author was classed as 'renegade'), and that
History of the Communist Party of the USSR, which I hardly
suspected was going to need quite so much revision as the
years rolled by. Apart from all this purely speculative activity,
we tried to keep up with the war news as well, certain that
Allied victory would be our victory too. Of course, practically
speaking, we did very little, but it was enough to have put
us in prison, or in Tarrafal, for several years.

But there was going to be an Allied victory, that was clear.
The opposition in Portugal began to revive from the long
discouragement which followed the Spanish Civil War. We
thought the defeat of Fascism in Nazi Germany would bring
in its train the defeat of the Fascist regimes of the Peninsula
as a matter of course. Had not the Spanish Blue Division
fought for Hitler? Had not Salazar been photographed beside
the picture of Mussolini which occupied a place of honour
in his study?

The Portuguese at this time were scarcely even aware of
the fact that Lisbon was a capital of international espionage.
What they learned of the outside world came to them in
obviously censored news-reels, or from the successive waves
of refugees who, particularly in the reception-area round
Caldas da Rainha, had appeared in their parochially-minded

society. But the war accentuated the dividing-line between one part of the nation and the other. The official establishment, behind a façade of neutrality, was heart and soul with the Axis powers. The rest of the Portuguese, suffering and down-trodden, had made the Allied cause their own.

The Western embassies, first the British and then the American, now began to extend their propaganda services in Portugal. My friends and I got in touch with the cultural attachés and distributed tickets at the university for film shows at the British embassy's private cinema, the Estrella Hall. We also arranged programmes at various small working-class clubs, using a projector and films lent by the Americans.

This sort of thing might have been made for us. It awoke student and worker, it forced them to see what Fascist methods —the methods of our own Government—really were, and incited them to struggle for democracy at home. We were able enormously to strengthen and increase our links with other institutes and colleges, and when the MUDJ, the Junior Movement for Democratic Union, was formed a month or so later, these links were to develop into a powerful anti-Fascist student organisation.

The MUNAF, the National United Anti-Fascist Movement, was started, I believe, in 1942 or 1943, supposedly by Communists.[7] There had of course been changes in the Communist Party since 1941. It was profiting by the militant activity of Alvaro Cunhal, as from the laurels gained by the Red Army on the field of battle and the MUNAF gathered to itself the whole democratic opposition save the intimates of the former Prime Minister Cunha Leal. Several organised underground political

---

[7] Under General Norton de Mattos, the MUNAF controlled a vast network of committees all over Portugal, had adherents among the armed forces and a National Council drawn from all sectors of the opposition. Its Executive Committee consisted of Bento de Jesus Caraça, an independent Radical Progressive, Jacinto Simões, a Republican with connections among the democrats of the left; Manuel Serras, of the Portuguese Republican Party, foremost of its kind under the First Republic; José de Magalhães Godinho, of the Socialist Union; José Moreira dos Campos, an army officer and a liberal Republican; and Fernando Piteira Santos, the Communist representative.

forces were also still in being at this time—the old skeleton of the Portuguese Republican Party, which enjoyed freedom of action up to a point; the ineffectual Socialist Party, or SPIO, split into rival factions, frequently penetrated by the police; the recently-formed Socialist Union, whose members were for the most part opposition sympathisers drawn from the liberal professions; and finally the Freemasons, who had been behind the anti-regime struggles of the thirties.

The MUNAF held a meeting at Sintra, presided over by General Norton de Mattos, and the resultant manifesto was hailed with enthusiasm. It came from the clandestine press with a list of essential conditions for the establishment of democracy, demanding a clean break with the past and a whole new pattern of life.

I had, of course, no first-hand knowledge of all this, but echoes of the MUNAF preparations reached me from two different sources—my father, who was very close to the leaders of the group, and my fellow-students, who were kept in the picture by the Communists. Clearly there were two schools of thought within the movement, where some were planning the downfall of the Government by means of a putsch and others, professing the same politics, aimed at creating the right conditions for a popular anti-Fascist rising on a national scale.

Neither putsch nor rising had occurred, however, when the long vacation of 1944 came round, during which I met Fernando Piteira Santos at Caldas da Rainha. I had known him slightly at the university and had heard that he had since gone underground. He was a legend even then and a legend he deserved to be, of tenacity, courage and intelligence : he had given the supreme proof of true militant devotion by holding out under torture in prison. He was, it appeared, a deputy member of the Central Committee of the Portuguese Communist Party and sat as Communist representative on the MUNAF Executive. In fact, he was the party boss in this western region, as well as controller of its student group on the Youth Section.

Our encounter was for me decisive. It was he who intro-

B

duced, or rather 'attached' me, as the political jargon has it, to the local Party Committee in Caldas da Rainha. This cell was run by a carpenter named Manuel Duarte, with whom I quickly struck up a warm friendship.

They found me jobs to do. I bicycled round the district at night with Duarte. I held meetings in the villages, or at farms in the middle of nowhere, to give the peasants and workers simplified explanations of national and international politics in the context of combined anti-Fascist action. It was all very thrilling and once, near Obidos, I even found myself making a speech at the bottom of a manganese mine.

These were memorable years for the Communist Party, years of battle and hope. Never again was it to command so much spontaneous vigour, with widespread strikes to crown the programme. Among others, these included one in the Ribatejo in which the writer Pereira Gomes took a notable part.

By the time I went back to college for the 1944–45 university year, I too felt like a seasoned militant. I was still asking myself questions about the nature of Communism, particularly as to whether a dictatorship of the proletariat were really necessary, and what was to happen to the liberty of the subject; but the appeal of action and practical work was exciting, nevertheless.

During the year Piteira Santos held a conference of his most trustworthy officers, some twenty in number, from among the various faculties of the university. It was a day-long affair, shrouded in secrecy. At his suggestion, unanimously approved, I was elected to the committee of the Young Communist University Movement, with the basic responsibility for forming a united anti-Fascist student sector, to be run in conjunction with the MUNAF. The ending of the Second World War was favourable to projects of this kind.

We started to organise cultural talks as well as the cinema shows, and gained a large audience in the country as a whole by working regularly with newspapers and provincial reviews. It was now that my own first articles came out in the *República*, a journal which, despite the handicaps of censorship, did manage to be in some sort the mouthpiece of the opposition.

All these doings, which occupied me far more than the books I ought to have been reading, were focused on the end of the war and with it the end of Fascism in Portugal. Once more, however, I must admit that, practically speaking, we did not really see quite what was to bring the Government crashing down, nor recognise this vagueness as a serious chink in our armour.

The MUNAF had been attempting to organise Anti-Fascist Combat Groups (the GAC) and delighted students had welcomed the idea of these small, mobile offensive units with the task of arousing the length and breadth of the land to revolt. But the operation was cancelled after a month or so : some of the MUNAF leaders considered that the regime would topple of its own accord in any case when the Allies won the war, while others pinned their faith on the military coup then in active preparation. Others again feared the consequences of raising up a force that could not be entirely under their control.

V-Day, 8 May 1945, brought news of Germany's unconditional surrender and the end of the war in Europe. On that never-to-be-forgotten afternoon I was in the faculty lecture-hall at a class on the great discoveries when a friend made me the expected signal from the corridor outside. This was it. I jumped to my feet at once, interrupted the professor and called for no more work that day. The poor man was terrified and could not think what to do. A German sympathiser leaped up in protest : Portugal was neutral and had no business to celebrate something that was no concern of hers. The argument grew heated and though most of the hundred or so students present kept out of it, others were drawn in. The professor's only suggestion was that we should go to the Director's office to see about cutting the rest of the lecture. We dismissed this notion out of hand and urged everybody to walk out and consider the class at an end. Then we ourselves, half a dozen of us, left.

Waving Allied flags, we clattered away to the heart of Lisbon, where the Praça do Rossio was packed, and obviously

expectant. We were greeted with applause and soon had a
train of young followers. The police and plain-clothes men
were out in force, occupying strategic points and doing what
they could to stop crowds forming, but today they were correct,
almost polite, about it.

Suddenly we produced a huge Portuguese flag and began
to sing the National Anthem. The result was electrifying.
Within seconds there was a press of people round us, clamour-
ing for a triumphal march to the foreign embassies. It was a
sea of people, thousands upon thousands of them, chanting
'Victory! Victory! Liberty! De-mo-cra-cy!'

Next morning we saw to it that the colleges and secondary
schools were closed. The demonstrators who joined us were
of every class and kind. Where we went, they went. Again
we paraded before the American, British and French embassies. (There is no Soviet embassy in Portugal.) The thing took
on an undeniably political complexion. Now the cries were,
'Death to Fascism!' 'Free the political prisoners!' 'Shut the
camp at Tarrafal!' I had the impression that the whole of
Lisbon was out in the streets.

The messages we handed in to the Allied ambassadors were
very clearly worded. Embarrassed, the Allied ambassadors
returned their purely formal thanks and acknowledged the
cheering in a chilly sort of way. It is possible that even then
they knew that they were going to let us down; that they had
to make terms with the recent enemy and keep Salazar securely
where he was.

Chapter Two

Salazarism:
The True Picture

And so, in my third year at the university, the war was over and Salazar and his regime were faced with the defeat of Nazi Fascism. It is time to go back a little and see who Salazar was, and what was his regime.

Up to 1945 the Portuguese political system which we may, for convenience, call Salazarism, had a certain logic and life in it. After that date it was no more than an anachronism, unconnected with the march of events and indifferent to the clouds of menace which its long immobility had gathered round it.

The dictator was himself neither a doctrinaire nor an ideologist and belonged to no particular system or party. He had a few simple, almost banal, notions to steer by and came to power in 1928 at an unusually difficult juncture in the country's fortunes. Circumstances both at home and abroad undoubtedly made for his success, but much of it he owed to his own autocratic will. The will of Salazar was absolutely proof against the modern world and the needs of the nation.

He had neither family nor friends, led the life of a hermit and shunned the glitter of smart social occasions. But he climbed the ladder of power nevertheless, propelled upwards by the well-organised *integristas*, the hard core of the Portuguese Catholic Church. It was they who made Salazar the man of destiny. Cardinal Cerejeira, Primate of Portugal, who knew him well, has described him as having a feminine sensibility. He was a cold-seeming man who talked through his nose, lacked popular magnetism of any kind and could never address an

audience without a script in his hand. A colourless deputy of
the Catholic centre in Republican days, he soon resigned his
seat. As professor of Political Economy in the Law Faculty at
Coimbra his students found him inaccessible and distrustful.
Today it is hard to see how such a man could have ruled as
undisputed master of Portugal for forty years.

We might break the problem down somewhat and explain
it under different headings. To start with, he had the support
of the Church, the army and certain financial interests; with
the Spanish Civil War came the myth of his infallibility, with
some very clever propaganda to help it along; and there was
always that cold, purposeful will-power, allied to a talent for
manipulating and corrupting people.

Salazar used his power to make himself a kind of absolute
monarch. As Franz Villiers rightly said in his book on Portugal,
'*L'Etat, c'est lui*'.[1] He spared neither friend nor enemy and
would stop at nothing to achieve what he wanted. Impervious
to fresh ideas, incapable of discussion even in the privacy of a
cabinet meeting, he lived wrapped up in an immeasurable
pride.

The thirst for personal power and the demands of public
order as he understood them, led him to demolish all opponents,
not excepting those members of his own entourage who never
stopped saying how devoted they were. Salazar was a destroyer
of men and of consciences, and it will take a very long time
to fill the political void that he created round him.

Criticism he could not stand, however mild and well-
intentioned, and he imposed a long silence on the country by
his implacable censorship. With the aid of his political police
he shut down all possible centres of debate—parties, civil movements, cultural societies, study groups, everything. The result
was as tidy and quiet as a cemetery. Nor was the one party he
did allow, the National Union, permitted to extend in any way,
for fear his followers should outdistance him. For those four
decades the Portuguese press was probably the dullest in the
world as every day in the same old way it praised the perfect
merits of the man of destiny.

[1] *Le Portugal*, by Franz Villiers, Éditions du Seuil, Paris.

Certainly no one in the country had a lower opinion of his contemporaries, beginning with his supporters, whom he knew best, than had Salazar. He showed a constant and peculiar predilection for men of weak character, corrupt men, such as revealed by their behaviour some vice or imperfection. He shared, in fact, the Castilian temperament to be found among the old Inquisitors and, interestingly enough, he favoured the Spanish rather than the Portuguese custom in using his mother's family name instead of his father's, which was Oliveira.

He regarded Portugal as some sort of rural estate which had to be kept carefully enclosed against impure infection from other people's way of living. The world beyond had not the slightest appeal for him. It seemed, on the contrary, hostile and quite incurably foreign. He seldom left his native land and never visited the colonies, not even the Azores. The rich were more important to him than the lower classes and, provided that they did not interfere, he respected and served them like a zealous major-domo. He failed to notice the changes taking place, by sheer force of circumstances, in modern Portugal. The small degree of industrialisation, the slow spread of education in the wake of modern media, the awakening to the outside world brought about by the huge-scale emigration of workers and by the tourist trade, were so many ills that he could not prevent but which, in his view, presaged disaster.

The disinterest of the masses in politics and their apathy with regard to national problems, things that shock the foreign observer of today, have been deliberately induced. Portugal, let us not forget, has the lowest standard of living in Europe,[2] and people from the villages and the outskirts of the towns either exist wretchedly or go abroad to seek the minimum wage they cannot earn at home. Let us not forget that the intellectuals, too, have had to leave, or that if they stay they feel, as our one Nobel prize-winner, Egas Moniz, has put it, 'like exiles in their own country'. And that country, 'proudly alone' in Salazar's

[2] According to figures published by OECD in September 1971, the gross national product in 1969 was 600 dollars per head, as against 872 dollars for Spain and 950 for Greece.

phrase, is no less significantly having to wage a colonial war, unjust as it is stupid, on three fronts, in Angola, Mozambique and Guinea-Bissao. It all hangs together.

One may indeed ask how Portugal, with her *oito séculos de idade*—eight centuries of history—a brave, adventurous, forward-looking nation who, as Camões said, 'gave new worlds to the world', can have delivered herself into such bondage. To answer that disturbing question we must analyse what led up to the events of 28 May 1926.

The military revolt of that date has been claimed as a spontaneous national reaction against the shambles of democracy, whereas the people felt in 1926 as they did in 1910 when the Monarchy ended. National institutions were still as much monarchical as republican and they would not have defended them had they known how to.

The most widely differing elements supported the conspiracy. They included Monarchists of the deepest dye, Catholics and Republicans who disagreed with the reigning *democráticos* of the PRP, leading churchmen, even Radicals and Anarchists. As general background it should be remembered that the country was rudderless and disabled, ruined financially as a result of armed intervention in the First World War.

It was also in a state of grave crisis, facing problems of reorganisation and a great popular need for social justice. Complete liberty existed, but it was veering slowly into anarchy and the Republic had unfortunately no idea where to find men capable of carrying through the urgent necessary reforms. The political parties were mere rootless associations unconnected with the real life of the country, disorder mounted steadily and Parliament could do nothing to control it.

Such were the circumstances in which revolt broke out on 28 May. One knows what political intervention by an army means, however well it may intend, and that nothing can be looked for but more and worse problems as a result. Portugal was now to have a copy-book illustration of this truth.

Leading the movement was Gomes da Costa, a respected soldier of proverbial courage but a political weather-cock, quite out of touch with the age he lived in. The lieutenants and colonels at his back were power-hungry men with no experience of affairs, who had been plotting against the Republican order for some time.

And yet parliamentary democracy had given us close on a century of social, intellectual and administrative progress. One of the most fruitful periods of our history is that between 1834 and 1926. It includes the Constitutional Monarchy as well as the First Republic. But since 1926 we have been told that the nation is not yet ready for freedom and that the Republic is to blame for the disorder which, it has been proved, was actually fomented, to their own considerable profit, by hidden forces of economic and clerical reaction.

The sixteen years of the First Republic, from 1910 to 1926, were indeed very difficult, and the budget deficit especially provoked the horror of its opponents. And yet Afonso Costa[3] had balanced his budget in 1913 and the last constitutional Government of the Republic had a minimum deficit only. It was the military dictatorship which, in the two years from 1926 to 1928, increased it to the very verge of bankruptcy.

Much is also made of the rabid anti-clericalism of the Republic, its persecution of priests and the intolerance of its politicians. It is forgotten that religious peace had returned to Portugal long before 28 May 1926. The Separation Law disestablishing the Church was by then an accepted fact and a *modus vivendi* had been arrived at between Church and Government.

Certainly there were frequent changes of ministry between 1919 and 1926 and many second-rate men appeared on the political scene. This instability was accompanied by endless social agitation which the transient Governments could not cope with and which very often served as a screen for money-interests better left unspecified. It is not hard to see that hidden hands were pulling the strings behind the many strikes and outrages that took place, nor to detect the influence of what

[3] Afonso Costa was Minister of Justice in the first provisional Government set up by the Republic, and Prime Minister in 1913. He died in exile in Paris in 1937.

might be called an 'Economic Union', or daylight freemasonry of financiers and industrialists who could count upon Salazar as a heedful fellow-worker. There was, indeed, a close parallel with what happened in Italy before the advent of Fascism.

Salazar first came into the Government with the *coup d'état* of 1926, but the military junta refused to give him the powers he wanted as Finance Minister and in six days he resigned. Nobody paid much attention to this at the time, but in 1928, when the same military junta had plunged Portugal into administrative and financial chaos, the Prime Minister, General Vicente Freitas, recalled him to deal with the mess. In those two intervening years the Church and the 'Union of Economic Interests' had marked him for their own. He reassumed the Ministry of Finance and immediately imposed severe measures which were accepted without demur. Constitutional rights were suspended, public liberties suppressed and the parties, trade unions and most prominent political figures of the First Republic proscribed by the military dictatorship.

And what new notions did Salazar bring to the situation, with his *Sei muito bem o que quero e para ondo vou*—'I know quite well what I want and where I'm going'? They amounted, in essence, to putting the house in order. To do this the budget was to be balanced by cutting down expenditure and income increased by means of new taxation. Any decent housekeeper could have thought of it. Salazar, a classic economist of the pre-Keynes era, held fast to his orthodox principles : a balanced budget and back-to-the-wall maintenance of a strong currency.

On a public distressed and confused by two years of military chaos, these health-inducing monetary measures were not without effect. The property-owning and conservative classes, seeing in the new Finance Minister a pious character with a fixation about public order, felt safe again, and by 1932 the financial dictator of 1928 was dictator pure and simple. There were some sharp engagements by the way—plots, civilian and army risings, strikes and demonstrations, followed at once by purges and reprisals. But he was supported throughout by the bankers, the large landed proprietors and most of the moneyed classes. Catholic opinion was with him; what was more, many of the troops fought for him actively. The Salazar myth was beginning to take shape.

And as Fascism gained ground in Europe, voices were raised on all sides against democracy. Democracy was supposed to undermine the authority of the state and leave it weakened before the attack of international Communism. Also, the middle classes, in Spain and Portugal as everywhere else, regarded Fascism as a protective shield against the constantly increasing pressure of demands from the workers.

Though Salazar was from 1932 onwards the unchallenged fount of all authority, he never accepted the first place in the state, a fact that reveals one aspect of his tortuous nature. He was a retiring man. He turned away from the limelight to the shadowy seclusion of his study and sat there like an indefatigable monk, weaving his political web, working his attendant marionettes. He made use of mystery, intrigue, intimidation and reward, like dreadful weapons, from a distance.

He was a dictator *sui generis*; not at all on the Italian pattern, for Mussolini was the complete *condottiere*, exhibitionist, extrovert and orator, nor on that of Hitler. He was perhaps nearer to Franco, without the military brilliance. Neither *duce, fuehrer* nor *caudillo*, he managed to fulfil the dictator's role as plain Dr Salazar, Prime Minister.

A further difference was that he did not, like his rivals, seize power by his own efforts. It was offered to him on a plate by the soldiers, who found the arts of government beyond them : Portugal had known dictatorship before the dictator came. He had the backing of no personal political party in the strict sense of the term. The National Union was for him a result, not a cause, of his ascent and helped him neither to reach nor to keep his position. No mass-movement compelled him to the pseudo-reforming policy in which some Fascist regimes had indulged. Upheld by the army, the Church and the Union of Economic Interests, he came to power alone. The fact that he retained it was due more to inertia and fear of the future than to any active military support.

In 1933 the regime, having operated until then by decree,

sought to make itself politically and constitutionally acceptable. It was by decree that Salazar, as acting Colonial Minister, had forced through the Colonial Act which marked the end of the traditionally liberal attitude towards our overseas possessions and the beginning of the 'Portuguese Colonial Empire'; an Empire later to be shamelessly disowned, for political convenience, by the very man who had created it. Soon after this a Constitution was announced, to give the regime some semblance of legality. It was no longer the National Dictatorship, it was the *Estado Novo,* or New State. But the Constitution, drawn up by the Government, was ratified by a plebiscite in which all abstentions were counted as votes in favour.

Henceforth the regime was a unitary, corporative and imperial Republic, seeking to maintain a hybrid compromise between its own brand of representative system and the several patterns of Fascism then to be found in Europe. Here began disillusion for the Monarchists, who had thought that the dictatorship would pave the way to Restoration. The National Statute of Labour, in which certain corporative principles were set out for the first time, was copied almost word for word from the Italian *Carta del Lavoro*, while the imperialistic theories propounded in the Colonial Act stemmed similarly from those of Mussolini.

When the Spanish Civil War broke out, true Fascism became much more apparent. There was a strengthening of the sole authorised party, the National Union; the Portuguese Legion and the Naval Brigade were recruited as armed forces of political militia; youth was served with the para-military *Mocidade Portuguesa.* Corporativism was encouraged, not only as the accepted doctrine of the state, but as a half-way house between capitalism and Socialism, something that would help to resolve social conflicts. What it did, of course, was to lay the foundations of rigid economic control and help the big monopolies.

It should be remembered that a whole series of risings and revolts against the dictatorship in Portugal had taken place before the Spanish war. There were those of 7 February 1927, of 20 July 1928, the 1931 rising in Madeira and that in

Lisbon on 26 August of the same year, to note only the bloodiest examples. Working-class agitation was ruthlessly suppressed and, after the Anarchist-inspired strike of 18 January 1934, wiped out completely. Bands of exiles such as the *Liga de Paris* in France and the *Budas* in Spain, all holding Republican opinions, never ceased to work against the Government while plots were laid from time to time within the country itself, to be swiftly annihilated by the police.

The supporters of the regime were definitely minority groups, but the international situation lent them some degree of significance and force. And other factors, too, helped the system established in 1933 to take root and grow—the economic and cultural backwardness of Portugal, the ignorance of the masses and, above all, the absence of a powerful working class. Salazar was himself a meeting-point of the various right-wing schools of thought and his writings and speeches of the time display his hesitations as to doctrine, his opportunism and eclecticism.

The Constitution of 1933 echoed this attitude perfectly. The Republic was defined as an *Estado Corporativo*, with the principle of popular suffrage retained for elections to the National Assembly and the Presidency, although it would be abandoned for presidential campaigns after that of General Delgado in 1959. The fundamental freedoms were recognised, theoretically, in Article No. 8, but entirely cancelled out in practice by a series of decrees forbidding voluntary association and making the right of assembly dependent on the whim of the Minister of the Interior and of Civil Governors. The legislative power, supposedly shared between the National Assembly and the Government, was in fact exercised by the latter more or less alone. Finally, the President of the Republic might dismiss the Prime Minister at will, dissolve the Assembly and—again in theory—was answerable to the nation only. In practice, however, all power lay with the Prime Minister, who was solely responsible for Government policy and who appointed and discharged ministers as he saw fit.

It was a Constitution tailored by Salazar to suit himself, and when it came to ruling he did not bother overmuch with tedious points of principle. Constitution or no Constitution, he was the State; the perfect Police State.

His two main instruments were always the police and the censorship, both of which he directed in person. Through the security police he could impose a reign of terror and be rid of the most determined adversary, while the censorship enabled him to do as he liked with communications and blanket the whole country in silence. And that was all he ever knew about the arts of government.

In the early days of the dictatorship the security police, or 'Investigation Force', were brutal in the extreme. The tortures they employed were many and various. They manhandled people, beat them with whips and bull-lashes, used blinding lights, live electric handcuffs and so on. Those under arrest and awaiting trial could be kept for any period in the station-cellars or the special cells of the police prisons at Caxias, São Julião da Barra and Peniche or the Aljube prison in Lisbon.[4] Sometimes they went beyond violence to actual crime, as when prisoners 'fell' out of the windows at the police-headquarters in what had once been part of the San Carlos theatre in Lisbon, or disappeared mysteriously without trace. Salazar in an interview with the journalist António Ferro[5] justified the tortures practised by the political police as *safanões a tempo*, 'cautionary softenings-up'. The strain was made so unbearable for detainees that one old anti-Fascist veteran, Jaime Rebelo, slashed his own tongue rather than risk giving his friends away.

The only regulation for the treatment of detainees was that there were no regulations. An anonymous denunciation was

---

[4] See on this subject *Portugal Oprimado*, by Fernando Queiroga, published in Brazil in 1959. It was written almost entirely in the prison at Peniche, from which I smuggled the manuscript out in 1946. Its historical value is considerable, the author having gathered much of his evidence directly from the victims themselves.

[5] See the collected interviews published by Ferro under the title, *Salazar*. This is one of the books that helped to create the Salazar myth and as such is well worth reading. The author was paid in princely fashion, for his post of First Secretary in the Department of Propaganda made him a kind of Portuguese Goebbels.

enough to put you inside, with no legal time-limit, for just as long as the police felt like keeping you there. At the mere stroke of a pen, and without a shadow of preliminary proceedings, successive batches of prisoners were sent off to the Azores, to Guinea or São Tomé, to Angola or the distant island of Timor; and there they stayed for years, until the police felt like fetching them back again. Often it was then, and then only, that they appeared before the special court which, under military jurisdiction, dealt with political offences. My father, for example, was deported twice, first to Madeira and then to the Azores, where he spent a year in the fortress of São João Baptista at Angra do Heroismo, and was finally tried, and acquitted, on his return to Portugal.

The security police were completely reorganised after the attempt on Salazar's life in 1937. They had considerably overreached themselves in forcing 'confessions' from a group of Anarchists, whereas the judiciary police later discovered that the would-be assassins were different people altogether : a clear indication of what such 'confessions' were really worth.

Already in 1934 Salazar had decided to transform the Investigation Force into the Police of Vigilance and State Defence, or PVDE, and two years afterwards appointed to its head a pair of captains whose names can still produce a shudder, Agostinho Lourenço and José Catela. With them the sheer unsystemised brutality of earlier days gave way to the scientific brutality learned from the political police of Italy and Germany. Contacts between the PVDE and the Gestapo became so close that the notorious Kramer came to Portugal himself to organise the new units.

The concentration-camp at Tarrafal, in the most desolate part of the island of Santiago in the Cape Verde archipelago, was opened in 1936 and a large number of prisoners (especially any militant workers of anarchist or Communist persuasion) were transferred there from the Azores and metropolitan Portugal. Many of them died in that forbidding spot, others, after ten or fifteen years, left it with health permanently shattered. In the absence of medical supplies and the most rudimentary hygiene, they could not stand the climate and nearly all caught fatal fevers. Even the quinine their families sent them was withheld and what they endured was as bad as anything in Dachau or Buchenwald. There were, for instance, the infamous *frigideiras,* tiny cells roofed over with cement tiles, windowless save for a slit about twelve by sixteen inches that admitted little or no light, in which men were literally roasted under the tropical sun.

In 1946, Salazar modified the PVDE again, this time into the PIDE, or International State Defence Police. Its chiefs, having abundantly proved themselves, were unchanged. (This was a year before the camp at Tarrafal was shut down, although it was to be used once more for African nationalists in 1961.) A series of decrees, based on Nazi methods and authorised by Cavaleiro Ferreira as Minister, gave legal warrant to the arbitrary conduct of the police. The term of confinement before trial was fixed at six months—a long, six-month, polar night—and PIDE inspectors could now act as examining magistrates while investigations were going on. At the same time, special courts, known as *plénários,* were instituted to hear political cases and there was precise definition of the 'security measures' to be used against 'incorrigible delinquents'. These measures might be employed again and again indefinitely, and might in practice mean perpetual imprisonment. The PIDE, like the PVDE before it, could do as it liked in Portugal.

No official might be appointed to a state or municipal job without its approval; it could pay its numerous agents and informers, and offer royal rewards for spying, out of an almost bottomless fund which did not have to be accounted for. Its men were everywhere, in the ministries, the universities, the armed forces, Government offices and big businesses in private ownership. The system, once set going, rapidly bred an intolerable atmosphere of doubt and fear on all sides. Worse, once going nicely, it went on working beautifully by itself, with no need even to invent anti-Government plots to justify its existence when real ones were lacking.

The Portuguese people had no protection against the PIDE. Whatever it wished to do, they were at its mercy. In my student days, when I was imprisoned at Caxias in 1947, I found a dozen men who had languished there for twelve or fifteen years. They had either never come up for judgement or, as was the case with most of them, received light sentences which had expired long before.

In Portugal the police cannot be wrong and therefore anyone held on a political charge is by definition guilty. Police enquiries actually suffice as proof, and defending lawyers may not interfere while they are being made. There is moreover no comparison between the treatment of political and non-political prisoners. The former are dealt with far more harshly. When imprisonment is followed by an indictment—though for most this hardly ever happens, given that unlimited remand is itself a punishment—this is pure formality, a mock-up designed only to confirm what the police have done.

During the first two decades of the regime the security police used to beat everybody as a matter of course, either to terrify their prisoners or the better to extract confessions. People of all classes, not excepting senior officers and former Government Ministers, underwent this degradation. Later on they became more subtle and preferred the statue torture, in which a man is forced to stand upright for days at a time, or the sleep torture, when he is forced to stay awake. On both procedures I have first-hand evidence. I saw my friend the lawyer Albano Cunha with monstrously bloated feet and body crumpled with exhaustion after twelve days of 'the statue' in Aljube prison. I have defended many clients who have suffered both and can vouch for the physical and moral effect produced. I have twice endured the sleep torture myself, being kept awake at a police-station for four consecutive days and nights. I managed not to give way, but it is diabolic. I know how it saps the will and destroys the personality. They put you in an empty room with a warder, who is relieved every four hours. All he does is prevent you from going to sleep and point out that you will be allowed no sleep until you have confessed. And it can go on for two or three weeks, according to the resistance of the individual, and end in confession or collapse.

Everything in a Portuguese prison is designed to make the

inmate feel isolated and forsaken. During preliminary enquiries, which may last six months (and before 1946 could have lasted almost indefinitely), he is entirely in the power of the police and the law has no intention of checking on what they do. Obviously, then, this is when the worst things happen. A man is held in solitary, close confinement, out of all possible touch with the outside world, his family, lawyer, relations or friends, or with other prisoners. From the warders he hears only a word or two a day when they bring his food or make their rounds. Books and newspapers are forbidden and he often has nothing to write on.

For many years, more or less from the beginning of the dictatorship until 1965 or so, the close-confinement cells were known as *curros* at Aljube and as *segredos* at Caxias. The *curros*, which Lord Russell has stated were unfit for human habitation, were without windows and never properly lit. They measured some seven feet by four and had double bars over the doors. The furniture consisted of a board with a palliasse and a couple of old blankets, one mug, one plate and one spoon. Thousands upon thousands of Portuguese have been in those nightmare places since the dictatorship. Some have gone mad there. Others, at the end of their tether, have paid so high a price as the betrayal of comrades in order to get out.

Until I had occasion to describe them in a defence speech at a political trial I had never seen these dens myself; as was only to be expected, I was in them shortly afterwards, for twenty-two days. I recall a policeman with a grim sense of humour who remarked, 'Next time you're on about the *curros* in court it'll all be first-hand stuff, anyway.'

The erosive work of the police in stamping out anti-Government activity and frightening most of the population away from political life was complemented by pre-publication censorship. Indeed, the two were interdependent. But for the censorship the misdeeds of the police would have been promptly denounced and become in time impossible; but for police terrorism, the nation would never have put up with the censorship.

Thanks to preliminary censorship, however, the Government keeps tight control of all the news media. Furthermore, it alters the news as it feels inclined. Not only can it stop the publication of certain items and of any comment on them, but it also decides on the headings and the amount of space that any given piece of news is to receive in the press or on the air. Public opinion on any event, at home or abroad, is, in other words, moulded by the censor's office which kindly helps the journalists to amend the articles submitted for inspection. So devotedly, indeed, do its minions add to and delete, alter and mess about with, that the final result will often baffle human understanding. Nor do they control press, radio and television only, but books, plays, films and shows of every kind as well, not forgetting recitals of classical poetry, the lyrics of *fado* songs, the small ads. and the social gossip in the newspapers.

There is no defence against the cuts and bans and closings down. The ultimate decision on such things rests with the Prime Minister. He is the Supreme Censor, from whom the rest take orders, and the rest are, most of them, officers or priests of lower-than-average culture. For years certain books were banned automatically, as were certain expressions, and even words, which were considered subversive, and the names of certain people could not be mentioned in any circumstances. They were paying the penalty of silence, undergoing the civil death to which, in general, all who opposed the regime were condemned without appeal.

Enough improbable tales and bizarre anecdotes exist about the Portuguese censorship to fill volumes. A land renowned for proud, unswerving orthodoxy has been known to make mincemeat of papal pronouncements, and even of encyclicals. Better still, there has been lopping and chopping of interviews with the dictator himself, since what is suitable for readers abroad is not necessarily good for the public at home.

Censorship and political police between them have had a debasing effect on the average man in Portugal; the same effect, in fact, as that of the Inquisition which undoubtedly caused a national decline from the sixteenth century onwards.

For future historians it will certainly explain the long continuance of Salazarism; a continuance paid for with the
nation's soul.

Salazar had been against the Spanish Republicans long
before the Civil War. He had demonstrated his sympathies
by giving every assistance to rebel army officers who came to
Portugal for refuge and was not niggling with aid when the
struggle was at its height. During the war he launched the
country into an anti-Red crusade which afforded splendid
opportunity for settling accounts with Republicans on his own
doorstep; and he raised the *viriatos* as an expeditionary force
of over 20,000 men to fight with Franco's troops under Botelho
Moniz.

Despite this unequivocal stand, however, he indulged in
non-intervention with consummate skill when it came to international affairs. The neutrality in question was a mere façade,
used by various of the great powers as a weapon with which
to crush the Spanish Republic, and while Salazar professed
himself neutral he knew well enough that the fate of his own
regime was bound up with that of Fascism in Spain.

The Nationalist victory was a death-knell for the democratic
opposition in Portugal, and it is true to say that Salazar ruled
as he pleased from 1939 to 1943, with no organised adversary
to worry about. Portugal was isolated from the free world,
shut in upon herself with the sea on one side and Franco
Spain on the other; and this was so throughout the Second
World War.

It was the dictator's boast that he, the architect of neutrality,
had averted from his country the horrors of that war, whereas
in fact it was Hitler's notion of strategy and the course of the
fighting that saved the whole Peninsula from Nazi invasion.
Moreover, he had played a double game. Portugal, with her
colonies in Africa, could not easily evade her obligations
towards Great Britain, her traditional ally, yet the regime was
ideologically much closer to the Axis, and he himself believed
almost to the end that Germany would win. The ambiguities
of the policy he later referred to as 'juridical neutrality' were

made plain in any case by such deplorable episodes as his failure to check the Japanese occupation of Timor.

After the Allied victory he tried to make the most of his services to England and America, with special emphasis on the cession of a naval base in the Azores. It is as yet virtually impossible to uncover every twist and turn of Portuguese diplomacy during the war, but Salazar swung back and forth between the Axis and the Allies as opportunism prompted, keeping all the time within the bounds of his British alliance and of the 1939 Iberian Pact with Spain, which was renewed on 29 July 1940, soon after the fall of France.

Some years ago, under the auspices of a committee presided over by the former Minister of War, Santos Costa, a White Paper on Government policy in the Second World War was issued by the Portuguese Foreign Office. Not surprisingly, it omits all reference to the strange case of General Marques Godinho. As Governor of the Azores during hostilities, the General received from Santos Costa, who was then in office, a whole series of letters giving details of military measures to be taken against the Allies. He was arrested later for conspiracy against the regime and in 1947 died mysteriously in prison. His lawyer, Adriano Moreira, then a protégé of Marcello Caetano, brought a charge of manslaughter against Santos Costa and was himself arrested as a result, at the same time as were Godinho's widow and son.[6]

I too was in prison just then and met him there. His story was that Santos Costa had got rid of the General in order to recover the correspondence, with its proof of the pro-German attitude of the Government. He was given several days in the *curros*. Then the case against Santos Costa was dropped and the PIDE having laid hands on the letters, Moreira, the son and the widow were released. Just how they laid hands on them

[6] Adriano Moreira's political career has been a varied one. He passed for a progressive in his student days and after the war drew nearer to the opposition democrats. But later he was Under-Secretary of State for the Colonies and Salazar made him Colonial Minister in 1961. He was once counted among the old dictator's possible successors and appears today as a leader of the 'ultras' of the extreme right.

is hard to say, but the General's son said it was Moreira who told them where to look. Certainly the latter's political opinions changed from one extreme to the other and he went to the Colonial Ministry before many years had passed.

No more than six months after Stalingrad, Salazar felt it expedient to cover himself in case the Allies won. Some say that he merely agreed to give freely what would have been forced from him had he raised the slightest objection; but be that as it may, in August 1943 he granted use of the bases in the Azores to England, thus ensuring her a wonderful strategic position in the Atlantic, and extended the same rights to the Americans at the end of the following year. Yet his sympathies never changed. He had the flags half-masted when Hitler died.

But that was a farewell gesture, his last tribute to the Nazi chief before setting about his great shift of policy. The Portuguese people might be unable to felicitate him as one of the victors, but he was going to show them how well they had done out of neutrality. Placing his own interpretation on the word 'collaborator', he now sought to convince the Allies that he, too, had collaborated, but with them. His point was that this collaboration had been more useful than anything he might have done by imitating the Republic on the previous occasion and putting an army in the field.

It was a sad and solemn Salazar who addressed the National Assembly on 8 May 1945. His subject was the end of the war and his speech a collector's item, short and grave. Twice he said, 'Let us bless the peace', and 'Let us bless the victory' once. He did bring himself to state that he rejoiced to count England—and England only did he mention—among the conquerors, winding up the discourse on a note of measured anxiety, with thanks to God and prayers for the new masters of the world in their desperate need of guidance.

Ten days later he delivered another speech to the same hearers. In it he asserted, quite seriously, that the one true version of democracy was that established by him in Portugal. We heard the term 'organic democracy' for the first time.

As the opposition slowly began to rally, Salazar, without

changing essentials, proceeded to adapt himself to the new climate and hastily to trick out his totalitarian regime in democratic colours. He had the support of sundry foreign Governments and of the Vatican under Pius XII, and no ideological scruples. On 7 October he asked the Portuguese people who, as he reminded them, did not like elections, to make the sacrifice and go to the polls, there to vote for the single-party candidates standing for the National Assembly. Voting, he explained, was an important duty; everyone should vote. And after a dictatorship of twenty years the avowed enemy of popular suffrage now undertook to hold free elections, 'as free as they are in the free land of England'.

All this the opposition believed. Not, of course, the glowing promises; but the opportunity seemed so splendid, so much in accord with the way the world was going, and they believed in that. They believed the Allies, with their talk of driving Fascism from the face of the earth. They believed that Salazarism would drop, like rotten fruit from the tree. And that was where they made their big mistake.

Chapter Three

Lost Opportunity

If there was a conviction in Portugal at the end of the war
that Allied victory meant the automatic overthrow of existing
institutions and the coming of democracy, the democratic
leaders, for their part, were sure that Salazar would not be
easy to get rid of. He would have to be forced out by violent
popular, military or foreign pressure.

Between May and August 1945, when hostilities were over
in Europe and the Far East respectively, the opposition made
active preparations. The three major powers were calling for
brotherhood-in-arms in a common cause, but the nations knew
nothing of the manœuvres of interest and influence the Allies
conducted so cautiously behind the diplomatic scene; nor had
Churchill at the Fulton conference yet sounded an alarm in
his famous words about the iron curtain that had fallen across
the continent, 'from Stettin on the Baltic to Trieste on the
Adriatic'.

The MUNAF was working underground, co-ordinating the
various sectors of the opposition. Its newspaper, which survived
for very few numbers, was significantly entitled *National
Liberation*. But already there were differences of opinion as to
how the liberation was to come about. Members of the old
Republican and Liberal parties, and the Socialists in general,
all agreed that the army, which had done so much to create
and to maintain the political situation, would have to be called
in to end it. The Communists on the other hand thought
military coups were dangerous things to play with and concentrated on working-class demands, hoping in this way to foment
a national anti-Fascist rising.

There was in fact a wave of strikes in 1944 and 1945 and

the workers had produced some remarkable leaders—men such as Alexandre Dinis, better-known as 'Alex', whom the police battered to death in the open street. The masses, however, remained to an extraordinary degree apathetic and unforthcoming, though this was hardly to be wondered at when savage lessons over the years had eventually taught the boldest to be prudent. Also, strikes were illegal and to cease work was, and still is, a crime that carries very heavy punishment. In the artificial scarcity at the end of the war, with speculation and a scandalous rationing system that left nobody short but the poor, the Communist Party could sponsor strikes on a fairly large scale. Jorge Botelho Moniz, who had commanded the *viriatos,* was in charge of reprisals in the Ribatejo, where several hundred strikers were arrested and penned like cattle in the bull-ring at Franca de Xira. But strikes in themselves were obviously not enough to start the process of bringing down the regime.

The Labour victory in Great Britain, with its promise of social advance and the transformation of the British Empire, brought new hope to the democrats in Portugal. I know with what tremendous joy I heard that Churchill's Government was out and Clement Attlee at the helm, for now, I thought, we should see how Socialism might be achieved by democratic methods, without going through the stage of proletarian dictatorship. Later, observing Ernest Bevin's foreign policy, especially his condonation of the Fascist regimes of the Peninsula (and ignorance of current events in Russia and in the people's democracies made this much harder to forgive), I was to revise my opinion of the Labour Party.

By now everyone believed that the regime was on the brink of collapse. The liberal professions, the army, Government officials, young people, even the more politically-minded of the working-class, spoke out almost openly against it. The feeling of fear had practically gone, although, of course, few except the Communists were victims of repression at that time.

The end of Salazarism nearly came with the big civilian and military plot of August 1945. This was headed by General Norton de Mattos, a former Masonic Grand Master and president of the MUNAF, and had supporters everywhere, including the District Commands of the army. We were on holiday at Luso, with messengers in and out of the house all day and my father busily occupied at the heart of the whole thing, for he was an old friend of the General, who trusted him completely.

Whether every political strand of the MUNAF was aware of what was happening I do not know. I rather think not, and should indeed be more inclined to say that the Military Committee in charge, under a senior officer named Miguel dos Santos, had no sort of contact with any of the political committees. There was even some attempt to keep the Communist Party out of the picture altogether, although one important group of officers involved was predominantly Communist.

At the very last, the venture misfired. There were unforeseen postings, hesitations, a failure of nerve on the part of the service leaders. Deep disappointment ensued, especially among the civilian element. And yet, paradoxically, this very disappointment was to give rise to the Movement for Democratic Union, the MUD.

Its principal promoters, Teófilo Carvalho Santos and Mário de Lima Alves, were both lawyers, and both had known of the August-September plot. When Salazar made a speech promising that candidates in the legislative elections might introduce and explain themselves and their policies to press and public, these two decided to try their luck and apply for permission to hold a public political meeting. This was a fairly simple aim, one might suppose, but it was a bold one for the time : to realise how bold it is enough to recall that there had not been a single legal anti-Government demonstration for twenty years. But Salazar had openly pledged those free elections, 'free as in the free land of England', so why not see whether he meant what he said? Such, at least, was their line of reasoning. Both men were under forty, members of the generation that had just gone up to university when the dictatorship began; that had taken part in strikes and protests and manifestations of every kind against Fascist rule; the generation that had seen the Spanish War. It had played no first-hand part under the First Republic but felt itself the heir of that Republic's patriotism and idealism and believed that the future of Portugal depended on the triumph of democracy.

The application, supported by a certain number of signatures, had by law to go before the civil authorities in Lisbon and signatures were not easy to obtain. This was the sort of thing which led—terrifying thought—to repercussions. In the end only eleven people agreed to put their names down, and nearly all of them belonged to the generation of which we have been speaking.

To the universal amazement, the request was granted and no immediate vengeance fell upon the signatories. All unbeknown, the country had entered upon what Salazar called a period of *liberdade suficiente*, or 'sufficient liberty'. Henceforth, once in every four years, the censorship was to be modified in the pre-election month and candidates would be allowed to appear as such in public, always provided that they did so separately and not in groups and made no use of banned political organisations. Once the time of sufficient liberty was over, the entire opposition was expected to vanish from the scene and the police would quell, forcefully, any attempt at resistance.

In forty-eight hours, not without difficulty, the organisers found a hall and someone willing to take the chair, and polished up the text of the propositions they wished to submit to the Government. As no theatre- or cinema-manager wanted to risk hiring his premises, they had to take the small hall at the Almirante Reis Republican Centre, which seated scarcely more than two hundred. Their chairman was Barbosa de Magalhães, a Minister under the First Republic and a Law professor at Lisbon until they retired him in 1940 for having disapproved the signing of the Concordat with Rome. Mário de Lima Alves made the one speech of the evening and introduced the petition, which was adopted by acclamation.

It took courage on the part of opposition sympathisers to attend that historic meeting on 8 October 1945. At the age of twenty, I was excited, fearful and enthusiastic all at once. There was an oppressive atmosphere; the secret police were posted round the place, visible and watching. The document Lima Alves read out was temperate to a degree. It criticised the dictatorship and put forward a list of minimum necessary conditions (never to be granted), for the holding of free elections. These were : freedom of the press, freedom of assembly and to disseminate propaganda, permission to found political parties or movements of a political nature, proper supervision of electoral registers and the counting of votes, and an amnesty for political offences. When the imperturbable voice went on to demand the suppression of the camp at Tarrafal a thunder of applause broke out. Everyone signed the petition at the end of the meeting.

When the press reports appeared next morning the country awoke from its long slumber. On all sides, in Portugal itself, in the Atlantic islands and in Africa people arranged gatherings, to keep the impulse going. With the less rigid censorship the papers had something interesting to say at last, especially the *República* and the *Diário de Lisboa,* which were snatched up as soon as they went on sale. In the Praça do Rossio in the middle of Lisbon the little newsboys were shouting, 'Salazar on toast! Salazar on toast!' at the tops of their voices. Unless one lived through that time and felt the general, popular enthusiasm, in the streets and at the opposition meetings, one can have no notion of just how strong the thirst for freedom was. Writers, professors, artists, scholars, intellectuals of every complexion, high officials and modest employees, signed the MUD membership lists by tens of thousands. Many of them told reporters quite openly that they wanted democracy, and the reporters published what they said. The nation was beginning to breathe, to show clearly that it did not want Salazar. These were bitter days for the regime and to the dictator, who had never acknowledged the faintest shadow of opposition to his own will, they must have brought one of the greatest disillusions of his life.

The Democratic Union flooded across Portugal in the course of a few days. Committees were set up spontaneously in every provincial capital, in the main towns and many villages. Recruits poured in and overwhelmed the eleven men who had called the original meeting at the Almirante Reis club. They were inundated. No one had any political training or experience, there was no nucleus of leaders, no legally-constituted political body in support. There was not even an office with typewriters and telephones. Everything had to be improvised.

A temporary headquarters was set up in Mário de Lima Alves's office in central Lisbon, and I went along with some of my friends to see what our student organisation could do. This was the beginning of the juvenile branch, the MUDJ, probably the largest youth movement in Portugal.

As the election campaign progressed it became unhappily obvious that Salazar was anything but willing to agree to the essential points set out in the MUD petition. Because of this the various opposition sectors decided they would advise people not to vote, and so invalidate the entire procedure by making it an utter farce. Time, they thought, must work for the democrats in any case.

Seen in the light of later events, this was not a good idea. In 1945 the electoral registers had not yet been finely combed by the police, while the great majority of public officials, in the psychological climate of that post-war period, were in favour of change and would have voted against the existing Government. Moreover, these being the first elections held by the dictator, the art of falsifying them had not come to its fine flower. At that stage, we might have got a few opposition deputies into the National Assembly, and—who knows?—have shaken the whole system.

But one thing Salazar understood a good deal better than did the still-deluded opposition, and that was the supposed need to legitimise the regime in the eyes of the Allied Governments. He knew perfectly well, in fact, that the Western Powers would never interfere in the affairs of Spain or Portugal. As far as they were concerned, any coat of whitewash would do so long as it deceived international observers and covered the hue of reactionary policies. Also, Salazar and Franco, mortified at having assisted the losers, seemed all the easier to manage these days, and ready to oblige the new lords of the universe without making too much fuss. The Western Governments demonstrated a terror of freedom and of what democracy might lead to in countries other than their own. They saw the period of political instability that was likely to follow the advent of democracy in Spain and Portugal as a threat to the strategic necessities of a world-policy based upon two rival power-blocs. In this they were mistaken, but in fear for the present they sacrificed the future of two nations. There now arose, to fit the circumstances, a suitable legend of Salazar the kindly despot, fatherly and moderate, whose rule might be a trifle antiquated, but who was austere and thrifty and careful for his subjects' well-being. Franco had to wait a year or so longer before he was forgiven, but they pardoned the Portuguese dictator.

Salazar was also very skilful in using any errors the opposition made, and one of the worst of these was when the MUD Central Committee stopped its propaganda meetings ten days after the campaign began. This grave miscalculation checked popular enthusiasm and gave the authorities a chance to recover. The MUD leaders had, it seems, been approached by high-ranking army officers, who offered to intervene and over-throw the Government if electioneering were brought to an end. There was also a rumour that Cunha Leal and Colonel Lelo Portela were planning a big public meeting in the bull-ring at Lisbon, and the MUD people were alarmed lest control should slip away from them. Naturally, too, they wished the opposition to acquire a name for good discipline. What was more, the former Prime Minister, Cunha Leal, happened to be the opposition's *bête noire* just then, accused of having flirted with reaction early on in the dictatorship and of disagreeing on certain points with the PRP Republicans and the *Seara Nova* Socialists.

Another much-commented mistake had a catastrophic effect on public opinion, though the MUD leaders were not in this instance to blame. As we have seen, the Almirante Reis petition evoked support from its first reading, and names poured in during the days that followed. The MUD leaders were very proud of this fact and vainly asked the President of the Republic, old General Carmona, to set up a caretaker administration which should guarantee the freedom and unbiased conduct of the elections. For the first time ever, anti-Government spokesmen were officially received by the President, who seemed undecided and apprehensive. To give the request more weight, the Democratic Union then informed the press that its supporters already numbered 50,000 in Lisbon alone, which was quite true. It was this statement that Salazar exploited for his own ends like a cunning and unscrupulous politician, thus doing the opposition a great deal of harm.

With the assistance of General Júlio Botelho Moniz, he contrived to cast doubt on the figures quoted. Botelho Moniz, Minister of the Interior and brother of the *viriato* chief, did useful work by affirming at an election meeting that neither bullets nor ballot-papers would bring the regime down, and going on to suggest that the lists of MUD supporters be taken to his ministry for checking. The leaders of the MUD, fearing that the lists would be impounded, tried to deposit them with the Public Prosecutor, who refused to accept them. Considering it vital to offer public proof of their following, they then asked for safeguards before leaving them with the Ministry.

Mário de Castro, their lawyer for the occasion, obtained all possible undertakings from the authorities before he parted with the lists, but they were valueless. Without scruple, the Government went behind his back. The first victim was Colonel Plinio Silva, who, although serving in the Azores, was at once relieved of duty. The same sort of thing was soon happening to others in every walk of life and the process continued for years. All of us whose signatures were found were summoned in turn to face a long interrogation at the Ministry, two main objects of officialdom being to scare the opposition and let it be seen how much was known to the political police.

A number of MUD committees up and down the country later refused to produce their membership lists and an insidious campaign against the Lisbon committees hinted that the latter had deliberately betrayed their supporters. This was utter nonsense. The Lisbon lists were signed to help the cause and solemn safeguards had been given when they were handed over. It was the Government that acted so despicably.

The elections took place in November 1945, the entire opposition abstaining. In due course, with banging of drums and blowing of trumpets, official victory was announced. And a most peculiar victory, too, for the National Assembly still consisted, as it had done since the dictatorship began, of 120 deputies, all of the single party and all unconditionally creatures of Salazar. The farce was unlikely to deceive many onlookers.

Some days before the Government had reapplied its stranglehold to the press, and the censors were implacably at work again. The joys of *liberdade suficiente* were postponed to the next election. The rich went tranquilly on, treating the country as one large private estate; the opposition returned to its long calvary, to the hopes disappointed and the battles lost. As for the people, they resigned themselves to the fact that they either had to live in their own land as though under foreign occupation or emigrate *en masse*.

The anti-Government men disappeared into prison one by one, but the nation was by now anaesthetised and their cries of anguish could not in any way disturb its conscience. The curtain of silence dropped over Portugal.

Chapter Four

Unconquered Opposition

During our first instalment of 'sufficient liberty', which ended with the elections of November 1945, Salazar had once again displayed his lack of flexibility in politics, and how completely incapable he was of envisaging any kind of Government except dictatorship. He had proved, in fact, that he would never, for any reason, compromise. The opposition meanwhile was constrained as usual to be quiet, although, as the MUD campaign had shown, it represented the majority of the population and the cream of the intellectuals.

In the post-war climate and a country which, like Portugal, belonged geographically to the so-called free world, this situation seemed impossible. Few people admitted it could last when parties were being reconstituted all over Western Europe, and those of the various oppositions accommodated with the rest in the workings of democracy.

But in Portugal the severity of the Government put its opponents in an awkward situation. Sufficient liberty had been turned off like a tap, the press was gagged, the improvised offices of the Democratic Union shut down. How, then, could we legally continue the fight? Most of us thought the authorities would have to allow the opposition some sort of semi-legal standing. In the meantime, the committees formed by the MUD at national level refused to dissolve when the elections were over, for they felt their responsibility was to uphold claims that were still unanswered.

The political commissions which the MUNAF, as we have seen, set up before the end of the war were a pointless duplication, since they and the MUD committees were often run by the same people. The MUNAF, paralysed by internal squabbles as to what should be done and reluctant to work for out-and-out revolution, was to dwindle and die away round about 1949. And yet the MUD, as a quasi-legal body struggling for official recognition and therefore limiting itself to purely political ends, was justified only in so far as it could co-exist with a powerful underground, united and capable of oversetting the regime by violence.

Once a Government blocks every way in which it may be legally replaced there remains no alternative to violence of some kind, the *coup d'état*, the military putsch or the popular rising. The fact that the MUNAF was unfitted for such things reduced the MUD to a mere civil movement. It gave up, and wasted, its own cadres to feed the flames of opposition, but could not hope to be effective in the realm of practical action.

Some of my fellow-students and I, having joined the MUD, now set about forming groups of supporters in all the institutes and colleges of Lisbon. We also founded the MAUD, or Academic Movement for Democratic Union, and were going to hold a public meeting in one of the Lisbon theatres. The Government forbade this at the last moment, but the *Seara Nova* review brought out a special number with the text of the principal resolutions that would have been read out and adopted. It was during preparations for this meeting that I met the Democratic Union leaders, chief among them Bento de Jesus Caraça, a professor at the university, where his enormous political and moral prestige and unaffectedly compelling personality gave him a natural ascendancy over us all. He died in 1948, but was without doubt one of the most important influences upon me in the three formative years of our acquaintance.

It was necessary to co-ordinate activities in the three Portuguese universities into a single movement and we began the task with a two-day session at Coimbra : two days that left me horrified at the miserable, if not actually sordid, conditions in which most of the students there were living.

It did not take us long to realise the limitations of a university movement; students, after all, were a very small proportion of the youth of the country. On the other hand, the MUD committees knew of young workers nearly everywhere who wanted to meet and join us.

This being so, we decided to change the MAUD into the Youth Branch of the Democratic Union—the MUDJ—and to welcome democratically-minded youth of any ideology or social class. We summoned delegates to the capital from almost every region and, more or less secretly, arranged a conference attended by some forty young people, at which I presided. The reports we adopted on the living conditions of the younger generation were the most complete and objective study of the subject ever made up to that time in Portugal.

This conference elected a Central Committee, the members, of whom I was one, being nearly all students : Francisco Zenha from the Law Faculty at Coimbra, Júlio Pomar and Rui Grâcio, reading respectively Fine Arts and Literature at Lisbon, Mário Sacramento, a Coimbra medical student, Fidelino Figueiredo, also from Lisbon where he was studying Economics, and José Borrego, who read Architecture at Oporto. There were in addition a workman named Oscar dos Reis and a clerk from a business-house, Octávio Rodrigues Pato. The formation of Young Workers' Committees also went rapidly ahead nearly everywhere in Portugal.

In this the moving spirit was certainly Octavio Pato, an intelligent man with a flair for organisation and an inspiring devotion to the job. He was about my own age and came from Vila Franca, where he had been out on strike in 1944. When he joined us he agreed to work full-time for the movement— as, indeed, most of us did, while being students to all appearances. I installed him in my father's school, where he could be sure of food and lodging, and the two of us made a useful team in the early days of the MUDJ.

Later, in 1947, when the police arrested our Central Committee, Octavio Pato slipped through the net and went underground as a regular Communist : he had belonged to the party since boyhood. He was caught in 1962, by which time he was one of its officials, and tortured viciously. They kept him without sleep for twelve days and treated him with great brutality in the intervals of prolonged interrogation. But he behaved like a hero in prison and told them nothing. Despite our political differences, he asked me to defend him and the case was a landmark in the history of political trials in Portugal, for international observers were present when sentence was read and facts had come out about the methods used on prisoners by the PIDE.

Unlike the *Mocidade Portuguesa*, which was an artificial creation of the state, run by adult soldiers and civilians, the MUDJ was a spontaneous movement whose impulse came from the young themselves. It was also a unitary movement which struck root and became a forcing-ground for political leaders. There were very few who ever let it down. Some, perhaps, may have lost heart, but most carried on the struggle in face of all kinds of hazard—of gaol, or legal proceedings or economic pressure.

Several years later the MUDJ was accused of being a Communist off-shoot pure and simple, but although many of its leaders were *de facto* linked with the Communist Party, I can deny categorically that it was anything of the kind. And while it is true that an essential part of its energies came from that party, there were other sources, too. Those who controlled the MUD had just as much influence. Most of the members, indeed, subscribed to no definite ideology but were merely united against Fascism. In 1947 they had a dreadful time when a savage drive was launched against the MUDJ and hundreds of young people were arrested, interrogated and hunted down without mercy.

It fell to me to present the political report on general organisation at one of our congresses. We had come a long way already and made astonishing progress, and the report filled nearly 300 pages. It began with an over-all sketch of the position of youth in Portugal in its various economic, social and political aspects, then traced the main lines of our programme. Once amended and accepted, this document was to be published and the day before my own arrest I handed it for safekeeping to an economics student whom I knew, in case I went to prison. When I came out a few months later it was to learn that my friend had burned the whole thing in a fit of panic; a sad end for the record of all we had been doing for two and a half years!

MUDJ representatives sat on every local committee of the Democratic Union as liaison between the two bodies. The latter movement, it will be remembered, had been improvised in the space of a month and its provisional headquarters, shut down by the police after the elections, were spartan indeed : no staff, temporary or permanent, and not even the simplest office equipment. What little we had came from voluntary contributions and those in charge all had full professional lives to lead. It was for these reasons that we, the students, were called upon to be the backbone of the movement and to do constant practical work, aided in the task by some of the Workers' Committees, most of which were in Lisbon.

I was the first representative of the Youth Branch on the Lisbon District Committee, whose original chairman was Magalhães Godinho. He was succeeded by Gustavo Soromenho who, together with Antonino de Sousa, and the militant Communist Anibal Bizarro—the latter recently released from Tarrafal—was the real creator of Workers' Committees in the capital. These groups were organised according to occupations —railwaymen, building-workers, metal-workers, tram drivers, office employees and so on—with a devoted membership running into tens of thousands.

Apart from the Workers' Committees, the real foundation-units of the MUD were the District Committees. Others, too, sprang into being, formed voluntarily by women, artists, writers, economists, members of the legal profession, or by doctors. Among many more, there was a committee for the assistance of political detainees.

The Democratic Union's first big demonstration after the elections of November 1945, took place in Lisbon on the following 31 January, close to the Institute of Higher Technology and not far from the monument to the President of the First Republic, António José de Almeida. The procession set off, headed by an orderly body of students, to reach the National Assembly, but the police intervened brutally to prevent us. The political significance of this demonstration was clearly not lost upon authority and served, I believe, as pretext for renewed attacks against the MUD. Open repression would have been difficult, given the international situation just then, and a steady stream of blows at the vital spots of our organisation was presented as a campaign against Communist infiltration.

The original Central Committee was unprepared to wage a long war of attrition with the Government in defence of its legality; also Lima Alves, until now leader of the movement, was himself at war with nearly all his political allies over the proposed policy of most of the committees. But soon after, the delegates met and voted by a large majority that the Democratic Union should continue its activities as before, while adapting itself to the new conditions of struggle wished on it by the Government. That is to say, being neither banned nor recognised : there was a mere acceptance of our existence, coupled with unobtrusive never-ending harassment. All things considered, it was decided to choose a new Central Committee and here again I was the MUDJ member. The chairman was Mário de Azevedo Gomes, a professor of Agriculture who had held office under the First Republic.

There was a great deal of negotiation between the different sectors of the opposition before that committee was formed. Its members did not, properly speaking, sit as political delegates, since the MUD was a non-party union of the whole opposition, but they nevertheless enjoyed the confidence of various anti-regime parties and schools of thought. Bento Caraça, Manuel Mendes, Maria Isabel Aboim Inglês and Tito de Moraís were independent progressives closely connected with the MUNAF; Mayer Garção and Lobo Vilela represented Socialist opinion through the Socialist Union; Luciano Serrão de Moura was a Communist, replacing the writer Alves Redol, who had been the party's first spokesman with the MUD; Helder Ribeiro, another former Minister of the old Republic, was very near to the PRP, and Alberto Dias was a working-class Anarchist and had been an important figure in the General Confederation of Workers, banned since 1934. With a Catholic or a Christian Democrat we should have been complete, but the Catholics at this point were either lying low or supporting the Government.

The Central Committee began to function in June 1946 and for nearly two years, until the MUD was officially suppressed in March 1948, practically ran the entire opposition. There was unanimity among its members, despite their differences of ideology and temperament. They stood solidly together, all of them, at one in politics and united by personal friendship. Seldom can any opposition group have accomplished so much or got on so well.

We had at least one meeting a week, a sort of Shadow Cabinet to discuss what the Government did and prepare detailed reports on public administration. Much of what we produced was issued during the election campaign of General Norton de Mattos in 1949.

To assist the Central Committee there was a permanent Economics Committee which, under our auspices, investigated the workings of the corporative system. Their report laid bare the weaknesses and inconsistencies of the, still uncompleted, system the Government was imposing on the country, and included memoranda on ways and means of solving the economic problems of the nation. There was as yet no official Development Plan—the first version of that was to come in 1953—and no one in the Government dreamed of sponsoring any such policy. Salazar himself failed to see that industrialisation was needed. Deaf to all suggestions, he even said no to Marshall Aid.

In August or September of 1946 he applied for admission to the United Nations. The MUD Central Committee thereupon drew up a lengthy paper in which it analysed the record of the regime and declared, in essence, that only under a democratic Government had Portugal any right to join. This met with much approval in the General Assembly of the UN, but at home the Government reacted quickly. First, with the connivance of the censorship, there was a press campaign in the *Diário da Manhã*, official organ of the one authorised party, on the theme of high treason, always reserved for serious occasions. Next the police went into action and the eleven people who had signed the offending document—the entire Central Committee of the MUD—were arrested, judged and indicted. We were let out on the enormous bail of 100,000 escudos each, and the case against us was to go on for years. The most distinguished members of the Lisbon bar took part and many of the leading personalities of Portugal were called to give evidence. It was dropped at last during a political amnesty : the Government's usual way of cutting the Gordian knot when a trial grew too embarrassing.

Yet the Committee went on with its work despite its tangles with the law. Hundreds of circulars were sent out to branches all over the country, in the Azores, Madeira and the colonies. Any national event was criticised in detail as a matter of course. Equally as a matter of course, no word of what we wrote ever got into the papers, but we managed to distribute it ourselves.

The customary persecutions began again soon enough. Professors Mário de Azevedo Gomes and Bento Caraça, our chairman and vice-chairman, lost their university positions, and official intolerance produced ever more tension among the people of Portugal.

In October 1946 there occurred at Oporto the revolutionary attempt known as the Mealhada Revolt. It was led by Lieutenant Fernando Queiroga, who persuaded the armoured troops stationed there to join him. My father was deeply involved in this plot, which covered the central and northern parts of the country. But the other centres failed to rise and the armoured column which had done so turned south and ended up by surrendering at Mealhada, near Coimbra.

The following April, with key-men in the various barracks ready and waiting for action, another attempted insurrection collapsed at the eleventh hour. This was 'the 10 April Revolt' and among the many officers implicated were two Generals, Marques Godinho and Ramires, both of them war-time governors of the Azores, and an Admiral,

Mendes Cabeçadas, who had been one of the leaders on 28 May 1926 and first President of the Republic under the military dictatorship. Having nipped this conspiracy in the bud, the Government was able to lay its hands on numbers of senior officers as well as civilians by the dozen, including my father, who was then seventy. 1947 was in fact a most disturbed year altogether. There was working-class unrest in several parts of the country, primarily in Lisbon, where a strike at the naval dockyard in April set off a series of stoppages in the industrial district. Crisis hit the anti-Government students at the university when first the members of their Lisbon Academic Committee were arrested, then those of the Central Committee of the MUDJ. A resultant protest at the Medical School was quelled, ungently, by the police. Thirty or so university professors were dismissed and I myself spent four and a half months between the prisons of Aljube, Caxias and the Penitenciária of the capital. The MUDJ Central Committee, unlike that of the MUD, declined to be let out on bail. A case was opened against us and when I was released, towards the middle of August, my father had been in gaol for close on three months. Our family had to endure a dreadful time and my mother, though she bore it all with great courage, suffered more than anyone else.

I went back to working for the MUDJ, which was in the midst of reorganisation, and for the Democratic Union, still battling to establish its legality.

In 1948 we decided to celebrate the anniversary on 31 January with another demonstration to which all the MUD committees were invited and, through them, all the people of Lisbon. When the day came round we were every one of us arrested in our homes in the small hours of the morning and taken off to police headquarters. Here time went on and as they were evidently hesitating as to what to do with us, we suggested sending out for some food. This being permitted, we found ourselves lunching in republican sociability in the very citadel of the PIDE.

When dessert came round Professor Azevedo Gomes rose to his feet and said, with deep emotion, 'In what better place, on this anniversary day, could we have shown our unalterable loyalty to the cause of liberty?' Nobody had noticed the loud-speaker hanging on the wall, but from it a voice immediately yelled,

'You can take the lot of them off to Aljube! Now! Get going!'

And so the complete committee went to the cells for a month's enforced holiday; a fairly peaceful month, only slightly marred by worry lest our former heavy bail should now be forfeit. In the prison we encountered many of the Republicans arrested after the abortive rising of 10 April, my father among them. On our release at the beginning of March the police informed us that the MUD was to be suppressed once and for all.

In a dictatorship the legality or otherwise of any political party really depends on the relative strengths of Government and opposition. In the first years of the Democratic Union's existence the Government was compelled, by the international situation and the atmosphere within Portugal itself, to show some degree of tolerance, and of this the opposition did its best to take advantage. But if authority feared to apply its curbs too blatantly, it also sought to limit its concessions. This balance lasted until April 1947. Encouraged by success, the opposition risked launching a frontal attack, with increased popular pressure, lightning strikes, economic claims in indus-trial and rural areas, student protest, agitation among the intellectuals—the policy of the putsch. It was the failure of all these measures, together with changes in the international situation, that led the Government to pass to undisguised oppression.

We could, therefore, do nothing about the banning of the MUD. At the time I thought we could, but must admit that no one on the Central Committee agreed with me. Now, in the light of later experience, I see that we acted for the best, since out-and-out resistance could only have meant the end of us and of the trained personnel it had cost so much to assemble and form.

Before our joint arrest, however, we had already begun

preparations for the presidential election, due to be held in 1949.

The idea of General Norton de Mattos as opposition candidate for the Presidency came originally from António Macedo and was put forward by the Oporto branch on the grounds that here was someone likelier than most to attract all shades of anti-Government opinion. Personally, I should have preferred Professor Mário de Azevedo Gomes, whom I had known on the MUD Central Committee, but the General enjoyed organised political support, and that meant that things would not be too difficult, despite the ban on the MUD. Our objectives would be unaltered, only the label would change. We accordingly went ahead with our campaign arrangements, using the Democratic Union framework to set up election committees for the General. But the welding together of the various elements of the opposition was to prove harder than we thought.

Our first complications came from the PRP, the Republican Party to which, in theory, the candidate himself belonged and which was against having anything to do with falsified elections. But the General, still at eighty a man of driving energy and a marvellously clear thinker, brushed these objections aside. In his view the opposition entered its protest by the very fact of taking part. He could not agree to stand, however, unless assured that the attitude of the PRP was far from being shared by most of the Democratic-Social Directive and one-time Ministers and deputies of the First Republic. Professor Caraça, his right-hand man, therefore asked four of us to make a motor-tour of the country to muster the support of the leading members of the PRP for the candidature. It was an exhausting assignment as it turned out, but we came back with the signatures of all the Republican bigwigs, and Norton de Mattos accepted nomination.

António Sérgio was among those who thought the opposition should have found a man whose links were not with the past, however glorious, who would not be so inescapably identified with the First Republic. They would have preferred some

non-political serving soldier, unassociated with the days before
Salazar, as a better instrument for dividing the regime.

On the Government side the election raised just as many
difficulties. Marcello Caetano, chairman of the National Union,
the one and only official party, was supposed openly to favour
Salazar's becoming President, since this would naturally mean
the appointment of a new Prime Minister and the settling of
the succession problem. Had this happened, the regime would
have evolved gradually on constitutional lines resembling those
of the Fifth Republic in France. But Salazar, fearful as ever
of losing power, showed himself unresponsive to evolutionary
ideas of any sort.

President Carmona might be old and ailing; he might not
always see eye to eye with his Prime Minister, but he had
obligations to the regime and Salazar had no wish to dislodge
him. Rumour spoke of a hold he had over the President, of
an unexplained murder case hushed up—the famous Uceda
affair which had never been solved and in which one of
Carmona's daughters was said to have been implicated.

But if Salazar desired a man of straw in the President's
chair, this particular President and his nearest colleagues
offered a spectacle of bodily and mental abatement that verged
on the grotesque. Azevedo Gomes and I, presenting one of our
many petitions, saw him, surrounded by ancient soldiers and
civilians, at the palace of Belem. The impression of sheer
senility was quite appalling.

We established election offices for Norton de Mattos on the
first floor at his own modest address, but real work started in
late autumn, after the holidays. Then we got down to it,
in October-November 1948. The recognised campaign period
would not come round, of course, until a month before the
actual election, which was fixed for the following February.
The General put me in charge, and with willing aid from
the MUDJ we organised a kind of secretariat to keep in touch
with branch committees and do all there was to do. Professor
Azevedo Gomes was in charge of the political side and, our
candidate's personal opinions being what they were, his task
was not an easy one. He wrote most of the manifesto setting

forth the General's programme and it met with unanimous approval from the opposition. From Monarchists to Communists, they all agreed with it, those of no particular party or doctrine as much as our dissidents or the handful of Catholics in our ranks.

The initial spade-work was done in an atmosphere of semi-secrecy. We could issue no printed material because of the censorship and had no money for our simplest needs. At first Norton de Mattos wanted to circularise an appeal for funds to the richer supporters of the opposition but when this came to nothing we evolved the slogan, 'Give an Escudo for our Campaign' and the contributions, mostly anonymous, from ordinary folk, covered the essential costs. Our basic campaign text, printed on the posters beneath Júlio Pomar's portrait of the General, was, 'I stand for an opposition unconquered and unconquerable'. The phrase became legendary.

Norton de Mattos was rightly the symbol of an opposition that never went back on its principles and never acknowledged the dictatorial regime. Persecuted, arrested, driven into exile, deprived of his chair at the Institute of Higher Technology, he stuck to his beliefs and remained unfalteringly a patriot. He was without doubt one of the great men of the First Republic and had the necessary breadth and scope to be a Head of State. A pioneer in Angola, he had favoured the entry of Portugal into the First World War. He had been Ambassador in London, holder of high Masonic office and a determined plotter against dictatorship in all its forms, from the time of Sidónio Paes to that of Salazar.[1] Wide experience had given him a profound acquaintance with men and circumstances; he was as brave as a lion besides, could charm anyone when he felt like it and was endowed with a sense of humour and a relish for life unusual at his age. His over-riding interest was Africa, and the part the Portuguese could play there. He alone, perhaps, had foreseen the colonial problems in wait for us after the Second World War and he was certainly alone in realising how urgent was a policy of liberal reform. He didn't

[1] Sidónio Paes became dictator in 1917, and exiled Norton de Mattos. Trans.

know what an inferiority complex was and bore no ill will for the years of ostracism he had suffered from the earliest days of the regime. On the contrary, he looked down upon the politicians in power, beginning with Salazar, as on a collection of pigmies. He, better than anyone else, knew them for what they were.

For me, young and inexperienced, daily contact with a man like this was a continual education. But dazzled as I was by the General's personality, I remained less happy about his political behaviour. The candidature was, in his view, the culmination of his political career, a last service rendered to the country, and my comrades and I could not always accept his personal notions and tactics. To us the campaign was just one more chapter in a tale that began before the days of the Democratic Union and which would go on when the election was over. All this led to misunderstandings, especially towards the end, in spite of the unfailing trust and friendship that he showed me.

To break the silence surrounding our introductory work, Tito de Morais thought that something on the lines of Salazar's famous 'spontaneous' demonstrations might be a good idea, and so one night we booked half the seats at the National Theatre. Norton de Mattos sat in a box and was hailed and wildly applauded by his partisans as the lights went up for the first interval, the rest of the audience joining in. In the second interval, of course, there were plain-clothes PIDE and armed police all over the place, but no disturbances. The *Diário da Manhã*, organ of 'the' party, remarked tartly next day how very odd it was that so many opposition sympathisers happened to choose the same night to go to the same play. . . .

Before the campaign began, the trial of the conspirators in the plot of 10 April opened at the Santa Clara lawcourts in Lisbon and many distinguished adversaries of the regime came forward with their evidence. It was as though the regime itself were in the dock, as though there were being revealed a kind of common front against Salazarism in which even the President seemed to be included. One of the civilian defendants, Correira Santos, told how he had mentioned the impending military plot to Senhora Carmona, whose dislike of Salazar was proverbial. Her reply had been, 'Well, keep up the good work! I'll get on a horse and lead it if you want me to.'

Throughout the hearing one was conscious of the army's latent hostility towards the War Minister. Vindictive in the extreme, General Santos Costa had evoked as much, if not more, hatred among the professional soldiers by his unjust and high-handed proceedings than had the dictator himself.

I took General Norton de Mattos to the court to give evidence for my father at this trial. His speech was a masterly political indictment of the regime and the reception accorded him before he made it was, in fact, his first public occasion as presidential candidate. The assembled lawyers rose to their feet in respect as he entered, the defendants followed their example; then the public rose; and the judges, taken by surprise, did as they saw others do.

The campaign on his behalf was probably the least improvised electoral activity we ever undertook. Thanks to the MUD groups we had accumulated many detailed reports on the regime, the more easily obtained since some of our people were officials with access to confidential information. The whole thing therefore got off to a flying start, so much so that for the first fortnight the public expected an opposition victory and what Salazar later spoke of as a 'constitutional *coup d'état*'. But this was mere illusion. The repressive instruments of the Government were still in working order. It had its police and its Republican Guard, it could still censor news and manipulate elections, and all the cogs of the administrative machinery were properly oiled.

Nevertheless, the people of Portugal responded eagerly and fervently to the opposition's call, and this is remarkable when we remember that only three times between 1945 and 1970 were they really aroused: in 1945, over the MUD; now in 1949 for Norton de Mattos; and again for Delgado in 1958. Never before had there been anything resembling a tidal wave that looked like sweeping all before it. Compared with this, other opposition movements, even the biggest, were sporadic and limited to certain classes only.

The assemblies on behalf of the General in Oporto, Evora and Beja showed how deeply the anti-Salazarist feeling ran. Thousands of people would travel for miles and stand in endless lines to watch and applaud him driving by, as they did on the road from Evora to Beja. His car was slowed to a walking-pace and I can see one ragged woman now, sticking her head in at the window and shouting, 'Go on, old boy, get that bloody Salazar off our backs!' She was the very image of poverty and revolution and she spoke for the vast majority of the Portuguese.

And for a week or so Norton de Mattos did represent the possibility of a non-violent return to freedom. Every level of society, from intellectuals to businessmen and workpeople and the nameless, faceless folk of town and country—all were looking forward together.

Authority tried to damp this national feeling down. Demonstrations had to be held on enclosed premises, it impeded election-meetings with ever more form-filling and pettifoggery, took the microphones out of public halls, mutilated published notices. Arrests were made; people who came to hear us had their tyres punctured, as mine were at Loulé in the Algarve. Often our speakers could not get a word out.

One gathering, of all I attended, I shall never forget, a youth-meeting in the Avenida Theatre at Coimbra. It was packed to the doors, the one small space left empty being the box reserved for the official agents of law and order, on this occasion a lieutenant of the Republican Guard with an assistant. The shouts of 'Norton! Norton!' were mingled with cheers for my friend Zenha, perpetual idol of the Coimbra students.

I had come from Lisbon with a party and was representing the General, at his own request. A Government order forbade election-meetings to go on after midnight and when time was running out before all the speakers had had their say I turned to our official watch-dog (who was nobody I had ever seen before), and asked for half an hour's extension. The hitherto noisy audience froze in their places and a menacing quiet descended. The man thought a little, hesitated a little, and finally said yes. I called for applause at once and they all blazed into life again. The sequel came a year or so later when I was under arrest at the PIDE headquarters and heard from the second-in-command of that force, José Sachetti, that it was he who had been on duty at Coimbra that night : our unexpected hand-claps apparently got him into serious trouble.

As the campaign went on it became clearer that the Government was not going to yield an inch over the minimum safeguards which our candidate demanded if the opposition were to participate in the election. As well as by the intolerable activities of the censorship and the police, we were worried about falsification of the registers and in the counting of the votes. The National Union had copies of the electoral registers and policemen to deliver its voting-papers from door to door. The opposition papers, on the other hand, could not even be supplied in the regulation form or colour and were most difficult to distribute for the simple reason that, having no registers to work from, we did not know the names and addresses of those who were qualified to vote. And, by yet another Government artifice, voting-papers are not available at the polling-stations in Portugal.

Our candidate was pledged to withdraw if the minimum safeguards were not granted, and on this our whole campaign depended. We had no desire to take part in some electoral farce that would serve to legitimise the regime in the eyes of the world. Since Salazar persisted in yielding nothing, abstention it would have to be.

However, as the campaign proceeded, a great many of our supporters, misled by the crowded public meetings, favoured participation on any terms. To withdraw altogether, they said, would be too big a jolt to public opinion; better to get the nation to the polls and then demonstrate the fraudulence of the count. Norton de Mattos himself, especially after a tour in the Alentejo and a second meeting in Oporto, frankly inclined to their way of thinking.

But this was not the only rift among us. Towards the end of the campaign some of the General's adherents, and he with them, began to hesitate, far more seriously, over our united opposition front. The Government's main argument all these weeks had been the peril of Communism if the opposition won. Earlier on, the alarm had been Freemasonry, with posters of Norton de Mattos in his Grand Master's regalia, complete with apron; but this backfired when a *liceu* teacher named Rodrigues Direito revealed in a sensational speech that more than one pillar of the regime, including President Carmona and the Minister of National Economy, Ulisses Cortês, had been Masons too. After that, Communist peril seemed the more rewarding line to take, particularly as the Cold War in Europe was just then redoubling in intensity. To the mass of the people, groaning under Fascism, poverty and lack of human rights, such propaganda meant very little, but there were moderate sections of the opposition who hated Communism quite as much as Fascism, and among these it did have some effect. The *Diário de Notícias* came out at this juncture with a series of contemptible articles by the former Minister, Armindo Monteiro, with allegations of a Communist plot, financed, he said, by Italy. The Church, whose hierarchy was so disgracefully involved with the regime, played a large part in the witch-hunt that followed. Articles by Tomaz da Fonseca on the political implications of the miracle of Fatima offered, for instance, an ideal opportunity for exploiting people's religious faith and turning them against the opposition.[2]

Norton de Mattos sensed the danger here and tried to avoid it by somehow getting round the pledges he had made. He consulted his close friends, my father among them, as to what would happen if he set the previous unanimity aside and produced a strictly anti-Communist manifesto instead. This was the course urged on him by some of his District Committees, including that of Lisbon, and by certain of the moderate opposition leaders. They pointed out that a military putsch

[2] Many Catholics today doubt the religious validity of the miracle of Fatima, but its political implications are certainly beyond question. The traditionalist element of the Church had used it as a weapon against the Republic and, later, as an essential part of the anti-Communist crusade.

might well ensue, since fear of Communist pressure was all that held the army back from intervening against Salazar.

It fell to me to play a key part in this backstairs drama. From my father I knew of the General's intentions and felt obliged to warn Azevedo Gomes and the Central Committee of what was going on. The great majority would never understand the new manifesto. It would lead to public division in our ranks and betray the bonds and promises agreed on during our campaign preliminaries. Worst of all, it would mean that we had done what we should never do and bowed to the propaganda of the other side, baseless as it was. With the help of Professor Barbosa de Magalhães I managed to argue our candidate round.

As the police were pressing us harder and harder and we needed to mend our schism once and for all, we called a national meeting of delegates at the Republican centre in the Avenida António José de Almeida in Lisbon. It was a dramatic occasion. Norton de Mattos, in the chair, favoured taking part in the election even though our minimal conditions had not been agreed to, but most of the Central Committee argued against him and finally he had to give in.

There were only a few days left to the end of the campaign. The General went off to nearby Estoril, then home to Ponte da Lima in the north. From there he sent us, for publication, a deeply pessimistic statement to the effect that all hope of saving Portugal was dead, so far as he could see, for many years to come. The last forty-eight hours were spent in burning the office records, with the PIDE outside the building, waiting to pounce. There was a terrible end-of-the-party feeling. When this party was over we knew that Salazar would neither forgive nor forget, and his methods of revenge were anything but pretty.

The farcical election on 11 February aroused little popular interest. The PIDE men entered my house at dawn on the 13th. They had arrested me more than once in my bed by now and I had learned to keep a few things handy. I got away clad in pyjamas, found a taxi and took refuge with a friend. We heard during the morning that our principal campaign-organisers had been picked up, as well as hundreds of peasants in the Alentejo and Ribatejo regions, and some dozens of workers in Lisbon and Oporto.

I had to appear that afternoon to answer charges as a member of the MUDJ Central Committee, and so went peacefully to court and was duly arrested at the door. It marked the beginning of a very difficult time.

Chapter Five

Cold War

From 1949 onwards Portugal, a member of the North Atlantic Treaty Organisation, set about making herself presentable as a full partner among the nations of the West. The Cold War was on and it saved Salazar.

But the Portuguese democrats, divided and ill-informed, felt once again betrayed, without knowing quite who to blame for their unhappy situation. Some took one view, some another. Shut away, forgotten by the outside world (Simone de Beauvoir gives a most unsympathetic portrait of them in *Les Mandarins*), under the heel of an implacable dictatorship to which everyone was turning a blind eye, and powerless to do anything practical against it, those who opposed the Government did so in bitterness and impotence.

In 1949, during this more than usually trying phase, I went to prison for a fourth time. This meant, of course, that I could not take my degree. I entered Aljube gaol at the age of twenty-four in the unpleasing knowledge that I was making a perfectly useless sacrifice and that few people realised, even, that it mattered.

Echoes reached us there of despondency and rout among the opposition. One month after the electoral campaign for Norton de Mattos, all was silent, terrified disorder. Those who had been foremost to support him were henceforth the first to criticise, and the police, with their repressive measures, split our ranks.

I was still in that prison on my wedding-day, and I was married there. My father had been released some time before, after fourteen months' detention—disheartened, over seventy, his faith in politics destroyed by the 10 April fiasco. The family was finding it hard to make ends meet and my mother now showing symptoms of the disease from which she died in 1955. It was a dark outlook on every side.

The police tried to convince me in their questioning that it was pointless to resist. They were a confident lot, and included an old fellow-student of mine at Lisbon university. One of the PIDE, a man named Fernando Gouveia, would boast, 'The law doesn't come up as far as the third floor here'; the cells for interrogation and torture being on the third floor of the headquarters in rua António Maria Cardoso, and he himself one of the most notorious practitioners of his day. It was in those cells, during a dawn interrogation, that Farinha dos Santos told me, twirling his revolver, 'You needn't think anything happens to me if I kill you here and now, you little bastard. I say I floored you in self-defence, and everybody says, "That's right".'

Who could doubt it? Trained in Gestapo methods during the war, the PIDE were now on excellent terms with the Central Intelligence Agency, whose specialists they jubilantly claimed among their best technical advisers. Portugal had well and truly received her good conduct certificate from the Western democracies. What Max Gallo refers to as Salazar's 'second victory and absolution' had come through even sooner than General Franco's.

Our discords of 1949 were purely technical: the opposition split over whether or not to vote. But they concealed a deeper disagreement which had begun to emerge during that campaign. This was the fact that the world was now divided into two hostile blocs, and that was a division spelling the end of anti-Fascist union and with it the possibility of popular-front Governments. The Communists had already been forced out of the Governments of Western Europe.

There seemed to be no room any more for intermediate shades of opinion. I used to say at the time that Europe was a stage ahead of us. There, with Nazi Fascism vanquished, the democrats could split and splinter as they felt inclined, but we were not at that point yet. In Portugal we still had to be anti-Fascists before we were anything else, but the threat of war between those two blocs could not be ignored, even by those who, like myself, had always put their faith in peace.

Given my Marxist training and the way the struggle was going between the United States and the Soviet Union I should, had it come to a choice, have chosen the Soviet Union and never hesitated. I still believed that Russia was the motherland of Socialism. Her encirclement after the war, the incredible epic of her people and the imperialist machinations against her amply accounted, in my eyes, for the difficulties, deficiencies and mistakes in Socialism. Of the crimes that were then coming to light I never so much as dreamed. Tito had gone his own way in 1948. David Rousset and Albert Camus had made known the existence of concentration-camps in Russia. Koestler's *Darkness at Noon* and Jean-Paul Sartre's *l'Engrenage* and *Les mains sales* had all been published, but it would be years before I read them. Kravchenko's celebrated controversy with *Les lettres françaises* about his book *I Chose Freedom* had made not the slightest impression on me. All the answers, so far as I was concerned, were in another book, *The Great Conspiracy against Russia*, by Michael Sayers and Albert Kahn.

If I had any doubts, I did my best to stifle them, lest they somehow affect the struggle against Fascism. The fact of the matter was that I was searching, confusedly, for a third road, although everyone assured me there was no such thing, and that if there were it would only have served the aims of imperialism.

It was much later, on my first visit to Paris in 1951, that I discovered the doctrine of neutralism and became a regular reader of *France-Observateur*, which Claude Bourdet, Gilles Martinet and Claude Estier had started the previous year. Its programme so exactly matched my own ideas that Piteira Santos, whose jokes were famous for their sardonic tinge, used to say, 'You don't know what to think about politics for a week when the police confiscate the *France-Observateur*'.

Soon after the 1949 elections the democrats of Oporto, followed by some of their comrades in Lisbon, took the lead in founding the National Democratic Movement, or MND, as a natural extension of the MUD and of the support generated for Norton de Mattos. But times had changed, and Fascism was back in its stride. Also, though its fundamental tenets were the same, the MND was much more a party of the left.

Indeed, almost all the leaders of the MUD and of the Norton de Mattos election committee, known Socialists and Liberals, were non-members of the MND from the beginning. Some of them, grouped about Professor Azevedo Gomes, even set up a committee that agreed instead with the 'Atlantic' way of thinking, on the grounds that this constituted a stronger protest against Salazar's right of admission to the Atlantic Pact. From the two dozen signatures on their manifesto, they called themselves the Committee of Twenty-four.

It is not true, as the police so often claimed, that the MND represented the legal aspect of Communism. Things are not as neat as that. Certainly it was a unitary movement, for most of its members were indeed Communists or fellow-travellers, and the job of its leaders, who were more than once arrested and indicted, was made all the harder by severe oppression from the police and the fact that democrats of every tendency could see their political opportunities growing less and less. This, I believe, explains much of the narrow sectarianism, which was never to my taste. But I must admire them all the same, for they stood up to terrible persecution with courage and idealism.

I was in prison when their party was founded, so could neither support not oppose it. I was all for a unitary movement—something which, by providing the right conditions and thus assuring that the whole opposition would join in, might get on with the work in hand. But this didn't seem to be the idea, and it was, perhaps, a utopian state of affairs to hope for. I and those of my friends most closely linked with the MUD Central Committee decided to keep out of the MND and wait to reunite the different anti-Government sectors at some more favourable moment. So began, for me, a very long span of silence which was to last, with sundry ups and downs, until Humberto Delgado stood for the Presidency in 1958.

Up to 1949 the Communist Party had been leaping ahead,

in numbers and in actual influence, but now it reached the moment of truth. The tide began to turn. In Portugal, as in the rest of the world, the abrupt policy-changes dictated by Communist (which meant Soviet) world-strategy constrained the faithful to uphold some quite impossible party dogmas. Defenceless under the heavy hand of the police, the campaigns they engaged in were at times ridiculous and had little enough to do with any immediate interests of the Portuguese. The Communists were therefore exposed, with no one to turn to, when the PIDE got hold of them. And of course Portugal, like everywhere else at that time, had to have its quota of Tito-type renegades, its Rayks and its Slanskys. One such was Manuel Domingues, who belonged to the Politburo of the Communist Central Committee, accused of 'treason' and found dead in a pine-wood. The whys and wherefores of his fate have never been cleared up.

Immediately after the war the Communist Party had been a mass organisation, with a large following among the workers, intellectuals and young people. Now, however, the organisation closed in, became almost an esoteric sect, abandoned by its most active supporters. Plainly there were internal reasons for the changes it underwent and they in turn were mainly due to the attentions of the police. The arrest at Luso of the acknowledged leader, Alvaro Cunhal, then at the height of his influence, was a severe blow from which the party recovered with difficulty.

I was still in prison, too, when the verdict was given in the case of the MUDJ Central Committee, to which Francisco Zenha and I belonged. The purpose of the trial had been to declare our party illegal, but we had a brilliant team of lawyers and made a good fight for it. All eight of us, having signed a protest I drew up against some student arrests, were charged with spreading false and tendentious news, calculated to cause public alarm. True or false, we were sentenced to three months in gaol and five years' forfeiture of civil rights.

The banning of the MUD, and then this verdict against its junior branch, clearly indicated a widespread official drive upon the more or less legal movements hitherto tolerated as a sop to foreign opinion. The situation called for skilful defensive tactics; an open fight was out of the question and would have meant the loss of our best men.

The PIDE having failed to prove anything against me, I was set free about the middle of 1949 and was at once asked to join the Central Committee of the MND. This invitation is perhaps best explained, in view of my position in the Democratic Union and my election work for Norton de Mattos, by the fact that the MND was concentrated largely in Oporto, while in Lisbon no one who counted politically had as yet joined. For reasons already given, I refused; and as I could not logically approve the continued existence of the MUDJ without contradicting myself I crept out of that too, on tiptoe. One of the underground newspapers was to assert later that I had been expelled because I wanted to 'liquidate' people.

The breach was now widened between me and the Communist party. From being one of its white hopes, one of the post-war political leaders it had been backing (with offers of dazzling promotion into the bargain), I rapidly became, first an opportunist, then a renegade. Pressure of all kinds was applied to make me conform and return to the paths of righteousness and many of my personal friends stopped seeing, or even speaking to me, without explanation. When it was plain that I was going to stand my ground I was judged lost beyond recall and a campaign was launched to destroy me politically. Despicable attempts were made to influence my wife, who had been dismissed from the National Theatre Company in 1948 on the decision of the Ministers of Education and of the Interior, and whose reputation, both as an actress and an opponent of Salazar, was now enormous. How could she, my Communist friends enquired, continue to live and to make common cause with an opportunist? Much later I learned from one of the younger generation of opposition leaders that the case of Mário Soares was on the agenda at every single meeting of the MUDJ. 'They taught us to loathe you', he said. This was merely one among many examples of the spirit-of-Stalin intolerance that were to be found in Portugal.

Yet these bitter and difficult days were for me the best of all apprenticeships, for I was learning that a Socialism which rides roughshod over people and personal freedom is only a caricature. Also, I grew innured to external attack and injustice, convinced that, in politics, a man is destroyed if he allows himself to be destroyed, not otherwise. Little by little I shed my ideological prejudices and learned to think for myself and how to use my judgement before making up my mind.

Despite my reservations about the MND, however, I could not desert them in the hour of trial, or fail to demonstrate solidarity when they were under persecution. When their Central Committee was in custody I finally agreed to sit on their Lisbon Municipal Committee. It was a move I should regret.

The break came in November 1950, over an Armistice Day peace-demonstration. Let us recall that Russia, since the famous Stockholm Appeal for the Interdiction of Atomic Weapons, was seeking to mobilise all, irrespective of ideologies, who favoured disarmament and the use of negotiation; that President Truman had revealed the explosion of the first Soviet atomic bomb in October 1949; that hostilities in Korea broke out in June 1950. The world was learning to walk its terrifying tightrope on the brink of war. Peace-committees, all pointing the finger of accusation at America, sprang up in Portugal as everywhere else.

Attempts to gather signatures for a peace-petition ended in failure, but the MND still wished to demonstrate in the middle of Lisbon on 11 November. Our committee made it clear that we thought the plan absurd and were against it, but the muster was held all the same, although only a few people turned up and several of these were arrested.

There was to be an important meeting that night at the Republican centre in the Avenida António José de Almeida and my wife, who was pregnant, came with me. We could see numbers of police about as we drew near and on arrival found an audience consisting almost entirely of agents from the PIDE. There were at most a hundred genuine democrats present. The place looked set for some big detective drama; it might have been a scene in 'Z', the Costa Grivas film about the Greek situation that in so many ways resembled our own. In the circumstances, I consulted with the others as to the wisdom of going ahead, but the organisers were determined.

The speech I had brought with me was fervently pro-peace and as fervently against 'imperialist aggression'. It condemned the Atlantic Pact as an instrument of war and left no doubt that those who loved peace and democracy were dwellers to the East. It was a very definite, unequivocal speech and just what the PIDE needed to put me in the dock and behind bars for years to come.

I was saved by the unforeseen. As soon as I began the officials present intervened to tell me that I could not discuss peace in this subversive fashion. I went on for a couple of sentences, and they interrupted again. From the front of the house came applause, catcalls and shouting and I could see the PIDE men closing in. Two words more, and another interruption. This time I objected; since they were preventing me from putting my point of view, I should not speak at all. Then the police leaped on to the stage, just as I, too, leaped into the front row of the stalls to fling my arms round Câmara Reys, the editor of *Seara Nova*, an elderly man noted for presence of mind in a crisis. I slipped the speech into his pocket as I landed and that was all I could do before being hustled out by the police who, among shouts and protests, hauled me into the street and pushed me into a car. But the speech, the vital evidence, was missing. They could therefore do nothing and had to let me go at five o'clock in the morning.

After the fiasco of the Armistice Day affair I made some adverse comment on the leadership of the MND in committee and there was heated but inconclusive argument. About six months later, in the middle of 1951, the Communists formally sent me a copy of their underground paper, *Avante*, in which I was accused of opportunism and the democratic heads of the MND were advised to expel me from their counsels. Worse, this article was an outright denunciation at a time when the PIDE were coming down heavily on anyone with left-wing opinions, while the man who delivered the paper brought me a message that added savour to the situation : the big chiefs really thought I should stay in the MND.

I severed relations with it, needless to say. At the same time I also broke with the Communists who, in one of their frequent spasms of self-criticism, tried, in 1955 or 1956, to lure me back into the fold.

In April 1951 President Carmona died. He had become acting President in 1926, soon after the rising of 28 May, and had clung to power in the shadow of Salazar. He was a shadowy person himself though he probably had more influence than he was given credit for, at least in the early years of the dictatorship. He was always said to be a likeable man, the kind who never upsets anyone; he had a happy touch with people and there was a sort of distinction about him. From being a liberal and Freemason, with many connections in both Republican and conservative circles, he had ended up as Head of State in a savage and ultra-clerical dictatorship—a flexible man, and basically a man with no profound beliefs. His doctor, Professor Pulido Valente, gave me some extraordinary stories of the President at close quarters, many of which brought in Senhora Carmona, an impulsive woman of humble origin and a great talker. Much the stronger personality of the two, the President's lady was our Madame Sans-Gêne and the bricks she dropped provided some of the regime's livelier ancedotes. Like the rest of the family, so one heard, she detested Salazar.

Carmona's death, two years after the Norton de Mattos campaign, meant that elections must be held once more. Salazar himself had no wish to stand, though many of his partisans, Marcello Caetano among them, thought that he should do so. As he was to tell us later, in a quite remarkable speech, it was not a saint, or a genius, or a hero who was needed. This being so, he could safely step aside and appoint General Craveiro Lopes, a man who was none of these things.

Disbelieving and divided, the opposition was ill-prepared for the new electoral period. The MND, the MUDJ and the extreme left adopted as their candidate Professor Ruy Luis Gomes, while the choice of the centre fell upon the retired

Admiral Quintão Meyrelles, who had once held office under the regime but was now in opposition. Between these two factions many anti-Government supporters, myself included, preferred to remain neutral rather than stress our differences. It was, unhappily, impossible to light on any one candidate to please us all.

The Cabinet meanwhile disqualified Ruy Luis Gomes, 'the People's Candidate' as he was called, as being ineligible. The MND and MUDJ thereupon began to advocate abstention from the polls, and it must be admitted that there had been no enthusiasm for Gomes in Lisbon, since everybody knew he had no chance of winning.

Admiral Quintão Meyrelles, for his part, was no politician, but he had two real fighters on his 'Brains Trust' who set the keynote of the campaign, an engineer named Cunha Leal and Captain Henrique Galvão. Behind them and, one must say, a good deal more quietly, came the old democratic regulars, headed by António Sérgio and Azevedo Gomes, to give the necessary democratic warrant to the candidacy.

The Admiral conducted his campaign in a new way altogether. He did not excite the masses or arouse popular feeling as Norton de Mattos had done, but sought instead to prove dissension in the opposite camp and concentrated on the financial scandals of the regime, particularly those in which members of the oligarchy happened to be involved. And indeed these tactics were no less telling, for they brought the moral decadence of Salazarism into the light of day, and now the emphasis was not on its principles but on its unbridled commercial activities. He published a series of corrosive statements, based upon irrefutable fact, and reading them the nation lost all respect for its rulers and for Salazar himself. It began to see them as they really were—an unscrupulous and specially-protected gang who had grasped political for the sake of economic power and the good it would do them in business.

Salazar, of course, always managed to appear as someone to whom money did not matter, who was interested only in power. But he left that clique of vultures, monstrous and uncontrolled, to go on creating an inextricable web of political and economic connections and interconnections that exists to this day.

Quintão Meyrelles, working under grave disadvantages, did appreciable damage to the dictatorship by his appearance on the scene. Yet he had only a fortnight for his electoral campaign, only one meeting in Lisbon and none in Oporto, where official pressures were so strong that he could find nobody brave enough to let him have a public hall. Over the entire country the usual machinery had gone into action to hinder the free circulation of ideas and of election material, and every conceivable difficulty was put in his personal path. In the end he had no alternative but to withdraw and set out his reasons for doing so in a statement to the nation issued in July. Point for point they were the same as those of General Norton de Mattos when he, too, gave up.

The election of Craveiro Lopes, like all Salazarist elections was, in the strict sense of the word, a nomination. And to those Portuguese who allowed themselves the luxury of thinking it was now manifest that the chances of solving the situation by peaceful means were more or less finished. Popular agitation sank to its lowest ebb in face of police activity—and the mildest activity was enough. It was an ebb tide altogether for the opposition, and one which did not begin to turn until the campaign of General Delgado in 1958.

Some few people, António Sérgio for example, Azevedo Gomes and Jaime Cortesão, and some groups, mostly connected with the liberal professions in the large towns, did what they could to keep the flame alive; but the opposition as an organised and militant force was practically spent. Even the Communists, despite their party structures, never once troubled the regime, and the working classes seemed to have drifted off and to be fast asleep.

The years 1951–57 were for me a time of stock-taking and almost solitary endeavour. I had no party ties and was, as it were, refashioning my broad lines of belief and thinking everything over. I took my Arts degree in 1951, but as I could not produce a favourable PIDE report I could not teach and therefore embarked on a five-year law course, since I had to earn a living somehow. The PIDE in fact did me a signal service in thus forcing me to qualify, though I cannot suppose they meant to at the time.

Being deeply interested in public affairs, I set myself to weigh the problems of my country in search of some solution. I wanted to get beyond the theoretical plans, all so detached from the realities of national life, and find a breach, any breach, in the hitherto impregnable wall of Salazar's system. The dissidents, I thought, needed to rethink their whole strategy, and the study of Law gave me useful weapons for the undertaking.

I also tried to establish common ground with some of my friends who shared these aspirations, for I was politically almost isolated. In this way was born the Republican Resistance Group which was founded to consider, as a group, the troubles of Portugal. Several of our reports appeared in the clandestine press, as well as a series of pamphlets against the regime. One of these especially comes to mind, which Manuel Mendes wrote as a pastiche of Khrushchev's speech at the twenty-second Communist International. In it he imagined that Salazar was dead and, with considerable foresight, presented Marcello Caetano, at some National Union Congress, bitterly denouncing the errors and crimes of Salazarism. It caused quite a stir. Unfortunately, however, the Republican Resistance never developed into anything more than a solid group of friends who met to discuss the state of the nation and realised that we must have an active left once more, as distinct from a Communist party which could do nothing effective to bring about the end of Fascism.

It was as this group's representative that I agreed, round about 1956, to join the Democratic-Social Directive. Basically this consisted of Mário de Azevedo Gomes, Jaime Cortesão and António Sérgio. They were three of the greatest democrats we had, exercising an unquestioned moral and intellectual ascendancy over us all, and I grew closer to them than ever. I had always agreed with the political notions of Azevedo Gomes but differed profoundly on some points from António

Sérgio. But now I learned to know him better and admire him, and I became very friendly with Jaime Cortesão. Our special function was to make critical assessments of the most significant events in Portugal, usually by means of letters to the President. Elections to the National Assembly took place in 1953, and again in 1957, but political activity was so fitful that the majority of people never noticed them.

In 1953 the opposition submitted lists of candidates at Lisbon, Oporto and Aveiro, most of the names being those of liberal democrats. In Lisbon our chief candidate was Dr Cunha Leal, the engineer. The opposition tactic of withdrawal on the eve of the poll had aroused much disapproval on previous occasions, and this time we wanted to carry through to the end, even if we had to do without the basic conditions we had so regularly demanded ever since October 1945. As ever, the Government refused to grant a single one of them and the election result was therefore bound to be inaccurate. The official figures showed no more than ten per cent of registered electors as supporting the opposition.

Things were even worse in 1957. The opposition lists, compiled at the last minute, inspired no interest at all, for people had lost faith in them. Meetings and electioneering were minimal. The Government, with accomplished cynicism, made everything as complicated as possible and in the end the candidates thought it best to retire.

Such, then, were the lamentable circumstances of the country and of the opposition up to the time of General Delgado's presidential campaign in 1958. The Government was absolutely unyielding, absolutely sure of itself. Accepted by the 'free world', Salazar was represented at the United Nations, in the Atlantic Treaty Organisation, EFTA and various other international bodies. According to the *Diário de Notícias* the world at large had much to learn from him, and certainly it placed no obstacles in his path. Rather, it paid him some surprising compliments. Princess Margaret came, and then the Queen of England, General Eisenhower, Sukarno and the Emperor Haile Selassie; Presidents Café Filho and Juscelino Kubitschek came, in turn, from Brazil; General

D

Franco came, as did Atlantic Treaty deputations. There were international conferences in Lisbon. At home the opposition, fragmented and beaten down, powerless to organise or say what it thought, presented no grave danger. Employing what Delgado called 'expressions of tempered hatred', it confined itself to making the dictator realise that it was there. The police, while not unduly advertising their performance, were devoting themselves at the same time to putting his most obstinate opponents out of action and had, besides their battery of legal and repressive armament, notably efficient methods of getting at information. Furthermore, the main body of the opposition was paralysed by the split into two extremist groups, which we may call, for convenience, 'progressive' and 'pro-NATO', and saw no real prospect of forcing a change for some time to come.

The problem for the progressives was to know just how they could best combat Salazarism. By revolutionary means? But the advocates of revolution mostly took their cue from the Communist party and, with Franco Spain on one side and the Atlantic transformed into an American lake on the other (this being the epoch of Foster Dulles and McCarthy), the Communists told them to keep calm, that the hour for open attack upon imperialism was not yet; for that, at least, was what they meant by talk of the great anti-Fascist rising on some far-off future day. Fidel Castro, remember, was not to bring quasi-revolutionary orthodoxy back into the picture until 1959.

As for the Atlantic faction, for them the struggle, legal or otherwise, served as cover or at best encouragement, for ill-considered attempts at a putsch. Despite all set-backs, they had never given up the fight since 1926, and although their state of unreadiness often suggested an attitude of sheer levity, their fanatics and professional adherents were for ever in a ferment of revolt and always suffering casualties.

In the fifties there emerged a man who rose for a time to be Salazar's Enemy Number One. This was Captain Henrique Galvão, a former Government official and inspector in the colonial service, a former deputy and a former director of the radio station *Emissôra Nacional.* He was also a gifted writer and had been at one time much cherished by the dictator.

It is an interesting fact that nearly everybody who came over to the opposition from the other side did so through the patient persuasion of António Sérgio. For Sérgio was more than a brilliant thinker and an ideological champion; he was a permanent, non-stop conspirator too. General Costa Ferreira, Admiral Quintão Meyrelles, many Monarchists and some Catholics, Captain Galvão and, later, General Humberto Delgado, all moved into active opposition thanks to him.

After the rising on 10 April 1947 Galvão had testified before the military court on behalf of Colonel Carlos Selvagem, who was a friend of his. His speech on that occasion was brave and brilliant; nor was it an easy one to make, which meant that it was braver and more brilliant still. When he finished it I overheard him say, 'Well, that's the end of me, Salazar will never forgive me'. Salazar never did.

Not only did Galvão speak openly against the regime in that court-room; in the National Assembly he committed the far worse crime of attacking slavery in Angola. The colonial slave-traders, with their huge property- and business-interests, did not forgive him either. They had him out of the Assembly in short order.

He joined the opposition during the election campaign for Quintão Meyrelles and made no secret of it. Some of our communiqués bore the mark of his style. They pulled no punches and charged the establishment resolutely at its weak point, the crooked business deals. Galvão had served the regime. He knew his former friends better than anyone did and left them in no doubt of the fact.

Nor was he the man to stop once he got started, and was plotting against the Government before the campaign was over. The story was told of his missing brief-case which, containing plans for a proposed rising, disappeared from our election offices for twenty-four hours. When he was arrested some time later the PIDE dossier at his trial included photocopies of the documents found in it and Galvão, imperturbable as ever, maintained in court that they were all pure fiction; just a sketch for a play he had in mind.

His exploits, not least among them his subsequent escape from the Santa Maria Hospital, were the admiration of the whole opposition at this time. So, indeed, was his trial, one of the most extraordinary I ever saw. His defending counsel, Vasco da Gamas Fernandes, was assisted by dazzling shafts from the accused, who pulverised the entire tribunal with his answers and the virulent onslaughts he made on the regime. Galvão had many faults, some of them serious, but he had, too, the dash and inspiration of the old Portuguese adventurers.

They gave him a very long sentence and he proceeded to organise a conspiracy from the Penitenciária in Lisbon. Thanks to co-operation from some of the warders he actually ran a secret printing-press and sent out manifestos revealing Government scandals to the country at large, which promptly discussed them in private. This state of affairs, however, did not last. Once discovered, he and his auxiliaries were transferred, first to Caxias and then to Peniche. The head-warder, who had done most to help, yielded to police persuasion and killed himself.

The youngest General in the Portuguese army was at this date away in America, acting as the Government's military attaché with NATO. The democratic American way of life, as he afterwards declared, impressed him very much and he began to reflect on the fate of his own wretched country, under the longest-lasting dictatorship in Europe. He was especially troubled by the news of Henrique Galvão, a personal friend, and on his brief visits to Lisbon he had the courage to visit the prisoner at Caxias and at Peniche, which is more than most serving officers would have done. At Galvão's suggestion, he also met and talked with António Sérgio. Humberto Delgado was out of the general run of generals. We were to hear more of him.

Chapter Six

Delgado, the Prodigy

General Delgado came like a thunderbolt on to the political scene. His return to Lisbon from a first triumphal election visit to Oporto was greeted by a crowd of some 300,000 or more, while the Communist underground was referring to him in an issue of *Avante* as a 'Coca-Cola General' and a Fascist.[1] And yet very little was known about him. For the majority he was just a serving General with a Fascist background and the guts to come out against the regime by standing for the opposition as an independent presidential candidate. They also kept in mind his opening press conference and what he had said about Salazar : 'He goes if I'm elected.'

That catch-phrase, which his hastily-appointed advisers had thought unrealistic and wanted him to cut, brought most of the nation to his side. Two more points helped him to political success : as a General on the active list he could presumably count on the army; and he had been liaison officer in the United States, where he was evidently liked and trusted.

Psychologically these facts meant a great deal. After repeated disillusions the Portuguese had no reason whatsoever to believe in any election held by Salazar, but this time with a General as candidate, things might be different; the rules might be respected for a change. Also, if the Americans sent observers, as it was thought they might, the prospects of victory went soaring; it had been the Western democracies, after all, who turned traitor and saved Salazar after the war, and the Cold War of the fifties that had kept him where he was. . . . Moreover, the Communist attitude seemed almost to guarantee such

[1] Communists at this time firmly believed that the entire Coca-Cola organisation was a network of imperialist spies. Trans.

hopes. Their bitter enmity was a trump-card in Delgado's hand.
His initial success was due, I think, to a combination of
these factors. Equally important were his courage and his
modern-style campaign. From the very beginning he stood up
and proclaimed his policy in a way that earned him his nick-
name of 'the Fearless General', and a campaign based on
house-to-house visiting made him popular as nothing else could
do. Some years later, in a moment of mingled admiration and
dislike, Salazar spoke of him as a rabble-rouser of genius.

These unconventional methods meant, interestingly enough,
that those at the various party headquarters were perhaps the
last to understand what a prodigy he was. But the people
understood, straight away. Also—and almost instinctively—he
acted like a prodigy.

I remember Delgado on that return from Oporto. It was
round about six o'clock on a normal working day. Piteira
Santos had insisted that we should welcome him formally at
the station and, rather tepidly, I agreed. As we waited for
some of the others at our central rendezvous before going down
to the Santa Apolónia terminal, we noticed there was more
movement than usual in the same direction. 'What *are* they
doing?' I enquired, unable to credit that several thousand
people could be on the way to meet a man they had never
heard of a day or two before. But all the same, they were.

Afterwards I heard that the *Emissôra Nacional* had
announced in the afternoon that any demonstration was forbidden and would be severely punished. The authorities had
learned how things had gone at Oporto, where he had received
a huge popular welcome, and they were frightened. In the
capital, of course, news from Oporto was censored out of the
papers and no one knew what had happened there, so it was
in fact the alarmist official broadcasts which led to the biggest
and most remarkable demonstration I had witnessed since the
end of the war.

When Delgado, accompanied by a few of his friends,
reached Santa Apolónia the Republican Guard and the police
had already occupied the platform and only a handful of
democratic supporters were to be seen. It was the staff and

the railwaymen who poured suddenly out of the station buildings as the train came in and filled every corner as if by magic. The crowd was stuck outside, unable to move forward and the police diverted the General from his expected route. He acquiesced and then made the mistake of following one of their cars. The crowd, ignorant of what was taking place, grew restive and the rumours flew. Had Delgado arrived? Had the police got hold of him?

All at once they could wait no longer and began shouting to go to his election headquarters. The office was on the Avenida da Liberdade in the very middle of Lisbon and towards it there now moved a tide of humanity, orderly, gay and good-tempered, singing the National Anthem as it went and cheering for liberty and the candidate. One or two of us found ourselves in the forefront. Windows were flung open on our way and knots of people yelled encouragement. As we reached the business quarter the police, drawn up in the Praça do Rossio, opened fire at point-blank range. Bullets went whistling over our heads and into the windows of houses and shops. Then the mounted Republican Guardsmen charged into the crowd and there was a stampede, with screaming and tramplings underfoot and demonstrators scuffling with police. Many were hurt.

Thus, amidst passionate popular feeling and governmental violence, General Delgado's campaign began.

I first heard of him a few years previously when the schoolgirl daughter of a friend of ours came home wanting to know who he was. When asked why, she had said, 'Because there's a girl at school who says her father's going to be President when he gets back from America'. Coincidence or not, we all took this seriously and began to follow with some interest the doings of the General who seemed in those days to be such poles apart from us.

Holding high rank in the Air Force, at one time the youngest General in the Army, Delgado was a born fighting-man and had had a brilliant career. The Salazarist politics he imbibed had certainly not hindered his progress, as witness his appointments to the *Mocidade Portuguesa* and the Portuguese Legion and the Fascist slant of several things he wrote. Some of those who knew him personally found him authoritarian and conceited, while an inordinate exuberance and attitudes that were, to say the least, unpredictable, also failed to appeal. He had no sense of moderation. Perpetually in a turmoil, gesticulating wildly, he had his work cut out to make the democratic leaders like him.

But Delgado was brave and daring and honest, and could occasionally get through to people in the most amazing way. Unlike most of his fellow-officers he was a convinced Anglophile, had done a lot for the Allies and held a British decoration.

His intervention in the tragi-comic Azores incident during the war gives a glimpse of his character. The pro-German Government in Lisbon was terrified of losing the Azores. Out there in the Atlantic, the archipelago was a vital spot. The Germans were stepping up their submarine activity with the object of preventing the delivery of arms and raw materials to England from her Dominions and America, and the C-in-C Azores, General Ramires, got it into his head that there would be an Allied landing. He saw the enemy wherever he looked and since he was always revising his orders and testing his defences the troops could never relax for a minute. Then one night a sentry heard suspicious noises and beheld a strange shape in the mist. He called on it to halt. It did not halt, so the man carried out his orders and fired. Shots were immediately loosed off in every direction, sirens went all over the island. The secret emergency defence plan was put into operation without delay and HQ scurried to its prepared retreat, sure that invasion of the archipelago had come. Dawn revealed the enemy as one stray cow. But the C-in-C was emotionally unbalanced and the consequences might have been appalling.

In any case, Lisbon ought to be notified of the situation, and quickly; but what bold man was going to make a report like that? It was Delgado, on his way through from a mission in the States, who heard the tale and undertook the task as soon as he got home. He was nearly court-martialled for his pains, but Santos Costa, the Defence Minister, realised from the preliminary court of inquiry that he had acted correctly and hushed up the whole affair.

As we have said, Delgado was military attaché in Washington when he first met António Sérgio and before long they were like two plotters together. On his return to Portugal he began to criticise what he found there. Salazar was obviously told of this, and of the visits to Henrique Galvão in Peniche, and, as was his wont, he attempted indirect purchase. Plans were under discussion for enlarging the runways at Lisbon to take jet aircraft and Delgado was made Director-General of Civil Aviation. The post could have made him rich with very little effort on his part, but he was a man of absolute moral integrity and ignored the implications of the gesture.

The anti-Government leaders saw him as the mainspring of a revolutionary and military plot. They hoped his dynamism and firmness would prove a focus for the latent discontent in army circles, where he knew so many people and where Santos Costa was then so unpopular. Meanwhile, the opposition as a whole began to stir, for the next presidential election was drawing near. This was still by popular suffrage, although since 1949 all candidacies had to be approved by the Council of State, the supreme body consisting of the great ones of the establishment.

And the establishment had its problems, too. Even more than Carmona, Craveiro Lopes, as his term of office ran out, had had his differences with Salazar. He was an upright man, not over-intelligent, but one who gave serious thought to what he was doing and who considered it a duty to enforce respect for the office of President, an aim which his Prime Minister did little or nothing to forward. Everyone therefore knew that Craveiro Lopes would be seen no more and that manœuvres were already going on within the regime. Several names were mentioned. The Minister of the Presidency, Marcello Caetano, insisted that the right and fitting man was Salazar and the virulent quarrelling of his followers with those of Santos Costa —for the two factions were then at loggerheads—furnished a background to the atmosphere of intrigue. In the end, and once again, the dictator imposed the candidate he himself preferred, Admiral Américo Thomaz, his faithful head of the Navy Department, a colourless character from whom he could expect implicit obedience.

The dissidents knew they had to find somebody capable of dividing the enemy camp as well as of uniting all the shades of opposition. The Communists, weakened by repressive measures and feeling isolated, agreed with this and were willing to make large concessions. Their selection was the former Prime Minister, Cunha Leal, now a great controversialist and opponent of Fascism; they seemed to forget that they had before accused him of being reactionary. But, seeing that he would not have the undivided support of the entire opposition, he declined the offer.

The Democratic-Social Directive was very much against his candidacy. António Sérgio considered two points essential— the man chosen must be a soldier, for then the army would be sure to see fair play at the election; and he must have come to us from the Government side, the better to bring in others who had served the regime and later changed their minds. This idea did not, however, meet with unanimous approval, most of the group, myself included, preferring the distinguished historian Jaime Cortesão, whose prestige in opposition was unarguable and whose lengthy exile in Brazil had come to an end in 1955. He was, moreover, exceptionally gifted as writer, poet, playwright and essayist, with a rare conception of his duty as an intellectual. A Republican since his student days, he had sat in the National Assembly as a democratic deputy for Oporto and he, like Norton de Mattos, had done much to bring Portugal into the First World War on the side of the Allies. Gradually he had adopted the Social-Democrat doctrine, had helped to found the *Seara Nova* group and violently opposed the dictatorship from its very beginning. When he had to get out of the country, he went to Spain, and then, until the German occupation drove him out, to France. Back in Portugal, Jaime Cortesão was arrested, imprisoned for some months in the castle of Peniche and then forced to go and live in Brazil. When I knew him, on his return, he was a man of seventy.

But while in Lisbon we were arguing the merits and demerits of one candidate and another, and failing to make our minds up, a group of democrats in Oporto approached Delgado through António Sérgio and asked him to stand for the Presidency of the Republic. The General accepted without hesitation and the opposition was faced with the *fait accompli*.

The Communist Party and some of the left, especially in Lisbon, refused to confirm an arrangement as yet unapproved by the rank and file. Feverishly they cast round for an alternative candidate to replace Cunha Leal and as a last resort adopted Arlindo Vicente, a lawyer and an artist, if not hitherto very noticeable in the political field. Nevertheless, he now became third runner in the presidential elections of 1958. The Social-Democrats, faced equally with the ready-made solution, did not hide their opinion of Delgado's governmental past but decided to support him. The Republican Resistance was behind him from the first, Manuel Mendes was one of his keenest partisans, but it must be admitted that, because of ideological prejudice, it was late in the day when many of us —and here I include myself—joined in his campaign.

And a chaotic campaign it was to begin with, owing to the lack of experienced people on the management committees. Yet even so we raised more popular support than ever before, reaching and kindling large sections of the population to whom politics had previously meant little. There was such enthusiasm, such a wave of protest against the regime, as almost succeeded in sweeping Fascism out of doors. This was one of the few occasions when Salazar, in his forty years of dictatorship, was in real danger.

Delgado's campaign could fairly be called a national uprising, a completely unexpected collective phenomenon from which no class stood aside. And when the Bishop of Oporto circulated his famous letter of criticism a month later, to the honour of the Church in Portugal, which was until then wholly involved with the Fascist regime; when a Catholic opposition took shape and a not inconsiderable percentage of the army began to pay attention to politics, these things sprang indirectly from the emotional impact of the Fearless General's campaign.

A movement so widespread was sure to provoke strong reaction. The Government looked to its defences. The constitutional amendment of the following year, under which the President was to be elected by an officially approved college of voters instead of by direct suffrage, was an admission of weakness. As for us, our optimism was paid for with savage persecution.

The final meeting of the Delgado campaign was held at the *liceu* Camões in Lisbon and that same evening there was a particularly big mass demonstration. The air seemed heavy with menace and enough police were on duty to make the boldest think twice. The meeting itself passed off without incident but the whole town looked as though war had been declared. Delgado was very much on edge and I heard him say, 'I have an actual, physical feeling of danger. There's danger all round, but I don't know where it's coming from. Dreadful sensation.'

The police went energetically to work in the nearby streets. Thousands of sympathisers who could not get into the school were dispersed with blows and since they were less passive than they had been they fought back with unaccustomed vigour. The authorities showed the utmost brutality in return and this good middle-class district witnessed cavalry charges, gun-slinging and headlong panic flight. The Monte Carlo café was systematically wrecked when the police shot their way in to dislodge demonstrators. So ended, as it had begun, General Delgado's campaigning month in Lisbon.

Up to the very last he and his advisers had the usual misgivings as to taking part in the election at all. There were reasons in plenty for abstention—the restraints, annoyances and violations of every kind and, principally, the absence of any proper check on the actual count. But those electors who had done wonders in getting the ballot-papers round in record time were mostly willing to go on and vote and we ourselves wanted to follow the current electoral experiment through to the end.

The voting-papers bearing Delgado's name had been delivered to our headquarters too late for valid distribution and were, we could see, slightly different from those of the Government candidate. This deliberate variation naturally favoured the regime, for few public employees would risk proclaiming allegiance to the opposition in the very act of voting.

The first man to collect supplies, for the Ribatejo area, was Teófilo Carvalho Santos, and the PIDE arrested him at once. Thanks to the General's immediate intervention he was released in an hour or so, but the incident was enough to spread alarm on all sides and cause delays in distributing the papers just when time was running out and every minute mattered.

As far as Delgado himself was concerned, I could never decide whether he really wanted to complete the course. He was in an extraordinarily difficult position and beset with contradictory pressures on every side. Garrisons, air and naval bases were demanding his ballot-papers, while officers were speaking openly in mess against the Government and for the opposition as never before. Yet there was at the same time a high-level conspiracy afoot for a *coup d'état* which would avoid a fraudulent election.

Craveiro Lopes, at the end of his term of office, which ran from 1951 to 1958, had made up his mind to get rid of Salazar. But he did this after much hesitation, fearing to find himself unsupported or accused of acting from personal motives only, and would do nothing unless he could count on certain units of the armed forces. Negotiations were opened with Delgado, but those who handled them were not always entirely trustworthy. On the eve of the election the President waited all night for someone who was supposed to take him to the garrison at Santarém, where he was to announce the dictator's dismissal. No messenger came, however, and one of the chief conspirators betrayed the plot to Santos Costa. Several of the Generals, as I have reason to believe, had promised Delgado their support, and this is borne out by letters subsequently written by him to Botelho Moniz and other high-ranking officers. The truth of it all may possibly be known some day.

The week before the election he seemed a prey to contradiction, and absented himself voluntarily from a meeting at his headquarters where it was to be decided, finally, whether or not he should fight on. Then, without consulting his nearest advisers, he signed the Cacilhas Pact, so called from the small village of that name, by which the two opposition candicacies were fused into one and Arlindo Vicente stood down in his favour.

The pact brought no advantage to Delgado and enabled the Government to renew its old alarms about the Red Peril. Why, then, did he sign it? Only one explanation occurs to me : that, disappointed at the failure of the hoped-for military coup, yet aware that the whole electoral process required him to carry on to the end however unfair the result might be, he was dreaming of a general strike and a great mass-movement to force the Government into retreat. And all this, he thought, would come about more easily if the opposition closed ranks.

In the end the election took place, in perfect order, on the Government's terms. Manipulation, that is to say, assumed the proportions of highway robbery at the expense of the opposition, which had neither means nor opportunity to do anything about it. Observers, seeing the very large turn-out in comparison with earlier occasions, believed that most of the democrats must have voted. Even the official figures showed that Delgado received 25 per cent of the votes cast and he always claimed that he had in fact won. In any case the Government, admitting that the opposition commanded a quarter of the electorate, should have accorded it legal recognition. But of course it did nothing of the kind.

Delgado challenged the validity of the official figures and his solicitor, Fernando Abranches Ferrão, drew up a document listing the principal malpractices as so many reasons for the annulment of the election. Needless to say, he might have saved himself the trouble.

But whereas the anti-Fascist spirit collapsed when previous elections were over, this time it stayed alive in every class of the population. Delgado remained a symbol, a standard of revolt and a rallying-point for the struggle. His campaign-offices were closed, the censorship clamped down, the secret police laid hands on the opposition leaders and hundreds of their followers, but hope was not extinguished. The General wished to start a National Independence Movement—the MNI—but this, unfortunately, was not what was expected of him.

All the same, he was a thorn in the flesh for Salazar. Totalitarian governments are not supple enough to absorb such prodigies and can deal with them by violence alone. Yet before resorting to violence Salazar tried to persuade Delgado to attend an Economics course in Canada as a member of one of the splendidly-paid Military Missions. That is, he tried to buy him off again. Delgado said no. During the next few months he was removed from the Civil Aviation post, taken off the active list and finally relieved of his rank in the Air Force. For all official purposes he became ex-General Delgado.

He had no employment, he was under an ostentatious, twenty-four-hour surveillance by police agents who did all they could to provoke him; his every action was spied on. Delgado, we thought, was a man due for arrest at any minute or, worse still, we should hear of an 'accident' and he would have been assassinated. Then one day he learned of a demonstration to be held near his house in the afternoon. The warning came in time. Without delay, or even a word to his nearest associates, he went to the Brazilian embassy, a bare few yards from the PIDE headquarters, and there took refuge.

Chapter Seven

The Years of Hope

After earlier presidential elections hope of prompt reform had died away, but after Delgado's campaign it did not die. Rather, the struggle for democracy in Portugal had received new impetus from many new supporters, and this at a time when Salazarism was anything but healthy. It was no mere coincidence that Marcello Caetano, heir to the dictatorship, should choose this moment to withdraw from political life into twelve years' prudent retirement.

There was so much discontent, the leading political figures of the establishment were so thoroughly discredited, doubt as to Salazar's methods and what they were worth was so widespread, that nobody thought the regime could last for another decade. International conditions also seemed to favour change.

In the late fifties, we may recall, many things happened that looked like hopeful portents. Cardinal Roncalli became Pope as John XXIII in 1958 and published his famous encyclical *Mater et Magistra* in July 1961. In 1956, at the twentieth congress of the Russian Communist Party, Khrushchev announced the doctrine of peaceful co-existence which was to have its greatest days when Kennedy was President. The Common Market came into being in January 1959 and with it the prospect of a power in Europe to balance the other two blocs. In that same month Fidel Castro entered Havana in triumph, to demonstrate how a Fascist dictatorship might be overturned by appealing to national revolutionary sentiment alone. In Spain the technocrats of Opus Dei came to the front in 1957 and set in train the great changeover of 1960–63, when the target shifted from stabilisation to development.

But the fighting in Angola began in 1961 and Salazar was

probably saved, paradoxically, by the nationalist movements erupting in the African colonies. They brought a new dimension into the politics of Portugal for they made our problem an international one. And though opposition was more openly avowed because of the nationalist outbreaks, they also made any possible change of regime harder to envisage. The aim could no longer be a simple change of home politics; the whole structure of the state would have to be remade. At stake now were the country's future after forty years of Salazarism and her integration into the modern world, and things were much more complex. Changes so radical presented fresh and very difficult issues that were bound to affect the positions of Salazarist and dissident alike.

And indeed many who opposed the dictator felt some hesitation. It is not really surprising that the colonial war did in fact stabilise the regime to some degree, once people saw that no immediate defeat was likely. With the least politically-minded among them it was not even necessary to launch appeals to patriotism, while those who longed for change held back in view of problems manifestly so intricate and so very hard to solve. For this reason there was no serious revolutionary attempt in Portugal after the revolt at Beja in January 1962.

One positive result of Delgado's campaign had been to cause profound differences among the Catholics.

The Church until then had invariably supported Salazar. It was the main ideological pillar of the regime, securing it the doctrinal framework within which to develop. Not only was the dictatorship sure of the backing of the Catholic organisations, they furnished its most dynamic political leaders too. The same thing had occurred after Franco's victory in Spain, where the political force of the Church acted as the vital counterweight to the influence of army and Falange, but in Portugal there were aggravating factors. Here the sole National Union party remained an artificial and torpid movement that could never attract the mass of the people; and Salazar always thoroughly distrusted the army. Under him the political power of the Church was more or less un-rivalled.

There is another essential point to remember. Franco was a soldier by profession. He was the army; in him it saw itself personified. But Salazar, for all his years as War Minister, was still a civilian as far as the army was concerned, and at the bottom of him he despised soldiers. He was a man of the Church, a lay-brother, as it were, who had set his hand to the plough.

It is therefore true to say that Salazarism and the Church in Portugal were intimately intertwined, much more intimately than were Francoism and the Church in Spain. For decades the twin powers were indistinguishable. Shockingly so, for the Portuguese Church was always *integrista*, always sided with Salazar. There were rare exceptions in its ranks, but they only served to prove the rule.

For instance, in 1958, after the Delgado campaign, the Bishop of Oporto, Dom António Ferreira Gomes, felt called upon to write a letter to Salazar. In it he spoke for the first time of the urgent necessity to 'disengage' the Church from a regime he regarded as anti-Christian. Notably, he denounced the mumbo-jumbo of corporativism. At about this time, too, Lino Neto and António Alçada Baptista began to exert their influence in the cultural life of Portugal. The ideas they spread with such unwearying faith were those of what is called 'progressive' Catholicism, and there arose a body of Catholic opinion definitely opposed to the regime.

Also soon after the campaign there appeared an important memorandum in the form of an open letter to the Prime Minister. This was signed by some fifty Catholics in their capacity as such, and who included half a dozen priests. They censured the brutality of the PIDE, into whose conduct they demanded an impartial enquiry. It was a polite letter, its appeal was expressly to militant Catholicism and it ended by condemning the use of a political police force in a state supposedly inspired by Catholic belief.

The Brazilian ambassador, Alvaro Lins, himself a well-known author and literary critic, also wrote a letter, this time to the Cardinal-Archbishop of Lisbon, to report a PIDE atrocity; and he wrote as one outraged in his Christian convictions. From the embassy window his wife had seen a prisoner thrown from the third storey of the police headquarters and left to hang on the electric cables for hours until he died.

The fifty Catholics naturally received no answer from the Prime Minister; or rather, he left the PIDE to do the answering for him in practical fashion and to prepare a case against the signatories. With the Bishop of Oporto, who happened to be out of the country, he dealt by preventing his return, so forcing him into what was to be nearly ten years' exile. No hint of public protest came from the hierarchy, not any least gesture on behalf of the wronged prelate. It was only because the opposition would not let the matter drop that anything was heard of it at all.

Later on things changed. The Church under Pope John passed through the great revolution of the Second Vatican Council and the Church in Portugal, burdened though it was with its weight of reactionary tradition, could not stand quite outside the general movement, even had it wished to do so. True, the hierarchy, with the exception of the Bishop of Beira in Mozambique, remained impervious to any modernising thought. But all the same, the leaven was beginning to work.

During the months before Delgado went to ground in the Bazilian embassy I got to know him better. As I have said, he wanted to start a National Independence party, and when he asked me to I lent him my office for an important meeting. I did not attend this myself, however for, seeing how badly its objectives were defined, I could not consider his proposal practical politics. Neither he nor his nearest collaborators seemed to have decided whether they were to contend with political weapons for legal recognition, or simply to serve as a screen for more or less revolutionary activities. Delgado was alone and, once the stimulation of his presidential campaign had passed, he felt the need of a party behind him which

might, as an organic force, balance either Communist influence or that of the Democratic-Social Directive.

The Communists, oddly enough, proclaimed themselves
willing to join such a party at the time. Obviously they were
hoping to form a united front, something on the lines of the
MUD, where they would furnish the motive power and by
means of which popular enthusiasm for Delgado could be
turned to their own ends. In thus expecting him, with his
revolutionary dreams and his fighting spirit, to be the figure-
head or banner-bearer for any such movement, they mis-
judged him badly.

For himself, he was already more than disappointed in the
Communists, whom he thought too law-abiding, and lacking
in what he understood by revolutionary ardour. The Social-
Democrat group and its 'paper-work opposition' also aroused
his wrath; submitting forms by the thousand was not his kind
of political warfare. Nor could he abide to see opposition
eminences like Azevedo Gomes or Jaime Cortesão treated
with the respect they deserved, and always called them
'bearded wonders'.

The National Independence idea came to nothing and as
time went on Delgado's political potential, which was considerable, fizzled out as the result of mistakes not always of
his making. And he himself was not a politician. He was a
man of action, prepared to play his part at given moments
now and then.

Our first open-air parade after the so-called elections was
held on 5 October 1958, anniversary of the founding of the
Republic. I had a lot to do with the arrangements and I suppose I could say, with all due modesty, that I taught him on
that occasion the basic rules of street-demonstration. The
meeting-place was to be the Alto São João cemetery in the
eastern part of Lisbon, where democrats were to pay the traditional republican homage to the heroes of the Republic. Drawn
by Delgado's presence, a dense crowd packed inside and the
police did not dare interrupt the speakers. When it came to
leaving, however, we found the gates were locked and we
were prisoners. After much parleying a small side gate was

opened and we were allowed to trickle out by ones and twos.

In the square beyond, invigilated by a strong force of police, was another crowd of those who had been unable to get in. They cheered on catching sight of the General, and just as he emerged some men ran up to him with shouts of 'Viva Delgado!', hoisted him on their shoulders and set off. From where I stood beside him I could see what they were trying to do and yelled, 'General! General! Look out, they're PIDE!' He punched himself free of his pretended well-wishers. By now the crowd had broken through the gates and spread into the square, which was cleared by a charge of mounted men. The people managed to form again further on, but they had no focus without Delgado and he was nowhere to be seen. Later, however, he appeared as arranged at a window overlooking the square, with some of the opposition leaders, to receive a delirious greeting. The frantic police had to use hand-grenades and tear-gas to disperse us.

Delgado's presidential candidacy awoke some interest in our opposition among political circles abroad. Important newspapers began at last to pay attention to Portuguese affairs and to cast a critical eye on the Government. The *New York Times* carried articles in this sense by Benjamin Welles and *Time* magazine, which took the same line, was unobtainable on our news-stands for several years.

This seemed a good moment to ask Aneurin Bevan and the head of the British Liberal Party, Jo Grimond, to visit us. Both accepted. We also invited Pierre Mendès-France, who said he had not time and refused. Bevan, Pietro Nenni and Mendès-France were then regarded as the leaders of Social Democracy in Europe and had taken part in a memorable three-man debate, organised by Jean-Jacques Servan-Schreiber and published in *L'Express*, on the future of democracy and Socialism on the continent.

The Government was claiming that the opposition as an organised political force had ceased to exist after the elections, and Bevan's coming at our invitation would certainly help to prove how wrong they were. For this reason we had to plan his visit with the utmost care, and I was asked to draw up a detailed programme and show it to Delgado. 'Good.' 'Go on.' 'Yes, that's fine.' Curtly, he signified approval. I came to a point where the suggested procedure was, 'Bevan, accompanied by General Delgado, will leave his hotel in central Lisbon at six in the evening, and drive in an open car to lay a wreath on the Camões statue. This is in one of the busiest squares in the town and he will be making the first public appearance of his visit. Even if the programme is kept out of the newspapers, as we may assume will be the case, we can ourselves ensure a big-scale demonstration, with a large attendance of democrats.' Delgado looked thoughtful, then asked,

'Who's going to stop the PIDE provoking trouble? Or even an assassination attempt?'

'I don't think there's any real answer to that,' I said. 'Some of us can walk by the car and stay round you, not that that's a proper protection. We simply have to take the risk, there's nothing else for it.'

'Very good, very good,' said the General briskly. Another moment's thought, and then : 'Couldn't we get somebody to throw tomatoes at Bevan? Show him what Fascism's like in Portugal?'

Deadlock. It was the former officer of the *Legião*, come suddenly to the surface.

But in the end we had none of these worries, thanks to Salazar. When the air-tickets were already on their way he announced that Bevan and his wife would not be allowed to enter the country. For this charming gesture he furnished the painfully silly excuse to the press that Bevan spoke only English, and so few Portuguese could understand that language. . . .

These years after the General's campaign were full of political ferment. The workers were presenting more and more claims for social justice and there was a widespread outbreak of purely political strikes as soon as the elections were over. The fishermen at Matosinhos near Oporto were particularly resolute and inspiring. In June and July the Communist underground caused stoppages almost everywhere, while the big May Day manifestations of 1959 led to savage bouts with the police and ended in a great many injuries and arrests.

But still the hope of change persisted. For the first time after an election the people did not lay down their arms. This the Government realised and set itself to deal with, calling as usual upon the PIDE. But the PIDE was not quite all it had been. Two happenings had contributed to destroy its legend of invincibility. Henrique Galvão had made a sensational escape from custody in the Santa Maria hospital in Lisbon; and Alvaro Cunhal, in company with some others, was similarly out of the fortress of Peniche.

Captain Galvão had been in prison since the early 1950s and was under twenty-four-hour police supervision while in hospital. But yet he managed to get away, complete with everything he possessed—manuscripts, books, even a tame sparrow he had made a pet of. He was given asylum shortly afterwards at the Argentine embassy.

The flight of Cunhal and his friends was more spectacular still. Peniche is an old walled township on a narrow peninsula jutting into the sea, and the single approach-road is checked by the police. The prison itself is the inner part of the eighteenth-century fort at the far end of the town, patrolled by Republican Guards. Conditions are severe in the extreme; Peniche is the quintessence, as it were, of all Salazarist concentration-camps, and virtually escape-proof. Alvaro Cunhal and his companions escaped.

These break-outs considerably damaged the prestige of the PIDE and the general gratification they afforded, even among those who took no interest in politics, is indescribable. And a year or so later there were two more, to underline the fact that the security police was losing some of the old efficiency. In December 1961 a group of important Communists got out of the fortress at Caxias, in the armoured car Hitler had presented to Salazar during the war and which was kept on the premises; and in 1969 Herminio da Palma Inácio, a revolutionary leader of the LUAR (the League of Union and

Anti-Fascist Action), then the best-guarded and most closely-confined prisoner in Portugal, slipped from the custody of the PIDE in Oporto.

The night of 11 to 12 March 1959 saw preparations for a rising against the regime. Owing to hesitations at the last minute it came to nothing, but it had important results all the same. The dozens of officers and civilians arrested appeared a year later before the military court at the Santa Clara prison in Lisbon and their trial, in which I took part in a professional capacity, became famous in the annals of political hearings in Portugal.

It should be clearly understood that the plot in question was quite unlike any previously-attempted putsch. The idea behind it was different, and different people were directing it. This was a young man's plot and the young men concerned had most of them come into politics during the Delgado campaign. Some were Catholics, others had begun life as Fascists, and yet there was non-Catholic support from democrats of various shades of opinion for the Catholic-inspired conspiracy. At the head of things on the civilian side was a Merchant Navy officer and one-time president of the Catholic Youth Movement named Manuel Serra, who had done devoted work for Delgado. He was the pattern of a romantic revolutionary, full of noble mysticism, but his organising talent was unfortunately less than his powers of persuasion, which were remarkable. The military side, though Major Pastor Fernandes was nominally in command, seems to have depended primarily on Captain Almeida Santos, who had been a leader of the *Mocidade Portuguesa*. He was tragically assassinated later and his body found buried in the sand on the beach at Guincho, near Caxias.

The plot had many prominent supporters besides those whose names came out at the trial, and they included senior officers of the armed forces. The police discovered some of the facts but for political reasons preferred not to reveal all they knew. Almeida Santos was very close to the former President Craveiro Lopes, who was certainly involved, and also had contacts in the Defence Ministry of General Botelho Moniz. But Salazar had an invariable technique with military plots. The army itself was left alone, only some of the instigators being charged, for the sake of the information they could be made to disgorge.

The conspiracy of 11 March failed, although the National Republican Guard and the PSP—the Polícia de Segurança Pública—among others, were prepared to help and it should have succeeded easily. Failure was due to lack of decision on the part of the military leaders, their reluctance to assume responsibility, and to serious faults of planning. Nevertheless the fact remains that, with all those weeks of work and several hundred people in the secret, the PIDE knew nothing until the very last.

The trial made it obvious that some of the service conspirators had had doubts at the eleventh hour as to where their duty lay. One CO who had noticed odd things going on in his own command and perceived with surprise the arrival of officers from other units, not usually on his strength, had sat up talking about and trying to unravel the plot until the early hours of the morning. Once he saw that it was neither likely to go into operation before breakfast nor get very far when it did—for it amounted to little more than unaccustomed unrest at some of the barracks—he advised his visitors to go away before he had to put them under arrest.

Humberto Delgado, meanwhile, was still in the Brazilian embassy. The Portuguese Government would not recognise the fact of his political asylum nor, therefore, issue him a safe-conduct to leave the country. But Alvaro Lins, the ambassador, with a courage beyond praise, dug his heels in and refused to concede to the very severe pressures exerted. Valiantly he defended Delgado's rights and in the end wrung from Salazar permission for him to travel freely to Brazil.

The fiftieth anniversary of the Republic fell in October 1960, and the opposition seized the occasion to plan several activities as demonstrations against Fascism. Inspired by Jaime Cortesão and aided to a great extent by Mário de Azevedo Gomes, 'our Professor' as we called him, we now began to compile our *Programme for the Democratisation of the Republic.*

The regime had been used to point out, in every electoral campaign, that the opposition was a mixture of dissident groups, incapable of producing a common administrative scheme and drawn together from time to time solely in an effort to destroy the Government. But this diversity, far from being a sign of weakness, showed that we were strong and vital. In Portugal the question had always been, and still is, how to mount a united, or at any rate a co-ordinated, operation against our only real enemy, which is Fascism. If we are to do it without any one set of notions coming to dominate the rest, then we must have clear definition of the aims and objects of each component group, and guarantee to each its autonomous organisation.

The Programme, then, was no minimal outline, limited to generalities which the whole opposition could accept. It embodied neither pact nor debate between the holders of differing political and ideological beliefs. Such was not the object. It was not intended as a straight declaration of principle but, primarily, as a definition of a coherent policy of the centre left that could stand as a valid alternative to the Fascism of Salazar. It tried to show that here were people who thought on European lines and were capable of taking the reins into their hands. The object was, in other words, to disprove official propaganda in all its absurdity of 'Fascism versus Communism and Chaos'.

The Programme was not a blueprint for a putsch or a revolution, as the police later said it was. All we wanted was to demonstrate that sensible men could implement a new and cohesive policy in every department of administration, and in this respect nothing like it had been seen before in Portugal.

The original idea came, very largely, from the Republican Resistance people, actively assisted by our Professor. But though the compiling team, of whom I was one, was avowedly left-wing, the Programme was not therefore the exclusive instrument of our own theories. The liberal Republicans, the

Social Democrats and the *Seara Nova* Socialists—men such as Nikias Skapinakis and Rui Cabeçadas—all adhered to it and the final compromise had not been reached without difficulty. We had had to appeal to technicians in official organisations or in the Ministries for classified information, and there were many political problems, notably over the colonies. The first draft took several months to finish and was not made public until May 1961, at a press conference held in Acácio Gouveia's office. The PIDE knew nothing of this beforehand, but next morning they arrested Acácio Gouveia, Gustavo Soromenho and me. The sixty-two others who had also signed the Programme were picked up and imprisoned one by one. I received the maximum six months, subject to sentence.

The preliminary enquiries themselves took six months and I was convinced for all that time that sentence would be delayed for ever. It was the official image that was going to suffer, after all. But eventually, thanks to pressure from the opposition candidates in the 1961 elections, our Programme was printed in full in the daily press and we were then let out on bail. An amnesty was accorded some years later.

The Programme is, I think, not bold enough on certain points and on others, overseas policy for one, is definitely behind the times. But broadly speaking its propositions were realistic and courageous and if adopted might have saved the country from the mess it is in today. As the first serious outline of democratic possibility it will stand as an important milestone in the political life of our nation at a most difficult juncture.

Nineteen sixty-one was the year of the big slide. All sorts of factors which had been developing in different directions for a long time now coalesced; things began to happen suddenly and the regime was beset with trouble everywhere. In January Henrique Galvão pirated the liner *Santa Maria*; some two months later war flared up in Angola; General Botelho Moniz, the Defence Minister, attempted a *coup d'état* soon afterwards and in that same month of March there was a Government reshuffle, Salazar adding Defence to his responsibilities as Prime Minister and appointing Adriano Moreira

to the Colonial Office. From May to November the Democratisation Programme was being circulated and those who
signed it going to prison as a result. In the October-November
election campaign the opposition first raised the question of
self-determination for the colonies, and in the latter month a
plane of the national airline, TAP, was hi-jacked in mid-air.
The invasion of Goa, Damão and Diu by Indian troops lost
us Portuguese India; and the Beja rising occurred on the last
day of the year.

These events contained enough dynamite to overthrow any
government in any country whose public opinion was blessedly
free; but Salazar survived them all. What thinking politician,
faced with so many knotty problems, but would have felt
some touch of misgiving and either resigned or at least consulted those of other political persuasions? He should have
sought, in coalition, for the best solution possible. The future
of Portugal was at stake, the future of generations yet to come.
There should have been a referendum on the Government's
African policy. But the dictator did not think so.

In the general climate of anti-colonialism after the Second
World War it was not exactly difficult to forecast the rise of
African nationalist movements in our colonies. Anyone who
expected us to be immune because our native populations were
backward or because we cherished legal fictions about 'Portugal Overseas', was either a crass fool or a hypocrite. But the
Prime Minister was uninterested in the overseas territories.
To him they were a long way off and far beyond his ken. In
all his years of power he never once dreamed of visiting them,
to learn more about them or to study their needs at first hand.

From 1951 onwards, not without much holding back and a
good many difficulties by the way, the Government did make
some apparent modifications in its colonial policy. This was to
prepare for Portugal's long-delayed entry among the United
Nations in 1955 when, as Salazar himself put it, they let her
in as 'small change'. Lisbon was attempting to right some of
the more flagrant wrongs and paying special attention to the
colonies. But the constitutional amendment of 1951 by which
these were abruptly transformed into Overseas Provinces, and

the Empire became One Multiracial and Intercontinental State, deceived nobody. The regime saw the overseas question as mere police work and thought that native aspirations were to be stifled by such oppressive methods as were employed at home. Even before hostilities began it was quelling revolts, strikes, protest movements and mutiny in the colonies with extreme violence of which no news was allowed to reach the public in Portugal. The revolts were foreshadowings of what was to come, but authority refused to consider negotiation and slurred over the real problems. Responsible sections of the opposition of course heard nothing, until the war broke out, of the many sickening things that had been done.

We shall analyse later the colonial policy into which Salazar dragged us after 1961, at a time when the old European powers had broken the trail by assisting their subject peoples, with more or less good will, to independence. Portugal, a colonial power who was herself a colony for the economic enterprise of other nations and increasingly dominated by foreign capital, made it her idiotic boast that the wind of change might blow on her in vain.

Towards 1960 General Delgado reached Brazil. In contact with Portuguese exiles there, and later with Henrique Galvão who was by then in Argentina, he attempted to reorganise his National Independence Movement by the injection of revolutionary ideas.

Events at this time are very hard to disentangle. In Brazil Delgado had a veritable hero's welcome, receiving the honours and respect that were his due as leader of the opposition in Portugal, and the political atmosphere was all in his favour. With the minimum of address he could have turned to account the immense fund of sympathy there for the democratic cause in Portugal; he could also have taken his opportunities with the Portuguese expatriates, traditionally conservative though they were, and set on foot a great liberation movement. Unhappily he did neither of these things, but let himself be drawn instead into profitless argument and personal dispute. His prestige was diminished as a result, he was led to make some disconcerting statements and publicly to support some rather odd opinions.

He and General Herrera, President of the Spanish Republican Government in exile, signed a pact of mutual aid between the two oppositions—an interesting departure, but of small practical import. He joined a lodge of exiled Spanish Freemasons at São Paulo. And it was now that the *Directôrio revolucionârio ibérico de libertación*, the Iberian Revolutionary Directorate for Liberation, or DRIL, made its appearance, claiming, at least to begin with, to have his approval. The famous attack on the *Santa Maria*, hailed by one Italian journalist as the greatest publicity stunt of the century, was carried out in the name of the DRIL.

It was in January 1961 that the Portuguese liner, with hundreds of passengers on board, was seized by a handful of bold adventurers, diverted from her accustomed route and, romantically rechristened the *Santa Liberdade*, headed into the South Atlantic, hotly pursued by ships of the British and American navies. Obviously a feat that courted attention. I remember spending days crouched over the radio listening for news, and how *Santa Maria* bulletins came through in every language you could think of. There seemed to be no other news at all. It is easy to imagine the fury of Salazar, used as he was to enveloping silence, at this unseasonable attention drawn by Galvão to Portugal and her Fascist regime.

But the perpetrators of Operation Dulcinea, as they called it, denied that they had set out to gain publicity. What, then, was their object? History gives no certain answer. There is no doubt that the attack was carried out by Spaniards as well as Portuguese, while some said that the master-minds were two Spanish majors, Sottomayor and Junquera, both veterans of the Civil War (I met them later in Brazil and very peculiar characters they were), and that Galvão took nominal command only because the vessel involved was Portuguese. Also the plan as first conceived was to 'rescue' not one but several ships. The abandonment of this scheme at the last moment for lack of means was supposed to have led to differences between Galvão and the Spanish majors.

There was much guess-work as to where the *Santa Maria* was going. Was she bound for Angola, where the nationalists made their initial attack on the prison at Luanda on 4 February? Some people saw a connection between the two incidents, since they happened at more or less the same time. Personally I did not agree; those concerned were as far apart in ideology and politics as they were in physical distance and unlikely to have synchronised so well. Then was she headed for the Canaries, there to land the exiled Spanish Government? No. The small force had insufficient troops for such an enterprise, even if they were expecting outside aid. Or did Galvão and his companions merely wish, as they claimed, to go to Brazil and there profit by the sympathy of the new President, Jânio Quadros?

But if the motives were obscure the operation was politically fruitful and did more than most things to show the world at large what the Portuguese regime was really like. Now at last the international press paid some attention to our troubles.

For most of its readers the man behind the *Santa Maria* incident was General Delgado, lending his authority as head of the opposition. In fact Delgado seems to have been kept in touch with events by the pressmen and, never one to allow encroachments, to have quarrelled with Galvão in the end. The most active members of the opposition thus split into two rival groups and the consequences were disastrous for us all.

Long after this, at the beginning of 1970, I happened to be in Brazil, where Galvão was in a mental home. I had spoken to him only twice in my life and never particularly approved of his political activities. But he was alone, old and ill. He had fought like a lion against Salazar after all. I was there in the country, and I felt I ought to go and see him. I found him in a bare room, lying fully dressed on his hospital bed. He could remember nothing, asked me for a cigarette, and then, with the saddest, most forlorn air, enquired why he was in prison. He wasn't, I said; he was here to be looked after. 'Then why don't they let me go back to Portugal?' he persisted. So I said yes, he probably could go, now that Salazar was dead; dead to all political intents and purposes, I meant.

He sprang up immediately and shouted at me, 'That's a lie! He can't be dead. I'm the one who has to kill him!'

Contrary to belief, the attempted *coup d'état* of General Botelho Moniz in March 1961 was not a result of what had happened in Angola. Ever since Delgado's presidential campaign conspiracy had been hatching among the armed forces. With increasing frequency officers and NCOs, dissatisfied with the regime, kept urging their superiors to some sort of action. Their superiors were the more inclined to listen since they knew they could rely on Marshal Craveiro Lopes if favourable opportunity arose. His anti-Salazarist feelings were notorious and he himself discreetly encouraging.

Military discontent, as we have seen, began to focus against Santos Costa. It was in order to nip conspiracy in the bud that Salazar, as soon as the presidential elections were over in 1958, decided to replace Santos Costa as Minister of Defence by Júlio Botelho Moniz, whom the army would have forced upon him in any case.

For the old guard of the opposition the very name Botelho Moniz was an offence. It spelled the Spanish War, the *viriatos* and the 'industrial mobilisation' of 1944 when strikers were herded into the bullrings. But these and similar horrors were associated with Júlio's brother Jorge and it was in fact Júlio, Minister of the Interior in 1945, who was now called in to allay the prevailing unrest in the army. He had been a Fascist, like the rest of his family, but in the years that led up to his becoming Minister of Defence had evidently been moving, warily, into disagreement with Salazar. Delgado told me that when he was promoted General he turned to three others who were gazetted at the same time with the words: 'We've got to the top now; it's our duty to throw Salazar out.' That pact was never fulfilled, but one of the four was Júlio Botelho Moniz.

More than a single conspiracy was brewing among the armed forces, however. There were several, centred on different people—generals and colonels, or more lowly captains and lieutenants. Often the various groups were unknown to each other or at most made transitory contact through common friends. But it is true that evident links existed between the plot of 11 March 1959, the attempt of Botelho Moniz and the Beja rising, apart from other, lesser-known intrigues, and this despite the fact that varying aims made each a separate enterprise.

It is not easy to make out exactly what happened over the abortive coup of Júlio Botelho Moniz, for those chiefly involved have not yet spoken and there may be deliberate distortion in the accounts we have. It seems that the Defence Minister, assured of support from air, sea and land commanders in bringing down the Government of Salazar, urged the President to give the word; that Américo Thomaz asked for twenty-four hours to consider; and that this was time enough for the dictator, warned of the affair, to weed out his High Command and Cabinet and to dismiss Botelho Moniz from his post.

Meantime the opposition was not idle. After several years of internal dispute we felt we should now co-ordinate and reinforce our efforts against Salazarism. What was needed, we thought, was some kind of co-ordinating authority in the provinces and so were created the *Juntas patrióticas*, which were to become the *Juntas de acção patriótica*, or Patriotic Action Councils.

From the outset the Department of Political Justice, accepting the PIDE reports, looked on this movement as no more than a screen for the Communist Party. Anyone proved to belong to a Patriotic Junta was immediately liable to over two years' imprisonment with an automatic extension under the notorious 'security measures'. The police, however, were absolutely wrong. The purpose of the Juntas from their beginning in the winter of 1959–60 and right up to the establishment of the Central Junta in Algiers some three years later, was always to unify and gather in all the opponents of Fascism, and among their Liberal Republicans, Freemasons, Catholics, Social Democrats, Socialists and Communists, the latter were very far from being in a majority, especially in the higher echelons.

E

The movement was short-lived; Government oppression saw to that. But it had revived the brotherhood of anti-Fascists as we had known it during the final years of the war.

I entered the Aljube prison in May 1961 and was later transferred to the fortress at Caxias. There I was kept until 4 November, which was the last campaigning day for elections to the National Assembly. I could not, therefore, take part in the political preliminaries of those elections, nor follow them closely. Only one daily newspaper was allowed me, the semi-official *Diário de Notícias*, which hardly mentioned them. But I knew all the same that in some places, notably in Lisbon and Oporto, the opposition had produced combined nomination lists and done some brave electioneering. On 6 November its candidates petitioned the President for a change of government and next day—five days, that is, before the poll—they all retired for the customary reason, lack of minimum democratic safeguards to ensure a free election.

By now the country was at war. Reaction to the rising in northern Angola and the terrible ensuing massacres made the atmosphere during the campaign even more tense than usual. Some of the dissident candidates declared themselves in favour of self-determination for the native African populations and held the regime responsible for the outbreak of hostilities.

This campaign was also marked by the first incident of a kind that would become familiar. Herminio da Palma Inácio forced the pilot of a TAP plane to alter course in mid-air and flew over Lisbon and other parts of Portugal scattering leaflets which attacked the whole electoral farce. Palma was an amazing character, famous for having sabotaged aircraft at Sintra in 1957 and for a dashing escape from the Aljube prison in the following year. This hi-jacking of the TAP plane was his return to revolutionary activity after a decade and more of exile in Brazil and the United States.

December of 1961 was especially eventful. Several leading Communists, as we have seen, got out of Caxias on the 4th; and only those who have spent long months in that fortress gaol and know the grim and rigorous conditions there can appreciate just what a spectacular stroke that was. It was also a humiliating stroke for the PIDE and reprisals were inevitable. On the 16th José Dias Coelho, a sculptor and a militant Communist, was murdered in the street at Alcântara. He had, as I heard from a witness whom I met during the elections of 1969, been shot repeatedly in the back as he fled from his pursuers.

And this same month was to see the end of Portuguese India. After fifteen years of pigheaded diplomacy and propaganda, of futile challenges to the Republic of India, of violence and cruel repression—a particularly bloody example being the treatment of the *satyagrahi* demonstrators in 1954 and later —our enclaves of Goa, Damão and Diu were occupied with little or no resistance. It was a walkover for the Indian troops and the Portuguese surrendered unconditionally.

On the eve of the invasion Salazar, who was then Minister of National Defence, telegraphed to General Vassalo e Silva, the Governor : 'I contemplate no truce and I wish no Portuguese to be taken prisoner. No ship is to surrender. Our soldiers and sailors must conquer or die.' He also added. 'The struggle must continue for eight days at least, to give the Government time to mobilise international opinion as a last resort'.

But in this he failed. He was willing to contemplate the killing and wounding of hundreds of men and a holocaust of Portuguese troops so that the world might marvel watching; and that idea was more of a failure still. Rarely can there have been so great an absence of political foresight, such ignorance of what was going on abroad or such sheer, megalomaniac infatuation; and the result was manifest disaster. The national pride was abased, thousands of officers and men were captured and territories that had known the Portuguese presence for five hundred years were gone for ever in dishonourable and undignified loss. All this the country had to endure when her legitimate human and cultural interests could have been protected by peaceful negotiation.

As the American magazine *Time* put it, the rival forces

killed fewer enemies than did bottles of hard liquor. The most reliable statistics, it noted, gave a total of forty dead and wounded for both sides combined. *Paris Match* carried an enormous photograph of General Vassalo e Silva, faint with fatigue, over the caption 'True Apostle of Non-Violence'. The whole world laughed at the Mussolini-type bluster of the Government in Lisbon; but had that Government listened to the cooler counsels of the opposition things could have been different.

The question of Goa, or rather, of all Portuguese India, went back of course to 1947 when Great Britain under a Labour Government granted Indian independence, though the first murmurs in the Portuguese territories were raised a year earlier by Tristão Bragança da Cunha, Karkodhár and Rama Krishuam. These three were sent in consequence to Portugal, kept for three months at Peniche and then under surveillance in Lisbon. Integration of the enclaves with India was not then envisaged. The programme was for an independent state to be linked with both India and Portugal.

But in 1954 relations were broken off between the Republic of India and Portugal and the situation grew very serious. In Paris, twelve months before, the government of Mendès-France had negotiated the transfer of Pondicherry, thus adding a further important precedent to what Britain had done already. But still Portugal continued blind and obstinate. A ferocious campaign was launched against the peaceful *satyagrahis*. In Goa hundreds of people were thrown into prison. Salazar's reasoning was of the simplest : that Nehru, having claimed so often to be a pacifist and being so universally admired as such, would never dare resort to violence.

From 1954 onwards the opposition pointed out the danger of this deliberately unrealistic attitude. António Sérgio, who was himself born in Goa of European parents, caused a stir by publishing an open attack on what he called the Government's discriminatory and undemocratic policy. A similar statement was sent to the press by the MUD central committee under Ruy Luis Gomes. This declared that the problem of Goa could be settled only by negotiation based on the principle of self-determination and, although naturally censored, earned them several months in gaol.

The enclaves of Dadrá and Nagar Aveli were invaded in the summer of 1954. Salazar, thinking he might resolve what was an essentially political affair by recourse to legal quibbles, appealed to the International Court at The Hague, which gave its verdict on 12 April 1960. The glad tidings of official victory were proclaimed from the housetops; a little foolishly, it seems.

The whole machinery of government went into action on Portuguese India. Money was poured out on propaganda, diplomacy and armaments. Costly and belated schemes for economic improvement were put in hand, so that Goa spent its last days of Portuguese dominion in a state of artificial euphoria. Mining production was stepped up, the port of Mormugão developed. Thousands of Portuguese had to do their military service in India. And the whole thing finally collapsed in thirty-six hours.

That no proper plans were ever made for resistance in case of Indian attack is proved by the *chouriços* business, the Affair of the Sausages, the tale of which I had some years later from Major Reis himself, who assured me it was true. With the Indian troops poised to strike, the Governor of Portuguese India sent a cipher telegram to Lisbon with an urgent request for anti-aircraft ammunition—code-word *chouriços*. The job of delivery fell to Major Reis, piloting a civil aircraft of TAP, cargo and destination being alike unknown until he read his orders after take-off. His plane was the last to reach Goa. The invasion had already begun when he landed, and begun with an attack on the airfield, so his personal welcome was a grenade splinter in the leg. The airfield, harbour and all communications-centres were primary objectives, which meant that the defenders were out of contact from the start; they could get no news and they had no arms. Their joy at the sight of that plane coming in with the much-needed munitions was indescribable, as was their disappointment when the boxes were unloaded. Lisbon had despatched *chouriços*, sure enough.

A true story, and one that shows how unready were our troops in India. The Government treated the subject of the enclaves like a poker game. It bluffed, and it lost.

Salazar never disclosed how much money had gone on the operations, nor was it ever established who had been responsible for what. The humiliated soldiery, Vassalo e Silva at their head, came home almost by stealth on their release. Some of them demanded that the officers accountable should be court-martialled, but even that consolation was denied them. True, there were bowler-hattings, but all enquiries were held *in camera* and the censorship saw to it that nothing ever leaked out.

The invasion of the enclaves could not be justified on legal grounds, so much is evident, but, as the Italian journalist Gianino Carta wrote in the *Corriere della Sera* on 19 December 1961, 'The Portuguese position was morally untenable. The use of force is wrong, but more so is the anachronistic doggedness of Salazar, clinging to his microscopic colonies in the Indian Ocean sixteen years after the independence of India.'

But that is what Salazar never even wished to understand. Small wonder then that international support, as he himself acknowledged in a speech on 3 January 1962, should fail him when he needed it.

During the night of 31 December 1961—at two in the morning to be precise—a mixed group of soldiers and civilians attacked and seized the barracks at Beja, provincial capital of the Alentejo in southern Portugal.

Once again the moving spirit was Manuel Serra. He had been held in the Santa Maria hospital after the failure of the rising of 11 March, escaped, sheltered for some months first in the Cuban then in the Brazilian embassy, and finally rejoined Humberto Delgado and Henrique Galvão in Rio de Janeiro. A few months more, and he came secretly back to Portugal to prepare Delgado's return. It was as the General's personal representative that he launched the opening stage of the plot, leading up to the revolt at Beja.

Delgado had given him a free hand and in eight weeks, and chiefly with civilian aid, his revolutionary ardour had attracted dozens of convinced supporters who longed to strike a blow against the regime. The sad thing is that they were in no way equipped for this kind of action, which was meant to begin by an assault on the Beja barracks, spread throughout the south and culminate when General Delgado appeared to take command. Serra hoped that Delgado's presence, together with statements to be put out on the southern radio station he expected to occupy, would sufficiently counteract the loyalist Government forces and so crush any will to resist. All that remained would be a triumphal march to Lisbon.

It was not as impossible as it sounds and one may even attribute its collapse to too much enthusiasm, too few difficulties. Those involved were over-confident of their own powers of improvisation, too ready to believe that nobody would be on the Government's side.

The original date of 1 December was changed to the 8th. Then plans had to be postponed at the last minute, when the conspirators were already at their posts. It was now that Piteira Santos, in his role of liaison officer, must have introduced Varela Gomes to Manuel Serra. Captain Gomes was a serving soldier who had stood at the last elections. He was fond of action, devoted to the cause and his commission was in danger as a result of his emphatic opposition to the regime. He agreed to take over.

As I have said, of several plots in being at the time there was not one that came to anything. But Varela Gomes, who had a great many contacts, quickly got his team organised and, once the military had decided to act, the civilian element of course had less to do. It was in fact no longer necessary to attack the barracks at Beja at all, for Major Vasconcelos Pestana, son of a former Republican Minister, would be quite ready to open the gates himself.

Humberto Delgado in Morocco was ignorant of what was actually happening. Impatient to begin, he did not see why the attempt had been more than once put off and his impetuous nature made the drawn-out wait unbearable. Without telling anyone, he resolved to make his own way to Portugal. Suitably disguised and accompanied by his faithful secretary, a Brazilian woman named Arajarir Moreira Campos, he crossed the frontier on a false passport and slipped through customs with his uniform and sub-machine gun in a suitcase.

He arrived in Lisbon on the 31st and there calmly proceeded to telephone sundry people, all of whom were being watched more or less closely by the police. He wanted to get hold of Manuel Serra, who was nowhere to be found. By the time he ran to earth a friend who could put him in touch with the chief conspirators he had missed them : Serra and Varela Gomes had left for Beja. As soon as he realised that the plan was going into operation that very night, Delgado decided to reach the scene as fast as possible.

At Beja meanwhile everything was ready. Varela Gomes, with four or five others, entered the barracks. The officers on duty accepted the situation and offered no resistance. The commanding officer, Colonel Calapez, had gone to bed but was alarmed by the sound of Serra's revolver going off as the civilian contingent scaled the wall. When Varela Gomes appeared to demand that he support the revolt or become a prisoner like the rest he replied by firing at and seriously wounding him. He then took flight.

The night, apparently, was as black as ink and it was pouring with rain. No one knew exactly what was going on but the shots in the barrack-yard heralded a terrific exchange between the guard and the attackers and two men were killed.

With Captain Gomes out of action and Colonel Calapez escaped to alert the headquarters of the Republican Guard, the conspirators were left in an awkward predicament. Two of them would have to get Varela Gomes out of the place and into Beja hospital if his life were to be saved and the others soon realised that the whole operation was at risk, for in the prevailing confusion they could not hope to raise the garrison. Everyone stayed where he was and waited for daylight. Calapez, having warned the Republican Guard and the local police, got in touch with Lisbon. The garrison at Evora, many of whose officers were implicated in the plot themselves, set off to crush the rising.

By the time Delgado reached it, Beja was a town at war. He could not get near the barracks for the encircling guardsmen and police and it is a miracle that he was not recognised and arrested at the road-blocks.

When, thanks to Colonel Calapez, the news came through, the Under-Secretary of State for War, Tomaz da Fonseca, left at once for Beja. He arrived as dawn was breaking and the apparently loyal detachment from Evora was about to go into action. Fonseca went forward and somehow, though how has never been explained, was killed by these Salazarist troops.

The final reckoning, then, was three dead, several wounded, dozens arrested and dozens of conspirators on the run. Those in the armed forces who knew of and sympathised with the plot, and without doubt they existed, made no move. The drama of Beja sank into silence very soon. It was the last military revolt against the dictator in his lifetime.

Chapter Eight

Story of a Crime

'I risked everything and I lost it all. Family, friends, money. I'm finished. And my God, I'm lonely.'

I was visiting Delgado in hospital in Prague in 1964. He sounded like a man in despair.

He had been in a Czechoslovakian clinic for some time, after an emergency operation for strangulated hernia. They had shaved his hair off, which made him look thinner than ever. He had aged since last I saw him, when he took refuge in the Brazilian embassy five years before.

He recovered himself after that first outburst and began to speak in his usual lively fashion. He was convalescent now and out of danger, but it had been, so he said, a near thing. They were doing all they possibly could, but he didn't know the language and felt very isolated. His surgeon had nothing but a few words of English and the nurses could hardly work out what he wanted. But the Czech Government was treating him as a Head of State and, worried about the inevitable rumours in case he had a relapse, was inviting selected friends of his to come and see how he was cared for. This was what brought me here. All Delgado could think of was his family. Were they safe and were they being left in peace? When I got home I should, I assured him, tell them he was well.

He was then, early in 1964, president of the Patriotic Junta for National Liberation, founded in Lisbon some years previously. After Beja he had gone back to Brazil, to return once more towards the end of 1963 and set about preparing for a revolution. He had been in Prague for the second conference of the Patriotic Front, at which he had agreed that the struggle should be a united effort. He planned to move next to Algiers, for President Ben Bella was offering all kinds of facilities to the Portuguese dissidents.

More and more people had been exiled for political reasons and many of them were beginning to believe that legal ways of combating the regime were more or less exhausted. The only thing now was root-and-branch revolution, organised from abroad; and many devoted anti-Fascists preached the examples of Cuba and Algeria. The revolutionary Junta, they said, should be the driving force, with the Front to represent the political power of the united left. Here all revolutionary currents ought to find a place and even the Communist Party might join in some day. Thus the Front would come to resemble the *Front de liberation nationale* in Algeria or the '26 July' party in Cuba.

I never thought that such a revolution would do in Portugal, which had to follow the political patterns of Europe, but the notion raised long speculative discussions among the different anti-Fascist persuasions. The Communists, naturally, did not agree at all, for they always considered themselves as the one and pre-eminent revolutionary party, despite the fact that their great day was perpetually postponed. The Front, as they saw it, was nothing but a practical catchment area for such sections of opinion as fell outside their own net.

But General Delgado was a revolutionary empiricist and speculative discussion had slight effect upon him. For him the Front was a means of creating the political support *his* revolution needed, just at a time when he felt himself more than usually cut off, and it was not long before the leaders of the Patriotic Front began to differ as to the proper course to follow. Also, as the movement grew stronger abroad, its branches in Portugal went steadily downhill.

The few months in Algiers had proved enough to bring about ideological, political and even personal friction, sometimes of the silliest kind, between Delgado and nearly everybody in the Junta. He would by now have nothing at all to do with the Communist Party and craved immediate action. Advocate of the surprise attack or the bold stroke against the regime, he could not and would not realise what long slow toil had to go into thorough political preparations. The break came in the summer of 1964, when he refused to attend the Front's third conference in Algiers. A few days later he announced in *Le Monde* that the 'Portuguese Front for National Liberation' had had a meeting not far from the frontiers of Portugal. This was a phantom organisation he had conjured up himself and given the same initials as those of the Patriotic Front in order deliberately to cause confusion, gain publicity and cut the ground from under the feet of the leaders in Algiers. In Portugal, where news was difficult to come by, echoes of this conflict between the General and those who fought beside him aroused disquiet in opposition circles.

Knowing how isolated he in fact was and how little notice the country had taken of his calls for instant revolution, I could not think where his optimism came from. He must be counting on people I had never heard of, for though I was his friend I was not his out-and-out disciple. The last time I saw him was in September 1964, when we dined with Professor Emilio Guerreiro in Paris—in excellent form and full of faith in his destiny. Plans were making for Operation Oranges, a scheme for occupying Macao with the previously-obtained blessing of Red China, and there setting up a provisional Government which many of the United Nations would hasten to recognise. This project never looked likely to me, for how could Pekin be expected to approve? The dispute between Red China and Soviet Russia was by now a prime factor of international politics whose repercussions had reached Portugal; after a split in the Portuguese Communist Party two new groupings had appeared, the Marxist-Leninist Committee and the Popular Action Front, or FAP. Delgado's exuberant confidence must be based on something other than Operation Oranges, then at the tentative stage only. And indeed, though revealing none of his short-term plans, he did tell me how absolutely sure he was that Salazar and the regime had not long to go.

Twice during dinner he was called to the telephone and at about eleven o'clock he left to keep 'a very important appointment'. His farewell words to me were like a promise.

'Meet you in Portugal—sooner than you think.'
But Delgado's meeting was to be with death.

Several things suggest that the killing or kidnapping of General
Delgado had been planned long before by the secret branch
of the PIDE, or by some similar body. Peter Deeley, in an
article in the *Observer* of 26 April 1970, said that certain
members of the OAS claimed to have been offered £225,000
sterling for the murder. This would have been Operation
Beta, Operation Alpha being the projected assassination of
de Gaulle under the code-name of *Mont Faron*. Henri Leclerc,
a French lawyer on the committee formed by the Federation
of the Rights of Man to investigate Delgado's disappearance,
also received mysterious overtures from someone called Hoffman who said he belonged to the OAS and asked a large
sum of money to reveal what he knew of the attempt. The
European press, on the other hand, made much of the statements of Samuel Lehman, a Swiss legionnaire implicated in
the plot against de Gaulle; he who said that OAS men had
wanted him to kidnap Delgado, then expected on a visit to
Paris.

In 1964, soon before the General was assassinated, the
Portuguese writer Castro Soromenho, living in exile in Paris
and deeply involved with the Angolan nationalists, received
a warning from the French police. They had discovered a plot
to do away with him and four other prominent Portuguese
dissidents, including Fernando Piteira Santos, and advised him
to go into hiding in Brazil. And there was no doubt as to where
the orders for this plot were coming from. The French police
told him categorically—they were broadcast by the PIDE.
Castro Soromenho went to Brazil.

Another warning came from Victor Cunha Rêgo, an exiled
newspaperman and a personal friend of Delgado and Galvão.
He wrote to warn them that one of their 'supporters' in Paris
was a double agent whose mission was to have them both
murdered, and sent copies of his letter to other conspicuous
figures in the opposition. He had complete proof of what he
said and had lit upon some grisly preparations. There were

false papers, for instance, relating to the body of an American woman. A non-existent American woman was to die in the French capital and the papers would serve to take the corpse of a Portuguese anti-Fascist back to Portugal.

Delgado distrusted the regular opposition organisations and, coming late to the field of active politics, did not really know who was who in the battle. Differences of opinion, ideological or political, are one thing; the line that separates the true anti-Fascist from the unscrupulous adventurer is another. He had not enough experience always to recognise that line, and was the prey of people who claimed to be revolutionaries but who in fact made use of him against the established opposition groupings. Several of the men who first appeared about this time were of this sinister type : Mário de Carvalho and Ernesto Bisogno in Rome, Silva Martins in Paris or Henrique Cerqueira in Rabat, to say nothing of the enigmatical Ernesto Castro Sousa, or Sousa Castro, who was a straight police-agent.

Delgado considered himself, with reason, the chief representative abroad of the Portuguese opposition. But he reserved the absolute right to take final decisions without reference to the active members of the political associations behind him, and without even keeping them informed. It was thus his bad practice to choose his own representatives in various capitals of Europe and Latin America for their personal loyalty to himself, and they were all of them unknown to those who actually directed the opposition.

In 1962, after the failure of the Beja revolt, he had made public the details of his secret stay in Portugal—his disguise, the way he travelled round the country, the forged passport, which frontiers he had crossed on his inward and outward journeys, the photographs somebody took of him reading the *Diário de Notícias* in the middle of Lisbon, right down to the genuine PIDE stamps on the famous passport. It was not a wise thing to do, for it made a mockery of the police and could only infuriate them further.

To me this had always seemed the starting-point of the plan to kidnap him in Spain. He had entered his own country by clandestine means once, and so the police foresaw no difficulty in persuading the public that he had tried it again and been unmasked in time. This would at a stroke compensate them for the recent failure and rid them for years of a dangerous enemy, for Delgado had been judged, in his absence, morally responsible for the *Santa Maria* episode and a long prison sentence awaited him.

If they were to lay hands on him, however, they would first have to lure him as near the border as possible, and that meant Spain. Practical problems were few. They had been through the performance before often enough. We need only quote the case of Germano Pedro, whom they kidnapped at La Linea in Spain and smuggled into Portugal. Now all they had to do was make Delgado believe there was a military plot at home, with senior Air Force officers waiting to follow him. When he suggested that these officers come to Paris, the answer was, they could not; the police would be on their track at once, so conspicuous were they. They could, however, easily spend a day or two in Spain. Humberto Delgado fell as easily into the trap.

We may note in passing that the PIDE had tried to get him and Galvão to the Portuguese border just after the *Santa Maria* affair in 1961. Then the bait had also been a military plot but the scheme, with its rendezvous at Badajoz, had failed. But Badajoz, as though by pure chance, was named again as the rendezvous, four years later.

During the summer of 1964 Delgado, through a certain Mário de Carvalho, who was their agent in Rome, had been having more and more to do with a quasi-revolutionary group, supposedly working in Portugal. Mário de Carvalho was the spokesman abroad and he alone knew the real identity of the link-man who came out from Portugal and whom he introduced to the General as Ernesto Castro Sousa. The group, it is hardly necessary to add, was pure fiction, as were the plotters, their men and arms and meeting-places of which Mário de Carvalho wrote to Delgado. His letters, together with detailed states of the imaginary forces, were found among the General's papers in Algiers.

When he published his announcement in *Le Monde* of a gathering near the Portuguese frontier which was probably never held, Delgado had two main objects—to cause division among anti-Government supporters and to plant the suggestion that it would indeed be possible to have such a meeting in Spain, just across the frontier. Whether he meant to or not, he certainly gave the opposition a lot of trouble and endangered its work.

Therefore when he disappeared in Spain in February 1965 and the Patriotic Front confined itself to uttering its suspicions in sadly ill-judged communiqués, there was this precedent of the bogus meeting the previous summer to justify its behaviour, apart from any question of political differences within the opposition, or the General's mystifying train of conduct since. The ground in fact was well prepared for the false news subsequently put out by the Portuguese semi-official news agency ANI and the Madrid daily newspaper *ABC*, the purpose of which was to create confusion by making it seem that Delgado had never been in Spain but was in fact in Prague or elsewhere in eastern Europe.

During the latter part of 1964 the General progressively drew or was drawn away from many of the opposition groups in exile. In Algiers the quarrelling when he abandoned the Patriotic Front led rapidly to open warfare between the various anti-Fascists there, with Salazar's agents taking full advantage of the fact.

No genuine members of his Portuguese Front have ever been traced. I never found anyone who claimed to have belonged to it, even among those friends in Algiers who were loyal to him to the end. The only real names on that phantom roll were those of Mário de Carvalho, who was to put himself forward after Delgado's death as his political heir and General Secretary of the Portuguese Front, and Ernesto Castro Sousa.

Delgado tried to keep up his political contacts in Portugal, especially with people in the north, but these connections, which could have helped him to assess the true situation there and so detect the trap, now became extremely difficult to maintain. For example, he sent a message to his old comrade Dr Fernando Bandeira de Lima, who was spending a holiday in Paris in 1964, and asked him to come to Rome. The doctor had an unexplained telephone call on the morning he was due to leave, warning him of perils in store if he went; and the morning after that a stranger came up to him in the hotel lobby, casually mentioning that he was a PIDE man and producing an official card to prove it. Bandeira de Lima had been arrested and beaten up after the Beja revolt; clearly he preferred to return home without seeing Delgado and the object of the exercise was achieved. Humberto Delgado was cut off from those he trusted personally and who might have warned him of what was going on.

But on the eve of that last trip to Spain he must have begun to wonder, all the same. He asked his 'friends' in Oporto to meet him twenty-four hours earlier than the time fixed by Mário de Carvalho. They refused. It would be nonsense, they said, to change.

His devoted secretary Arajarir herself hesitated about going with him. However, she gave in when he insisted and applied in Algiers for a visa to enter Spain. This he advised her to do, for he evidently believed that her Brazilian nationality would protect her. He himself travelled as Lorenzo Ibañez, a Brazilian diplomat, on a faked passport provided by an Italian doctor named Ernesto Maria Bisogno. This man had collaborated with the Fascists under Mussolini, was a friend of Mário de Carvalho and as shady a character as you could wish to find. He died later in circumstances which have never been explained.

There is evidence that the Spanish police checked Delgado's entry into Spain and kept him in view as far as Seville. The commission of inquiry set up by the International Federation of the Rights of Man established that he left by boat from Ceuta, the Spanish enclave in Morocco, and landed at Algeciras during the morning of 11 February 1965. In Algeciras he posted a letter to Henrique Cerqueira, then went on to Seville, and arrived next day at Badajoz, where he stayed at the Hotel Simancas. From Badajoz he wrote some cards, postmarked the 13th. After that, nothing.

It was Henrique Cerqueira in Rabat who raised the alarm on the 23rd. He stated to the enquiry commission that General Delgado had told him that he should be back on the 16th, but that there was no real need to worry until the 21st. If he had not returned by then Cerqueira was to let his friends know. Then, if no news came within two days they could assume that he was either dead or in prison, and should alert the press.

Cerqueira is another of the curious people in the story. The fact that he was first with the alarm means nothing, since he knew that questions were sure to be asked sooner or later. In Paris, Professor Guerreiro had received a postcard, in Delgado's handwriting but signed Deolinda, which was his sister's name, and this proved his arrival at Badajoz on the 13th. Guerreiro waited uneasily to hear that he was back safely. On the 24th he decided to inform the Freedom Defence Committee of Portugal as well as the General's family and friends. And it was he who asked the Rights of Man commission to set inquiries going.

Meanwhile, Adolfo Ayala and some of Delgado's friends waiting in Algiers were also growing anxious. The General had left instructions that, if he did not get back, Ayala was to leave Algeria, having closed the office down so that no documents fell into the hands of the Patriotic Front. The few straightforward people who knew of the Spanish trip felt it quite possible that something terrible had happened.

Cerqueira's attitude after giving the alarm is most peculiar. He informed the commission of inquiry that Delgado said he would wait for a telegram from Carvalho, who was then in Italy, to say that all was well, and would then set out for Badajoz next day. And yet this throws doubt on the rest of his testimony, for when a trial was held in Italy he was to make furious efforts to exonerate Carvalho and prove him innocent of any connection with the arrangements at Badajoz.

Delgado's message to Guerreiro on 13 February was: 'I

think the thing will go through all right. I don't know when or whether I'll be back, though. Kindest regards, as ever.'

It must of course be realised that much of our knowledge of the affair comes from the Spaniards, who held a judicial inquiry under a judge, José Maria Crespo Marquez, specially appointed for the purpose. Given the circumstances in which this inquiry took place and the conclusions it came to, we do well to be cautious. It was officially opened on the afternoon of 24 April 1965, after the discovery of the bodies, but the press said nothing about the affair at all until it was mentioned in a telegram of the Spanish news agency EFE on the 27th. As an interesting detail, the police superintendent in Badajoz told the inquiry at midday on the 26th that, as far as he knew, Humberto Delgado had never been in the town, nor had anyone called Lorenzo Ibañez, with a Brazilian secretary. Yet the bodies had been found two days before.

General Delgado had actually left the Hotel Simancas in a hurry on 13 February, without taking his luggage or paying his bill. The management, it was later disclosed, had lodged a complaint with the police and sent the bags round to them. This meant that the police had actually known of his disappearance since the end of February. And yet they denied it, notably to the Rights of Man inquiry commission.

Before all this came out, however, a third, unidentified, corpse had been discovered in the neighbourhood of Badajoz, apparently in the first week of April. The Madrid *ABC* reported it on the 29th: 'A third body is also connected with the crime. It is that of a man, found about three weeks ago in the Abalã river near the Portuguese frontier, on the estate of that name between Badajoz and Olivença. It was naked and at first thought to be that of some gipsy or smuggler. Recently, owing to the insistent rumours concerning the disappearance of General Humberto Delgado and his having been in Badajoz, Interpol men arrived in the town and the corpse was exhumed. Death was due to some other cause than drowning.' Like Delgado, the victim had received a blow on the head. 'Rumours that the Portuguese leader vanished at Badajoz', *ABC* went

on, 'arose at the end of March, for it was there that all trace
of him was lost.'

The Spanish police had in fact known since February that
he had vanished, and had every reason to suppose that he
had been killed or kidnapped in Spain. Their judicial inquiry,
moreover, revealed some pretty conclusive details. For one
thing, they knew the chassis and engine numbers of the two
cars used by the criminals when entering the country on 13
February and when leaving it again, their work done, at dawn
next day. When I asked Judge Crespo Marquez how he had
managed to come by such useful information, of a sort not
regularly gathered at the customs-posts, he said,

'We were rather lucky, really. Keen men on duty that day.'

Up to the discovery of the bodies the attitude and silence
of the Spanish police were peculiar; as peculiar, indeed, as the
discovery itself. It may well have been the purest chance that
led two children to that macabre find on 24 April, but there
are some worrying coincidences about it all the same. Why, for
instance, should it happen on the very day that the Rights of
Man commission happened to arrive in Spain? One has the
feeling that the Spanish authorities changed their tune the
minute they knew it had established the fact that Delgado
was last seen in Badajoz on 13 February, and that it intended
to publish its report to that effect. Then, and only then, were
corpses mentioned.

The *ABC* for 28 April gives the following account : 'The
bodies were found about seven o'clock last Saturday evening
(the 24th), by José Feijoo d'Almeida and José Filipe Cayero,
aged thirteen and fifteen respectively. They were taking their
usual walk along a lane adjoining the road from Villanueva
to Valencia de Mombuey, about six kilometres from the former
village. This path lies within the Encinas del Espinar estate,
three kilometres or so from the Portuguese border. The boys
noticed some loose soil just off the pathway, but they thought
at first it was only a dead animal and were going on. After
talking about it, however, they retraced their steps, saw a
protruding human head and ran back home to tell their
parents.'

According to *Fechas* on 4 May, the children found not one body but two, lying some distance apart in a heap of turned earth from which one head stuck out. The Madrid daily *Arriba* gave details on 29 April: 'The bodies had been buried in the dry bed of a river, in hollows about fifty centimetres deep. The corpse presumed to be that of Humberto Delgado was in shirtsleeves, wrapped in a blanket, and had been covered with quicklime, earth and stones.'

Contemporary press accounts and all the available evidence seem to agree that one at least of the bodies was partly exposed, the head emerging from earth that had been dug over. Also, there was the quicklime. Whoever buried them, and added it, wanted them to disappear completely and was taking precautions against any stench that might attract attention. How, then, did they come to be found in a heap of newly-turned soil and why was one of the heads visible? That particular detail led a reporter to note that the way the bodies were left made it easy to discover them.

Early in May I went along that frontier road and saw the place. There were still traces of Arajarir's hair. The hollows were thirty centimetres deep at most. The spot is quiet, but not so isolated that someone would not pass by every day, which makes it unlikely that the bodies had lain there unobserved until 24 April. They had been taken there, or they had been partly exhumed after burial in order to be seen. Either theory is possible.

Curiously enough, as indicated in the Madrid *Gazeta Ilustrada*, the father of one of the boys had noticed nothing out of the ordinary on his daily rounds, although it was his job to look after the estate. And the local inhabitants seem to have been just as unobservant. It is, to say the least, abnormal that two superficially-buried corpses, one with the head sticking out, should lie unperceived for two months at the side of a public pathway within yards of a fairly busy road.

Another very odd detail is the fact that reports had mentioned from the first a gold ring with the initials H.D. on a finger of the male corpse; yet if the General were supposed to vanish the logical thing would surely have been to remove any such decisive indication. I ran into serious obstacles when I went to Badajoz to try to identify the bodies as his family's legal representative, but the ring was mentioned straight away. Next day I went to the Badajoz court with the General's widow and son, and though they were refused any means of identification and not even allowed to see the body, they were shown this ring, which neither of them recognised because it was a clumsy fake. Here there are two possible explanations. Delgado may have lost his own ring during his exile and bought himself another, or else we were seeing a last-minute device for labelling the body his. It is a relevant point and might have been cleared up had the interested parties had access to the dossier and been able to make inquiries unhindered. We could do nothing of the kind, however, and it will be more and more difficult to solve such points as time goes on.

I must admit that, lacking proper information and dependent on the suspect news given in the Portuguese press, I did not really worry for Delgado's life until 23 April, when the Rights of Man commission came to see me at my office. What they had to say convinced me that he had been either killed or captured after vanishing in Spain.

That March and April Delgado's family went through hell. Scarcely a day passed but some doubtful source produced a contradictory rumour to raise their hopes or plunge them into despair. I was not then actually in touch with them and all this came to me, as it were, from far away, as did the storm of argument that broke out among the exiled Portuguese opposition when the man who had been their presidential candidate disappeared.

The letters and appeals of Emilio Guerreiro; explanations from Mário de Carvalho; the ironies and omissions of the Patriotic Front in its maladroit communiqués, especially that of 23 March; the urgent appeal from the General's friends in Algiers on 12 March and the fighting and arrests when the office of the Front was searched; incredible statements from Henrique Galvão in Brazil—of these things I knew nothing at the time, and so could enter into the affair, and make a close study of it, with no previous prejudice.

It is not without interest to recall how I came to act for the family. On 27 April, when the news agencies announced that the bodies had been found (and in passing we may note that the Portuguese papers were mute on the subject for another two days), I called a meeting in Lisbon of the Democratic-Social Directive, for this was a serious fact of politics on which I thought the opposition should consider its attitude. In the absence of definite information it was not exactly easy to persuade my friends that we ought to produce a statement, but in the end they agreed on a petition to the Prime Minister, which I took to his offices at eleven o'clock that night. The document, which was noticed in the foreign press, asked, first, that the papers at home should be authorised to publish the findings of the judicial inquiry in Spain, together with those of the Rights of Man commission; secondly that, if the news proved true, the body of General Delgado might be brought back to Portugal; and thirdly that the Government should keep the country informed of subsequent developments.[1] It was a most moderately-phrased petition, but the authorities refused to grant our requests and not a line of it got into the papers.

Next day, the 28th, I called upon Maria Iva Delgado to tell her what we had done and offer our services in her appalling situation. The help she needed, she said, was not political but legal : Delgado's wife believed that politics had brought misery on her family and always had a horror of them. I accordingly became her lawyer and at once enlisted Fernando Abranches-Ferrão, Vice-President of the Law Society. We set up a committee of ten barristers, of varying political opinions, to assist us in this very complicated case.

The first thing to do was to get hold of any facts that could possibly help to identify the bodies. Abranches-Ferrão and I left for Badajoz late in the afternoon of 30 April, to find an

[1] The signatories were Acácio Gouveia, Artur Cunha Leal, Carlos Sá Cardoso, Carlos Pereira, José Moreira Campos, Mário Soares. Nuno Rodrigues dos Santos and Paul Rêgo.

unpleasant surprise awaiting us at the frontier : my companion was not allowed to leave the country. 'Orders from higher up', was the only explanation we could wring from the local PIDE chief, so back we went to Lisbon. It at least gave me the excuse for requesting PIDE permission for Senhora Delgado to come to Spain instead.

I crossed over alone on 3 May, she following some hours later with her son and daughter-in-law. The Spanish customs told me to report to the police in Badajoz and I was shadowed the whole time I stayed in Spain; 'to ensure my safety', so they said.

I had every difficulty imaginable in reaching Judge Crespo Marquez, and then he would not give me one scrap of information, nor allow me to see either the bodies or the photographs. In spite of all obstacles, however, I did manage to obtain a private interview for Senhora Delgado and her son. I then set off for Madrid. Without a Spanish lawyer to help, things were going to be impossible.

I had read in a foreign newspaper that members of the Spanish legal profession had written to the Rights of Man commission set up by the United Nations, asking that its inquiry be conducted by a committee of international lawyers whose impartiality was beyond question. Heading the list of signatures had been the name of a barrister in Madrid, Dr Mariano Robles, whom I saw as soon as I got there. We decided, and those who had signed with him agreed, to form a committee consisting of himself, Josefina Arrillaga and Jaime Cortezo Vellasquez Duro.

I was under no illusion that Spanish advocates were going to be able to cast any light on the Delgado affair. I believe that pressure of international public opinion alone can do such a thing in a case of political crime, especially when a state's police are implicated; that is what makes newspapers so invaluable. The International Federation of the Rights of Man, whose findings had just been published in France, had thus played a vital part in focusing attention on the matter. Its commission must be encouraged to go on with the work and collect as much evidence as possible.

From Madrid I went to Paris and Rome to consult with Henri Leclerc and Luigi Cavalieri, both lawyers who sat on this commission. I was equally anxious to hear what Emilio Guerreiro had to say, for he had been making inquiries of his own. These had received a great deal of space in the world press and fairly named Mário de Carvalho and Ernesto Maria Bisogno as persons involved.

I had no sooner arrived in Paris than I learned of a statement circulated in Madrid on 8 May and printed in the next day's papers. All it said was that 'the presiding judge had established the identity of Humberto Delgado, nationality Portuguese', and added that the long delay in identification had been due to the 'state of decomposition of the body'. But this changed everything.[2] The Spanish lawyers representing the General's widow and children were now entitled to take part in the proceedings and have access to the evidence, including that heard in camera. The Delgado affair entered a new phase.

The Portuguese official attitude at this time should not be forgotten. For all its seeming ignorance of and indifference to events, the Government was allowing only such items as suited it to appear in the press. The papers printed little beyond the approved news-agency material treating the whole thing as a matter of score-settling between rival cliques of the opposition. In other words, an attempt was made to shift the blame for a triple murder on to the opposition.

But once the bodies were identified the Spanish authorities revised their tactics, did everything they could to disclaim any part in the crime and did not hesitate to implicate the PIDE. Mariano Robles and I went back to Badajoz in June and this time Judge Crespo Marquez consented to see me. He did not, to be sure, authorise me to examine the evidence so far established, but the crime, he gave me to understand, was certainly the work of PIDE men, assisted by double agents in Rome. Just now, too, the international press began to publish facts that were anything but comfortable for the Portuguese police.

[2] See *Diário de Lisboa*, 9 May 1965.

The judge held a kind of reconstruction of the tragedy and allowed me to attend in a non-official capacity. We went to where the General was supposed to have been killed and one of the Spanish police officers said to me : 'The PIDE had a lot of amateurs on this job, I can tell you. Left their handwriting all over the place.'

It would have been sheer waste of time to tell him it was because they were sure of Spanish official protection.

In August, on my third visit to Badajoz, the judge informed me that Delgado's body would be at the disposal of his family when the police had finished with it. That of the secretary Arajarir was sent home to Brazil.

The family agreed with my suggestion that the General's remains be taken to Portugal, the condition being that there was no political demonstration when they buried him at the small village of Cela, near Nazaré. We made the necessary application, therefore, to Santos Junior, Minister of the Interior. He granted it a week later, adding in a postscript that the funeral might take place when and in such manner as he considered 'convenient'. To me these words had a sibylline ring and I again applied to know whether we might fetch the body home any time after 10 September, when the Spaniards were to hand it over. On the 6th he replied, to say : 'The return of the body on the date you mention is not considered convenient.'

The date we mentioned was in the holiday season, when political demonstrations are most easily avoided. Permission was in fact denied because the Government incorrigibly hated the Fearless General and the old animosity was displayed again in thus refusing him a grave in Portugal.

Abranches-Ferrão and I had an appointment with the Spanish judge in Badajoz on 9 September, to receive the body. Since we could not take it back to Portugal the family had agreed to temporary burial in Spain. Once more we applied to the PIDE for travel permits and left as soon as they came through, travelling by road with two other lawyers and Paul Rêgo, the journalist, who had been Delgado's close friend. At the frontier we were shocked to find ourselves arrested without explanation or delay and escorted back to Lisbon where, in spite of all I could say, the police confiscated my papers.

This provoked a wave of protest in international legal circles and stormy reaction from the Portuguese Law Society. The official excuse was that anti-Portuguese trouble had been expected near the border and it was to prevent this, apparently, that we were arrested and held for a fortnight incommunicado. Before releasing me they handed me my papers, sealed, and said how sorry they were that some inexperienced minion had been so 'regrettably stupid'.

In October 1965 the opposition took advantage of the electoral campaign to raise what it considered essential political and economic problems in a national manifesto which I read on its behalf at a press conference in Lisbon. We referred to the Delgado affair, declaring that the assassination of the Fearless General had been a premeditated political crime and that the Portuguese authorities had done everything in their power to impede the lawyers and the commissions of inquiry. We emphasised their having refused him a grave in his own country.

The manifesto made a great impression when it appeared in the papers. The Government, which had so far made no official statement on the Delgado case, felt obliged to give some sort of answer. It was Salazar himself who did so, when he wound up the election campaign on 5 November, and what he said was exactly what José Sachetti, second-in-command of the PIDE, had told me during my recent spell in prison. Delgado, according to this reading of events, had gone to Spain to organise a revolution, and anyway intended to give himself up to the Portuguese police if the revolution failed.

While the Dictator and the PIDE strove in vain to impose their version, the Spaniards for their part were doing all they could to appear as white as driven snow. A year after the crime, with its two, or possibly three, victims. the Spanish court presented its indictment in three investigation reports, bearing the dates 11 and 28 February and 28 March. In essence these documents give the facts as follows.

Delgado and the two Portuguese, Ernesto Sousa Castro and Mário de Carvalho, the latter of whom lived in Rome, were in Paris towards the end of 1964, when they decided on a further meeting at Badajoz the following February, to be attended by other friends in Portugal. From an Italian, a known bad character named Ernesto Mario Bisogno, Carvalho obtained a false passport with which the General entered Spain as Lorenzo Ibañez. Three rendezvous had been arranged in Badajoz—the station, the central post office and the cathedral. Delgado and his secretary, arriving on 12 February, booked in at the Hotel Simancas. They went to each of these three points without finding anyone, and enquired at the Tourist Office about the best way of getting to Olivença and Villanueva del Fresno.

During the night of the 12th four men 'of North African type' were also staying at the Simancas. The first pair were someone called Benezet and another, whose name nobody knew, the second consisted of Hazan Guy Isaac and an unidentified companion. All four were observed in the dining-room in confidential conversation with the General, who left next morning after breakfast. Hazan and the man with him then moved into the Pension Las Vegas, where they remained until the 14th.

Delgado went again to the post office and the station on the morning of the 13th but again drew blank and decided to leave the town. His secretary bought two tickets for Seville at the offices of the Estellesa bus company. He also booked a taxi to Olivença, though he did not go; and sent a card to Emilio Guerreiro from which it appeared that the pre-arranged contacts had failed, but there were signs that the plan might succeed nevertheless.

Also on the morning of the 13th four travellers passed the customs at Villanueva del Fresno into Spain. Evidence was presented to prove that they were Filipe Garcia Tavares and Ernesto Castro Sousa, both owners of Portuguese-registered cars—an Opel, EA 59-55 and a Renault, GD 86-23—and two men giving their names as Roberto Vurrita Baral and Washdeo Kundanmal Milpuri. The first three had Portuguese passports and Milpuri's passport was British. They were accompanied over the border by António Gonçalves Semedo, senior PIDE officer at the Portuguese customs-post of São Leonardo. He introduced Filipe Garcia Tavares to the Spanish officials as the Chief of Police in Angola and said the others were also friends. The four of them were going to Seville for the weekend and would be coming back the same way.

The Spanish inquiry, however, had revealed that all three Portuguese passports were false and that the British one belonged to a Pakistani who lived in Jersey and was safely at home on the dates in question. He—the real Washdeo Milpuri—had lost his passport on a visit to Lisbon two years before and, as the British Embassy confirmed, it had turned up in the hands of the police. The car-papers, too, were false, as were the registration numbers. Unable to pursue their inquiries in Portugal, the Spanish police had requested the Portuguese force to verify the identities of the passengers and had had no help at all. However, the report continues, it can be proved that the Opel was sold by the manufacturers to their Lisbon agents. The chassis number was 1/2346444, that of the engine 17/6514893. It can also be proved that, far from taking the Seville road, the travellers headed for Badajoz. They never went near Seville, nor registered at any inn or hotel on the way. They re-entered Portugal next day through the customs at El Rosal de la Frontera, in Huelva.

Early in the afternoon of this same 13 February a car pulled off the Badajoz–Villanueva del Fresno road not far from Olivença and parked out of sight behind a low hill. Soon afterwards a second car drew up and several people got out to join the first arrivals. When they drove away they left behind them a trail of blood, some unused 7·65 cartridges, some spent bullets of the same calibre and a book of tickets for a Portuguese sports lottery for Sunday, the 14th. The Spanish reports add:

'There is sufficient evidence to prove that the men, with their cars, who met at this spot were those who crossed the frontier with false documents at Villanueva del Fresno that morning for the purpose of kidnapping Humberto Delgado, who was brought here and killed when he attempted to resist.'

The date of 13 February matches that on which 'Lorenzo Ibañez' and his secretary quitted the Hotel Simancas, leaving their luggage behind. Some persons unknown afterwards went through this luggage in their rooms. As the bill had not been paid the police were eventually informed, and all efforts to trace the owners of the bags were unsuccessful.

A month later, on a hilly road near Villanueva del Fresno leading towards Portugal, but where there is no border-post, the bodies of a man and woman were found a little over two kilometres from the frontier, and identified as those of Humberto Delgado and Arajarir Moreira Campos. The former bore several wounds, the latter showed signs of suffocation and had presumably been strangled. They had been dead about two months. And two months before a shepherd and a male nurse had both noticed a Land Rover on this same road, across on the Portuguese side, whose occupants said they were shooting pigeons, though it was in the close season.

The evidence shows that the Badajoz meeting was known only to Emilio Guerreiro in Paris, to Mário de Carvalho and his friend Bisogno in Rome, to Cerqueira in Rabat and to 'a few friends' in Portugal, these last including Ernesto Castro Sousa who, it seems, later drowned himself in the Guadiana. It also appears certain that Guerreiro and Cerqueira tried to dissuade the General from what they considered a dangerous trip to Badajoz, while Carvalho not only pressed the idea but pointed out that his friends from Portugal were already on their way; and that he then concocted excuses for not going himself as he had promised.

It also emerges that Bisogno, provider of the false passport, went to Lisbon more than once, both before and after the murder, and that he was in touch with a known OAS chief named Jean-Jacques Susini. This must connect up with the offer of Lieutenant Hoffman, of the First Foreign Legion

Paratroop Regiment, to sell details of Delgado's death to Me Leclerc—an offer which came to nothing.

In consideration of the above facts the Spanish courts found the following persons guilty of premeditated murder : Filipe Garcia Tavares, Ernesto Castro Sousa, Roberto Vurrita Baral, Washdeo Kundanmal Milpuri, Hazan Guy Isaac, Benezet, Ernesto Maria Bisogno and Mário de Carvalho. Of these names, as we have seen, only the last two were genuine.

The second investigation report, dated 28 February 1966, dealt with a Moroccan citizen, one Elie Tapeiro, owner of a Lincoln registered in Venezuela in which Arajarir Moreira Campos had been killed. The Spanish authorities discovered that this man drove from Madrid to Lisbon on 22 February 1965 and there fitted an American number-plate : State of Virginia 983/880. He then returned to Spain, taking the Seville road. Instead of using the shortest way by El Rosal, however, he went over the frontier at Villanueva del Fresno on the evening of the 25th. Later he passed the spot where the bodies were found, then had trouble with the car and was forced to stop in Valencia de Mombuey and have it towed to the Parra Garage in Badajoz. There the Spanish police discovered it, with bloodstains inside and some strands of Arajarir's hair. Their conclusion was that since Tapeiro had been in sole possession of the car from its initial customs check in Madrid on 19 February until the 26th when it arrived at the garage in Badajoz, he must be guilty. This exact dating confirms the rumour that Arajarir was killed several days after the General, deliberately murdered as a troublesome witness.

A month later, on 28 March, came a third indictment, this time of António Gonçalves Semedo, captain of the PIDE frontier post at São Leonardo. It speaks of 'sufficient evidence' against Semedo, 'officer of the *Policia Internacional e de Defesa do Estado* who on 13 February, being in charge of the post at São Leonardo, accompanied four travellers over to Villanueva del Fresno, having previously inspected their papers and ascertained that one of them, Filipe Garcia Tavares, was Chief of Police in Angola. He introduced them to the Spanish police and customs officials, who made a note of their crossing and of the number-plates of their cars. Inquiries reveal that the personal documents as well as the car-registrations of these four men, already cited elsewhere as having taken part in the murders of Humberto Delgado and Arajarir Moreira Campos, were false.'

A warrant was issued, uselessly, for the arrest of António Gonçalves Semedo. Lisbon professed itself unable to force any Portuguese in Government employ to answer charges in a foreign country, and it has not been possible to find what had happened to Samedo since. But there is nothing to show that he did not continue with the PIDE and, as those who work for the police are protected by the police, any complaint brought against him in Portugal could lead exactly nowhere.

The case made by the Spanish courts is by no means complete, for many points are passed over unexamined, but it at least demolishes the Salazarist theory that Delgado met his end in some internal settling of scores among the opposition. Also it definitely implicates the PIDE.

The Spaniards without doubt knew more than they admitted, but included enough in their dossier to justify a trial. For such reasons of state as are easily imagined where Portugal and her neighbour are concerned, there was no trial; and the Captain-General, Muñoz Grandes came on a visit, said to have been in connection with the affair, and to hold high-level talks on its political consequences. With this in mind we may perhaps return to some of the questions raised in the Spanish investigation.

For one thing, it accuses several people who, though not the actual murderers—or not yet proved to be so—appear under their real names and are certainly among the instigators of the plot against Delgado. Thus we have Mário de Carvalho, Ernesto Bisogno, Elie Tapeiro and António Gonçalves Semedo, all of whom, we may be sure, could give a lot more information. And there are clues that might suggest fruitful lines of inquiry but which were never followed up because Portuguese officialdom refused to speak. For instance, particulars are known of the motorcars and number plates used. The number plates were false, according to the Portuguese police, since they belong to other vehicles—a truck and a taxi. Yet they have the chassis and engine numbers and know that the cars themselves exist and were sold by the Opel and Renault agents in Portugal. Had they wished to make serious inquiries they had every means of tracing both the vehicles and the owners' names.

The passport belonging to the Pakistani Washdeo Kundanmal Milpuri is important, too; the Spaniards say that one of the gang used it to cross the frontier on 13 February. Milpuri is an actual person. He states, and can prove, that he was not out of Britain on that date and that his passport went astray when handed in to the PIDE two years previously. What other explanation is there of this very odd circumstance save that the PIDE were directly implicated in the murder? At quite an early stage, when Milpuri's name was mentioned in the paper, an official at the British Embassy at Lisbon told me they had a metal tag given by the police to Milpuri when he took his passport in, so he could get it back after the routine checking. The passport being mislaid, the tag was kept as proof of ownership.

Another profitable inquiry might concern the Land Rover seen on the Portuguese side of the border from ten in the morning to midnight of 13 February. It would be instructive to know who owned it, who was in it, and why.

In the course of their inquiries the Spanish authorities summoned Guilherme Gião, owner of the Meado farm, on Portuguese territory, where several PIDE men spent the night of 12 to 13 February. There seem to have been an unusual number of police about, including an ambulance of the Spanish Highway Police, which pulled up for repairs at a garage kept by Jorge Mendes Quintas in Reguengos de Monsaraz. The crew went into a café to wait. They had been to Lisbon with two injured Portuguese and were on their way back. 'Traffic accident?' someone asked. 'No; shooting,' was the startling reply. Guilherme Gião, though called, never appeared in the

F

Spanish courts, yet he was seen in Spain not long afterwards in company with a Minister of the Portuguese Government and is known to be friendly with members of the regime.

Most illuminating of all is the case of the PIDE agent António Gonçalves Semedo, who was head of the frontier-post at São Leonardo. He, too, was repeatedly summoned but never saw fit to appear in Spain. During the inquiries and before they charged him as one of the murderers, he told the Spanish police that his odd behaviour was due to his having been 'misled': people had shown him forged police-cards and badges, and he hadn't realised. It was a naïve and unconvincing explanation. In any case, the Spaniards at the post had heard him chatting away to Filipe Garcia Tavares and asking him, among other things, how his wife was. Most curious of all, the Portuguese Foreign Ministry came to his aid by announcing on 23 April 1966, that he was not, under an agreement made in 1867, bound to go to Spain. An official note to this effect was issued to the foreign press, but no Portuguese paper had permission to print it. If the Portuguese Government truly wanted, as it said it did, to collaborate whole-heartedly in getting at the truth, why did it not advise Semedo to speak in the Spanish courts? And why was it so eager to exonerate its PIDE man, in the eyes of the public, from any responsibility in the Delgado affair?

The French, for their part, had made no objection when the Spanish judge wished Police-Superintendent Puzol to give evidence in Madrid before the court of inquiry into the General's death. Had the Portuguese Government been blameless it would have had everything to gain by following their example. It chose instead to be systematically obstructive, and to make damaging insinuations against Judge Crespo Marquez and the Spanish lawyers who acted for the Delgado family, even going so far as to publish threats in the newspapers to sue Mariano Robles.

All the available evidence clearly shows that the net which caught Delgado was woven first in Italy. The key-figures here were Mário de Carvalho and Ernesto Maria Bisogno, while the third man, Ernesto Castro Sousa, whose real identity has never been established, was equally involved.

That identity was certainly unknown to the Portuguese opposition and he must have been an *agent provocateur*. Mário de Carvalho, who introduced him to the General, has not been forthcoming on the subject and said he wrote to him *poste restante* at Lisbon. Emilio Guerreiro told the Spanish judge that he had never seen him but was sure that he existed, and that Delgado himself had told him that Castro Sousa was with Carvalho when they met in Paris. Guerreiro also stated that he had received a letter from Zurich, signed by a Spaniard named Carlos, telling him that the body found in the River Guadiana was that of the man known as Ernesto Sousa Castro. Anything that Mário de Carvalho said about this person, however, has turned out to be quite untrue. For instance, he declared at the Italian trial that Ernesto Castro Sousa was known to the Lisbon daily *República* and had taken part in the Beja revolt. On the authority of the editor of *República* and of Captain Varela Gomes, who led the Beja revolt, we can, I find, dismiss both assertions.

We now come to Ernesto Maria Bisogno, an Italian subject and former SS collaborator who had been implicated in the drug traffic and white slavery. Mário de Carvalho, as we know, introduced him to Delgado. He was a doctor, and by means of small personal services gained the General's confidence. It was he who arranged the false passport for the journey to Spain. Nobody in opposition circles had ever heard of him until Delgado produced him at the 'peace-conference' in Paris some time before the murder. Bisogno later went twice to Portugal on orders from Carvalho, but it is impossible to find out why. When the bodies were discovered he was missing for a while from his usual address in Rome.

Mário de Carvalho, the central figure in the whole plot, was also completely unknown to the opposition. He claimed to be a professor of chemistry; he claimed to have been exiled from Portugal in 1947; but no one has ever come across any organisation in which he was active, or learned of anything he ever did in politics. He is, beyond question, an adventurer and an *agent provocateur* whose statements up to now have been nothing but a tissue of lies. Who supplied him with the vast funds he bragged about in his letters to Delgado? Who were the revolutionary elements he said he could contact in Portugal? Who was he supposed to be working for in the imaginary conspiracy that baited the trap at Badajoz? There is only one answer that I can see. Directly or indirectly, the PIDE had been behind him all the time.

On 21 February 1965, when the murder had already taken place, Mário de Carvalho sent a letter to General Delgado in Algiers, probably with the object of confusing the trail, saying, 'Our friends have confirmed the rendezvous and something satisfactory has been arranged, I am quite sure.' He has never said exactly who these friends were, doubtless because they never existed.

Since Carvalho and Bisogno are the starting-points of the conspiracy and since both lived in Rome, I considered that one way of getting at the truth would be to open proceedings in Italy : no easy matter when the victims were a Portuguese national and a Brazilian woman, and the crime itself committed in Spain by Portuguese. But the case is in progress at the time of writing, although little has been done in the last few months.[3] There are difficulties, and they have been aggravated by the death of Ernesto Maria Bisogno, but I am convinced that, if it comes to anything, it must throw fresh light on the affair.

My announcement to the foreign press that I was having a new inquiry opened in Italy brought immediate reaction from Mário de Carvalho and Henrique Cerqueira. The latter sent me a telegram from Rabat, the gist of which was that I had no moral authority to act for the missing man's family and

[3] In April 1970 António Figueiredo in London started an international campaign for a new inquiry into the assassination of Delgado. A detailed account of all that had happened was given at a press conference held under the auspices of eminent British lawyers and politicians, and the demand was made that investigation be continued until the criminals are brought to justice.

that he now held me responsible for further delay in clearing everything up. This arrived on 6 March 1966 and in view of its tone I showed it to no one but the lawyers working with me on the Delgado affair and to our clients. And yet the *Diário de Manhã*, official paper of the unique party and organ of the Government, published the entire text of that telegram on the 12th, in a despatch, dated two days earlier, from the ANI agency in Madrid. Among other things this said that Cerqueira had accused me of belonging to the Patriotic Front. In Portugal the papers reprinted the telegram with the heading : 'Confused Incident. Friend and Companion of Delgado Brings Grave Charge against Portuguese Lawyer.' This, we may note, being the first time our own press had been allowed to reveal that any Portuguese lawyer had been engaged on the affair at all.

After sending a telegram of protest to the Prime Minister I did manage to get a statement published in the Portuguese newspapers, partly correcting the libellous article. This had obviously been written to cause trouble and confusion and of course made plain the links of Cerqueira and Carvalho with the semi-official ANI and with the Government. They had tried to disqualify me as the Delgado family's lawyer. They failed. The General's widow reaffirmed her trust in me and the Law Society intervened on my behalf.

Cerqueira went on claiming to be Secretary General of the 'Portuguese Front' which, he said, had no lack of ramifications all over the country. But this turns out to be untrue and he would not give evidence before the judicial inquiry in Spain. At first a supporter of the 'settling of accounts' theory diffused so widely in the Portuguese press, he afterwards began telling world journalists that Delgado was really in prison in Portugal and he could prove it. For some undisclosed reason he left Morocco in 1969 and went to London, where he tried without success to get himself declared a political refugee. Later the Portuguese consulate produced a passport for him and with it he reached South America.

I was going frequently to and from Madrid at this time, and formed the definite impression that the Franco Govern-

ment was very much divided as to what to do about the
Delgado affair. Shared ideology may have tended to clog the
normal progress of the inquiry, but the 'liberal' sectors, notably
in the Foreign Office and the Department of Justice, wished
to carry it through to the limit, so as to absolve Spain of all
responsibility.

The negative finding of the Spanish court complicated
things for us in Italy. The judge in Spain, treating the matter
as closed, sent a memorandum to the Portuguese Foreign
Minister in Lisbon and with it, as a document essential to
further proceedings in Portugal, his indictment of the Portuguese nationals. Yet, as Judge Crespo Marquez knew perfectly
well, Lisbon had already made it plain that there would be no
further proceedings. Dr Mariano Robles appealed for international support nevertheless. But what can international
organisations do when sovereign states close ranks to impede
the course of justice?

The Delgado affair might seem to be a distant memory by
now, one more unsolved enormity like the cases of Ben Barka,
Kider, Lumumba and so many others. But the Portuguese
people do not forget it and justice remains to be done on the
most nauseating political crime in the country's history. In
January 1970 the Spanish lawyers acting for the Delgado
family wrote to Marcello Caetano, our Prime Minister : 'On
the fifth anniversary of the assassination of General Humberto
Delgado, when the culprits have still not been brought to trial
in Portugal, we address Your Excellency in the hope that he
may produce to the Spanish legal authorities those persons
accused in the investigation report of 11 February 1966, in
order to establish who were the authors of the crime and their
accomplices.' To this the Private Secretary, Quezada Pastor,
replied on 3 March with the information that all inquiries so
far made had failed to produce evidence 'sufficient to incrimi-
nate any Portuguese citizen'.

The road remains blocked. There is no desire to come at the
truth, no desire to see justice done. Silence suits everybody
better. If the PIDE now employs António Gonçalves Semedo

under its new name of General Security Department, that fact makes him no less guilty. Seven years have passed and the General is still in a foreign grave. This quiet must be broken, the inquiry pushed through to its conclusion. Silence like this is murder all over again.

Chapter Nine

The Colonies

On 4 February 1961 an attack was made on two prisons at Luanda, capital of Angola, with the object of freeing Africans held there on political charges. Official Portuguese reaction was shattering—a butchery of several hundred natives. On 15 March armed rebellion broke out in the north of the colony and it was the white man's turn : several hundred whites were killed with unspeakable savagery and public opinion was appalled. The first act of a long tragedy had begun. Drugged by thirty-five years of dictatorship, Portugal was awakening, in stupefied amazement, to the horrors of her colonial war.

Catastrophe had overtaken the white inhabitants. Their houses were destroyed, their plantations burning. Urgent decisions had of course to be made and Salazar as supreme director of national policy, assumed the Ministry of Defence. Almost no information was released about events in Angola, but he announced his intention of sending aid, rapidly and in force, to the imperilled colonists.

He was facing a colonial struggle of a kind previously unknown, yet this decision of his was part and parcel of the policy of complete intransigence he had followed ever since the passing of the Colonial Act : a policy blind to the realities of the modern world and in which the hopes of the African races counted for nothing at all. Salazar's decision, dictatorial and in some ways irrevocable, settled the collective future of the Portuguese.

Up to the middle of the nineteenth century Angola was merely a slave-market where labour was easily come by and Mozambique, at most, a port of call on the route to India. Portugal took scanty interest in her African possessions until the Berlin Conference of 1885 and the subsequent division of Africa among the great powers.

Just how few Portuguese there were in Angola and Mozambique at the beginning of the present century is indicated by the figure of 12,000 whites for the two territories combined. Great efforts were made to increase their numbers but neither colony ever became thronging and populous, as was claimed. The fact was that the Portuguese, when they emigrated, had small wish to go to Africa. They preferred more inviting destinations such as Brazil, the United States, Canada or Venezuela; and latterly they have favoured Europe—France, Federal Germany, or even Spain.

There are today 450,000 whites in Angola, 70,000 of whom are stationed there as soldiers, and this is far fewer than the number of Portuguese who live in France.[1] The native population approaches the five-million mark. Mozambique, with seven and a half million natives, has 200,000 whites, including 40,000 troops.[2]

The 'pacification' of the Portuguese colonies is comparatively recent. The Dembos, a tribe estimated at 55,000, surrendered only in 1919 after fifteen expeditions against them. The empire of Ngungunyana, 'the Invincible', king of the Vatuas in Mozambique, finally yielded somewhere around 1897, while Guinea, which now has 800,000 natives to about 3,000 Europeans, excluding troops, was fully 'pacified' as lately as 1936.

There is no question but that the liberal Monarchy and the democratic Republic were particularly attentive to the colonies in Africa, their declared intention being to grant progressive autonomy and ultimate independence, as in the case of Brazil.

[1] 600,000 Portuguese emigrated to France between 1960 and 1969, in search of jobs and better wages. (See *Cabora Bassa ou l'impérialisme dans les colonies portugaises*, by Eduardo de Sousa Ferreira, published in Heidelberg, 1970.) At the present time there are some 800,000 there.

[2] The absence of reliable Portuguese statistics makes these figures doubtful, but they match those appearing in the international press.

And so at the end of the last century and the beginning of this there grew up a whole generation of magnificent colonial administrators to put into practice the ideas then prevalent in Europe. And when the old traditional name of Overseas Provinces was re-introduced for the *Ultramar*, it was done, not to deny the existence of a colonial Empire, but to emphasise the basic lack of racial prejudice in Portuguese colonisation.

When the First World War began the Republic was quick to foresee what effect the redistribution of zones of influence would have in colonial affairs and went in on the side of the Allies, mainly to keep our Aprican possessions out of greedy foreign hands. Such, in those days, was progressive thought.

The Republicans, with their generous ideals—which did not, of course, prevent them from being colonialists in the true style of the day—planned to make the African races step by step autonomous within an overall scheme of gradual development, and finally independent. But the dictatorship dropped the Republic's policy, and this is where what Salazar calls the 'historic responsibilities' of his regime come in. There was to be no more decentralisation with regard to multi-racial societies, no more phased autonomy. In 1930 Salazar, then temporary Colonial Minister, passed the Colonial Act by decree. Relations between the mother-country and the lands overseas began to be viewed in terms of an Empire, the Portuguese Colonial Empire; and the Overseas Provinces, called colonies once more, were colonies indeed. All such territories, in other words, became providers of raw materials for the profit of the big commercial companies exploiting their resources. Native labour was cheap and there was plenty of it. Thanks to foreign investment these companies, directed by a few dozen whites from metropolitan Portugal, were able to get the last ounce out of it.

The Empire that Salazar tried to build was ultra-centralised, ruled with his own firm hand from Lisbon in the interests of the homeland. But he had not the slightest notion of what Africa was really like and applied a policy of very marked racial discrimination. Government propaganda was largely designed to stimulate the nationalistic feelings of the Portuguese people whose destiny, so they heard, was to consolidate and spread the Christian faith—by force if need be. Fascist imperialism concluded a sort of Holy League with an aggressive, intolerant and inquisitorial-minded Catholicism for the aid and comfort of huge business interests whose spiritual aspect was not immediately obvious.

'Portugal is not a small country.' So ran the legend on an official map showing Portuguese possessions in various parts of the globe, and Lisbon at the heart of Empire. But the man in the street was not encouraged to go and live in any of these possessions. The former plans for colonial development, the projected multi-racial communities with their high degree of autonomy, had been shelved by the dictatorship. Henceforth the policy of the regime was to preserve the *status quo* and carry on a systematic exploitation of its territories. This furthered the interests of private business concerns and of government circles in Lisbon at the expense, if necessary, of those white residents who worked for themselves, independently of the great home-based companies. The experiment of giving the best land to white men to induce permanent settlement never amounted to very much and Lisbon, unaware of local problems, made no serious effort to better the conditions of the natives.

But the stir of African nationalism at the end of the Second World War galvanised the anti-colonial movement and the situation changed. The criticism of experienced men like Norton de Mattos, Paiva Couceiro, António Sérgio and Cunha Leal, suddenly made sense. Salazar, forced to choose between clinging to the old imperial myths or adapting himself to the new international scene, decided on a hurried revision of his African policy. The revision was a mere formality of course, imposed without consultation on the country, as he had formerly imposed the Colonial Act. Now the constitutional amendment of 1951 demolished the politico-legal fabric of the Portuguese Colonial Empire and replaced it by the Overseas Provinces again. Practically speaking, the colonial structures remained untouched. They had to wait until Portugal in 1955 was about to join the United Nations and under pressure from the international movement towards decolonisation, but even so there was argument about the change. Doctrinaires in office, including Marcello Caetano, rose in the *Câmera Corporativa*, or Upper House, to criticise the Government's modifications.

In the wording of things, however, change was immediate and radical. Those who had most enthusiastically supported the Portuguese Colonial Empire, both idea and reality, now held up their hands in horror if anyone mentioned 'colonies', while sneer and reproach were the lot of those who found the new-look vocabulary difficult to get used to.

The alteration was mainly for the sake of outside observers. Just as the *Estado Novo*, under the eyes of the Western democracies, had been hastily renamed an Organic Democracy in 1945 and gone on its totalitarian way notwithstanding, so it now termed its colonies Overseas Provinces, and the underlying facts of colonial life continued as before. Would the world allow itself to be deceived yet again?

In those colonies, those Overseas Provinces which were officially exactly the same as provinces at home, the population was still divided into three distinct categories. The whites were considered as first-class Portuguese citizens; the *assimilados* were Portuguese-speaking mulattoes and blacks to whom, in certain conditions, was granted the status of Portuguese, second class; and finally came the *indígenas* who made up the overwhelming majority of the black inhabitants. This disgusting system was in force until 1961 when the *Estatuto dos indígenas* was abolished as one of the first results of the outbreak of hostilities. The natives then became legally Portuguese citizens, but the human and sociological problem they represented could not be resolved by any mere decree. It rested upon ethnic, economic, social and cultural differences which nothing could wipe out but revolutionary change in policy and administration.

The obstinacy of Salazar over the African colonies matched his display over Goa, but there was now far more at stake.

In metropolitan Portugal the basically rural character of the people had assured the political survival of the regime; but here the famous 'gentle Lusitanian peace' always pointed out in such idyllic contrast to the turmoil of the emergent African countries, was the result of dire poverty, ignorance, superstition and tribal conflict. Nor were the colonies as calm or as idyllic as they appeared in the propagandist version.

Terrible things, for instance, had happened at São Tomé, the small South Atlantic island with its population of 2,500 whites, and 60,000 blacks brought across from Africa. Here in 1954, under the governorship of Colonel Gorgulho, a friend and protégé of the Minister Santos Costa, took place the notorious and bloody revolt of Batepa.

Between April and June 1955 the magazine *Présence Africaine*, in a series of articles entitled 'Massacres at São Tomé', told how thousands of natives were recruited in the other colonies—Cape Verde, Angola and Mozambique—for forced labour in slave conditions there. They described the savage beating of any who attempted to resist. The Portuguese press, forbidden to print a word, had to pass over these events in silence, but Manuel da Palma Carlos, who as a lawyer had come across the details, laid before the Supreme Court an account of how the natives were being treated: 'They are taken to the prison shackled together like cattle, never come out except to work and often wear heavy iron leg-chains.' It is known that on 6 February 1953 thirty of the forty-five men in one cell died of suffocation, and among other instruments of torture was an electric chair, used to extract 'confessions', from which no one ever got up alive. A thousand Africans died or disappeared at Batepa.

The PIDE went out to São Tomé on the track of a Communist plot said to have been reported to the Governor. But the Governor had been listening to fairy-tales. Discreetly, he was bidden back to Portugal, and there promoted by way of compensation.

At this time, too, another colonel, sent from the Ministry on an official investigation into the working methods of certain agricultural concerns in the island, vanished at sea on the journey back to Lisbon and not a line of his report was ever found. The half-caste officer with him died of poisoning.

There was never any core of armed resistance in the island itself, but the CLSTP, the Liberation Committee of São Tomé and Principé, was set up abroad. Its best-known leaders were Tomaz Medeiros and Guadalupe Ceita.

Things were no better in Angola, where the same ghastly conditions of work were the main cause of the rising in March 1961. Natives on forced labour overran parts of the north, leaving behind them a trail of utter devastation.

Among hundreds of Africans arrested by the Portuguese in 1959 had been some of the organisers of the MPLA, or *Movimento Popular para a Libertacão de Angola*, the People's Party for the Liberation of Angola. (This movement had been founded three years before and was one of several engaged in the fight against Lisbon and its spirit of colonialism; others were the Union of the Peoples of Northern Angola, or UPONA, which Holden Roberto created in Kinshasa in 1954, and the Angolan Communist Party, inaugurated in 1955.) More arrests followed in June 1960, when among the fifty-two *assimilados* thrown into prison was Agostinho Neto, poet, doctor and future leader of the MPLA.

These few facts will serve to show that the revolt of the black people spread gradually, while the forms it took grew more and more progressive. As for the Government, its ostrich-like policy was to deny facts of any kind by any means possible, as though problems ceased to exist as soon as no one was allowed to talk about them.

A great part of the revenue of Mozambique comes from the sale of black labour to South Africa and Rhodesia.[3] The traffic led to a revolt of Africans at Lourenço Marques in 1948, which was severely quelled; to dock strikes in 1956, when the so-called forces of law and order massacred forty-nine

[3] Mozambique derives one-fifth of its foreign currency from this trade: that is, from the sale, on average, of 400,000 human beings a year. See *La lutte de libération nationale dans les colonies portugaises*, by Mário de Andrade, in *La conférence de Dar-es-Salaam*, published Algiers, 1967.

Africans;[4] and to a rising at Mueda[5] on 16 June 1960 with consequent bloodshed and repression. From 1949 onwards several clandestine organisations were started in Mozambique. At Dar-es-Salaam in 1962 these were merged into one Mozambique Freedom Front, the *Frente de Libertação de Moçambique*, or FRELIMO. The founder and president was Eduardo Mondlane.

Guinea and the Cape Verde islands had their first nationalist group in 1954. Two years later this took the name of *Partido Africano da Independência da Guiné e Cabo Verde*, African Independence Party of Guinea and Cape Verde (the PAIGC), under the presidency of the agronomist Amilcar Cabral. A second party, the Guinea and Cape Verde Freedom Front, or FLGC, was founded at Dakar in 1959.

Thus a powerful underground movement, of a social and political nature, grew up in the 1950s, with sundry nationalist organisations established as a result. And the revolts and the more or less spontaneous mass-demonstrations were crushed, and the Government went on showing how perfectly it failed to grasp the meaning of events.

The cradle of African leadership was the Centre of African Studies in Lisbon, founded in 1951; that, and the Empire Students' Residence. Many of those who directed the freedom movements, men who were to be heard of after 1961, started out as militant anti-Fascists in the mother-country, connected with democratic bodies like the MUDJ and the MND. Such, for example, were Agostinho Neto, Amilcar Cabral, Mário de Andrade and Marcelino dos Santos, to mention only the most prominent among them.

Exposed to the iron rigour of Salazarist policy and with no prospect of official change in any democratic direction, the African nationalist movements tended to become autonomous, though the bonds of sympathy with anti-Fascist groups in Portugal were never broken. Moreover, before 1961 the opposition as a whole did not sufficiently realise that when

[4] See *Dossier sur les colonies portugaises*, published by *Vie ouvrière*, Brussels, 1970.
[5] *Idem.*

Salazarism ended decolonisation must of necessity begin. The truth is that the opposition could be heedless and fainthearted on this subject, and its opinions were ambiguous and hesitant.

African nationalists, then, began their own political organisations in the colonies, in metropolitan Portugal and abroad, but did not resort to arms immediately. This point is important, for it shows how enormously Salazar was to blame when hostilities actually broke out. The Anti-Colonialist Movement, or MAC, was the fruit of a conference on the progress of the struggle held in Paris at the end of 1957. Here for the first time it was stated that 'the freedom and advancement of our countries are independent of the social and political revolution in Portugal'. A peaceful dissolution of Portuguese colonialism was proposed and some two years later, when the MAC became the FRAIN, the *Front Révolutionnaire Africain pour L'Indépendence Nationaliste des Colonies Portugaises,* the new programme emphasised the peaceful means of non-violence and civil disobedience. The FRAIN would reply with violence only if that were used by the Government.[6]

Nineteen sixty was the great year for Africa. Mother-countries were granting independence on all sides, and if things went forward more smoothly in some of the new states than in others, still this policy of disinvestment was in marked contrast with that of Lisbon. It is hardly to be wondered at, therefore, that nationalist leaders from the Portuguese colonies should have changed their tone so definitely at a London press conference in December. 'By her savage repression and by her preparations for war in the colonies,' they said, 'Portugal leaves open to us the sole course of direct action.' Mário de Andrade, as spokesman, demanded acceptance of the right of self-determination for the peoples of the colonies; the unconditional release of all political detainees; the restoration of civil liberties, especially the liberty to found political parties; and the removal of all Portuguese forces and of the PIDE. Refusal to consider these demands puts responsibility for the colonial war squarely

[6] The nationalist movements in fact approached the United Nations in 1960–61 with a view to working out a peaceable solution.

upon the Government of Salazar. But the Government was in a hopeless quandary. How could it say the Angolans might choose for themselves when for thirty-five years it had been saying that the Portuguese might not?

The *a posteriori* arguments of the regime in defence of its colonial policy set out to prove :

(1) that the policy is upheld by the whole nation, 'without any argument', and that no other government, democratic or otherwise, could have acted in any other way;

(2) that since the African provinces are as much a part of the nation as is the Minho or the Alentejo at home, relations between Portuguese of differing racial origin are not the same as those obtaining in the colonial possessions of France, Belgium or Great Britain;

(3) that Portugal throughout her history has kept clear of the Spanish orbit and maintained her independence thanks to her development overseas. To abandon the overseas territories, in other words, would be to betray her historic mission. She would be risking her independence and Spain would benefit;

(4) that there is no colonial war, only a police operation. African nationalism, or 'terrorism' as it is officially known, is in fact an artificial phenomenon, a foreign importation, and the native populations are not remotely interested in it;

(5) that the Portuguese Government, in resisting the anti-colonial movement as inspired from Moscow and Pekin, is the foremost bastion in defence of the free world and of Christian civilisation in the Dark Continent.

For the public to whom they are addressed these arguments do indeed go far to justify the colonial war. And as some of them echo emotions that have been aroused by clever propaganda and others play upon fears and complexes not unknown among the Portuguese, they will repay close examination.

From the beginning of hostilities in Angola Salazar attempted to mobilise public opinion by the appeal to patriotism. Recruits, for instance, were required to punctuate their martial songs with cries of 'Angola belongs to us!'

The Government had a double line of argument to show it was pursuing a nationally-approved policy independent of any special economic or ideological interests : defenceless white inhabitants were under vicious attack and had to be protected, while our name was execrated in the United Nations and elsewhere. The great powers who were ready to accept the vile accusations that were being made were really wanting to profit by what was 'ours'—ours because we discovered it, were occupying it and held it by the sacred dictates of history.

The sudden eruption of the colonial problem caused difficulty and dispute among the opposition. The different sectors had varying ideas as to how the situation should be handled and what the eventual solution should be, but naturally nobody accepted what the Government said.

In the electoral campaign of October to November 1961, seven months after the combat began in Angola, the democrats, as we have seen, were holding the Government responsible for the outbreak of war. They also demanded recognition of the right of self-determination for the peoples of Angola, of the other colonies, and of Portugal.

The opposition has not yet come to agreement. Suggestions range from self-determination at some near or future date, to immediate independence. In 1961 it called for a referendum on African policy, to be preceded by a long period during which all political groups might discuss the question freely and on equal terms and decide on the best course to follow. It also demanded that details of the fighting should be released and public opinion thus kept informed.

The Government at first considered holding this referendum but in the end did nothing about it. Salazar thought that 'spontaneous' demonstrations in favour of his policy might be more effective and preferred to frighten his opponents with threats of high treason and alarums of a similar nature. Yet everywhere people talked, in spite of all restrictions. They discussed official policy so far, and some even of the least politically-minded began to realise what the colonial war was all about.

In March 1961 the Democratic-Social Directive sent several petitions to the Head of State, pointing out his responsibilities at the bar of history if he refused all dialogue and continued to arrange the country's future single-handed. But unfortunately approaches of this kind were known only to limited circles at home and news of them never penetrated abroad. There the voice of Salazar alone was heard, proclaiming that everyone in Portugal agreed with his colonial policy. During the legislative elections of 1965 the democratic opposition published a manifesto to the nation. This came out in the daily papers of Lisbon and Oporto and firmly condemned the colonial war, proposing a peaceful solution based on the principle of self-determination. The Government reacted promptly with a highly virulent campaign against what it called the treasonable opposition. I remember my friends advising me to seek shelter in one of the embassies when a great official demonstration was due in the Praço do Municipio in Lisbon. I was standing for Lisbon in the election. I had read out the manifesto at a press conference and was particularly desirable prey. That same evening a bomb was exploded by right-wing extremists near the house of another of our candidates Adãoe Silva. And yet despite all their announcements and the compulsory shutting of shops and offices, the rally had to be postponed for an hour because hardly anyone turned up.

As for the Catholics, a group of 101, drawn from the most representative intellectual and political thinkers of the capital, circulated a note affirming agreement with the democratic opposition. On the subject of the colonial war they spoke plainly : the defence of Christian civilisation should not be confused with the activities of a colonialism which the Pope had formally condemned.[7]

All the leading sections of our society, Communists, Social-

[7] This document, together with the manifesto, the text of our petition to the Head of State and a declaration drawn up by the democrats in Mozambique, was issued in 1965 in a pamphlet entitled *Oposição democrática*.

ists, Republicans, Liberals and Catholics, roundly censured the conduct of the Government in Africa, and this although there were so few ways for them to make their voices heard. Clearly it follows that Salazar's policy was no longer that of the nation. It was the policy of a dictatorial Government acting for the benefit of minority groups, themselves tied up with foreign capital.

The special nature of the Portuguese presence in Africa is another myth created by the *Estado Novo* to justify continued domination of the colonies. As the first Europeans to set foot on the Dark Continent, the Portuguese, so the official theory went, possessed an inborn aptitude, as did no other nation, for understanding and civilising the African. This amounted to a claim that the blacks of Angola or Mozambique must feel themselves to be as much Portuguese as anyone in any of the provinces at home.

This thesis, flattering as it is to the pride of Portugal, fails to stand up to the most cursory examination. Such of the natives, and they are unfortunately few, as have the slightest degree of culture of their own, do not feel in the least bit Portuguese. They feel Angolan, or Mozambican; they feel they are people of Cape Verde; while there is, too, the great mass of those who have no 'national' sentiment at all and simply belong to one tribe or another.

The attitude of Portugal towards her colonies has varied from time to time and place to place. Guinea and São Tomé have always been, and still are, areas of exploitation in the hands of big agricultural and commercial firms. There were attempts, relinquished by the *Estado Novo*, to make Angola and Mozambique into white settlements on a huge scale, and there are signs that this idea may be due for revival. Macao, of course, is no more than an *entrepôt* on the doorstep and at the mercy of China; how much at her mercy was demonstrated by the inglorious events of 1967, when Pekin issued orders and Lisbon unconditionally complied. As for the Indonesian island of Timor, it has very little to do with Portugal.

So where is the special nature of it all? Historically the conquests of Portugal in Africa and India have been as brutal as those of anyone else. In Africa, from the very beginning, the first thing any Portuguese ever attempted was to make slaves of the blacks.

And colonial history has not been written from the African point of view. Historians have concentrated instead on describing, somewhat rhapsodically, the exploits of Portugal. Afro-Portuguese literature presents the facts in quite a different light. If the truth were known, the only special feature of Portuguese dominion compared with that of other Europeans has arisen from the material and intellectual poverty of her settlers and the economic underdevelopment of a homeland, which is in turn the prey of major powers. It was not Christian brotherhood, as we are asked to believe, that led the illiterate peasants and old lags who settled the hinterlands of Angola and Mozambique to put themselves on a level with the natives; it was simply that they were almost as poor as any native there, and quite as uneducated. Wherever they went, the Portuguese swamped small local business, and occasionally small-scale cultivation too—things which more advanced colonial powers left to the native traders and farmers, though the better-developed regions were, it is true, administered according to the classic concepts of colonialism.

Today, when the conflict has become an international question, Angola and Mozambique tend more and more towards independence on the pattern of Rhodesia.

There are some theorists of nationalism who say that loss of the colonies would mean the end of Portugal as a separate country; that political union with Spain must be the inevitable result. Those who think like this also add that we are in any case more an African than a European nation.

Much has been heard in the discussions of the last few years of this Africa-or-Europe choice, as though Portugal had no alternative, if she wishes to remain independent, but to continue her African policy and hang on to her colonies. Politically and economically this is nonsense, but it does more for the regime than any argument advanced so far, for the people as a whole are deeply suspicious of Spain.

Yet Portuguese independence can hardly be called a political issue in the world today. She has possessed it, within more or less stable boundaries, for eight long centuries and no one in Europe now is seriously going to question a fact so well established. Spain, attempting to overhaul her time-worn institutions and bring herself, as she must do, closer to the rest of the continent and into modern ways, must bring to the task a democratic frame of mind; automatically she must reject imperialism and approve regional autonomy. The problem of Portuguese independence is of another sort; the current question is how the national resources are to be used for the people's benefit.

The Government in Lisbon can support its arguments with neither logic nor history. War in the colonies is in fact mortgaging the national resources, for we are having to borrow money from abroad. In order to preserve an increasingly shaky sovereignty, we allow foreign capitalists the use of our ports in Africa and are in a fair way to becoming the subordinates of South African imperialism. In that projected invincible white bastion to the south we shall play the part of ever poorer relations, while our African commitments will continually prevent us from taking our rightful place in Europe. Worse still, we are making Spain our go-between with the European countries. Why else should Marcello Caetano have had his talks in Madrid in June 1970?

For all these reasons the Government's policy, African and domestic, is one of national abdication and contrary to the real good of the people. In brief, its aims are to strengthen the small coteries which serve the foreign financial interests in Africa by channelling to them the profits from the exploitation of its riches; and to delay the social revolution at home that would turn Portugal into a modern country.

Until the war began, Lisbon never wasted a thought on the colonies and their development. Now the wry joke goes that the whites of Angola should raise a statue to the terrorists in token of deepest gratitude, for there has been amazing progress since—roads built, schools, hospitals and airports opened, natural resources surveyed and worked. The priority-system may leave much to be desired, but more has undeniably been done in eleven years of combat than was dreamed of in decades before.

As Salazarist repression grew worse in the colonies after 1961, so inter-racial relations deteriorated until the barriers were almost insurmountable. Anyone from metropolitan Portugal who has spent a year or so in Portuguese Africa will know what I mean. In São Tomé, for instance, where all was apparently and, for a colony, untypically calm, a friend said to me,

'Watch the negroes watching us when they think we can't see them. Look at their eyes—you can see the way they hate us.'

The unyielding attitude of Portuguese authority, and then the war, have shocked the African peoples. Now the Portuguese is everywhere the enemy, the coloniser ready with his curbs and controls, different as things were not so long ago. Moreover, with decolonisation spreading as it is in Africa, it is pure lunacy to think that we can, as it were, put our own colonial populations in quarantine and keep them from infection.

Plainly the Africans, who have been trained fast in order to keep pace with the needs of a developing society, are in fact an embryo army of qualified persons prepared to rise in revolt against Portuguese rule or to pick the right moment to declare their hostility. The *fazendas*, the great estates in northern Angola, are real armed fortresses. Let us make no mistake about it—the way this war is being waged, there will soon be no intelligent African who sides sincerely with the Portuguese. If, while claiming to be anti-racialist, we are thinking of anything on the South African pattern for our colonies, we may as well recognise here and now that we are heading for disaster.

The freedom movements are undeniably influenced by the emergent, and especially the neighbouring, African nations. It is equally obvious that these movements are supported in

Socialist countries and wherever anti-colonialism is strong and active. It is, of course, the Portuguese and their blind, pigheaded Government who have compelled the African nationalist to look abroad for the help he needs. Nor is it from humanitarianism or idealism alone that Sweden, the Netherlands, Italy and other countries of the West have shown their fellow-feeling. They show it because this is how their people think; this is the trend of history.

And so we come to the final argument of glory—what the regime calls the glory of being the bulwark of the free world in Africa. Though how the 'free world' (an equivocal expression in any case), comes to be protected by a basically reactionary and undemocratic order is rather hard to see.

Colonial theory as advanced in Lisbon has always tended to embarrass the Catholic Church, to whom Africa matters a great deal, especially with the Protestants there in force. In principle the encyclical *Populorum Progressio* of Paul VI condemns colonialism outright, though the Portuguese governing classes feign to know nothing about it and the Church certainly manages to adjust itself without much difficulty. It is not easy to forget overnight all those conveniently-calculated arrangements that helped the Church into a privileged position in the colonies, nor the sympathy it has shown to Salazarism. In any case, the white hierarchy in the Portuguese possessions[8] can scarcely claim any longer to be guardians of the purest Catholic faith in Africa—a faith imposed, moreover, at the bayonet's point—since the Portuguese clergy were not allowed to go to Kampala in July 1969 when the Pope himself attended the episcopal congress there. Significantly, too, he gave the African nationalist leaders a private audience in Rome the following June.[9]

[8] Angola enthroned the first black bishop in the colonies, Eduardo André Muaca, on 31 May 1970. His position is a delicate one and his career has been very different from that of his comrade and friend, Father Joachim Pinto de Andrade, who is once again in prison as I write.

[9] See the article on 'Tension between the Vatican and Portugal' in *Le Monde*, 5–6 July 1970.

Obviously the Portuguese Government can count on powerful support from the West for its policy in Africa; it could not have waged so costly a war for ten years without foreign assistance. But that policy has nothing to do with defending the free world, with democracy or Christianity. It has everything to do with something quite different—imperialism.

The colonial war broke out in Angola in February 1961, spread to Guinea at the beginning of 1963, to Mozambique in 1964; and its exigencies have forced the Government to give absolute priority to questions of defence. Army estimates have grown larger and larger over the last few years and since 1969 account for 52 per cent of the national budget, though the official figure given is somewhat lower. The period of compulsory military service has been extended to four years, occasionally to four and a half, and many officers have been obliged to do successive tours of duty in Africa.

Full information is not available, for the Government takes good care not to release it all, but trustworthy sources nevertheless confirm that the country has never had fewer than 150,000 men on active service, between 70,000 and 80,000 being stationed in Angola, between 40,000 and 60,000 in Mozambique, and 30,000 in Guinea-Bissao.

The African nationalist fighters have nothing very spectacular to show for their efforts, since it must be admitted that the Portuguese troops, at least in Angola and Mozambique, contrive to keep life normal for the settlers, especially in the large towns and near the main centres of development. From the business point of view it might even be said that commercial enterprise has increased in the colonies as a result of the war. But it is equally true that there are large areas of nationalist influence despite the so-called 'pacification' and that some centres of population are under nationalist control.

In Angola there exists a huge, officially-designated 'unsafe' zone, while African nationalists claim to hold a third of the country and to be fighting set battles with Portuguese troops in ten districts : over an area, that is, of 877,000 square kilometres, with perhaps 2,700,000 inhabitants.[10] Of the three nationalist parties in action there, one is the GRAE, or Revolutionary Government of Angola in Exile, the former UPA, or Union of the Peoples of Angola, under Holden Roberto; this operates chiefly from bases in Congo-Kinshasa. The second is the MPLA under Agostinho Neto, based on Congo-Brazzaville for its operations in the Cabinda region and in Zambia for those in the eastern part of the country. Third is UNITA, the National Union for the Total Independence of Angola, led by Jonas Savimbi. It claims to have a headquarters actually in Angola since being expelled from Zambia in 1967 but seems to do very much less than the others.[11]

In Mozambique the mainspring of the nationalist movement is the FRELIMO. A rival party, the COREMO, or Mozambique Revolutionary Committee, was founded in 1965, but has achieved little enough so far. From its headquarters in Dar-es-Salaam the FRELIMO professes to control one-fifth of all Mozambique—the provinces of Cabo Delgado and Northern Niassa in particular—and a total population of 800,000. The journalist Basil Davidson states that he attended the second FRELIMO congress, which was held in liberated territory, and that 150 delegates from various parts of Mozambique were there. The FRELIMO went through a difficult time when Eduardo Mondlane was assassinated in February 1969,[12] but things were apparently reorganised later when

---

[10] See *Rapport présenté par le président du M.P.L.A. à la conférence internationale de solidarité avec la lutte dans les colonies portugaises,* and *Lutte de libération dans les colonies portugaises,* published in Rome and Paris respectively in 1970; both by Agostinho Neto.

[11] See Paul Whitaker on 'Arms and the Nationalists' in *Africa Report* for May 1970. Another view is offered by Jorge Aliceres Valentim in *Qui libère l'Angola;* according to this book, published in Brussels in 1969, the main effort for Angolan freedom comes from the UNITA. Similarly *Le Monde* for 5–6 July 1970 says that 'UNITA activities in eastern and central Angola appear to be on an ever-increasing scale.'

[12] *Le Monde* said on 5–6 July 1970: 'The FRELIMO has been upheld from the first by the Makondes tribe whose chief, Kavandame, surrendered to the Portuguese in 1969. It claims to be in control of a third of the country and maintains guerrilla activity in the provinces of Cabo

Samora Machel assumed command on the military side and
Marcelino dos Santos on the political.[13]

It is perhaps in Guinea-Bissao that the freedom movements
have most to show. Here in 1955 Amilcar Cabral, Secretary-
General of the PAIGC, at the head of a band of militants,
established a very strong political and fighting group.[14] According to what he himself says, Cabral is in control of two-thirds
of the rural area of the colony, approximately 15,000 square
miles and 600,000 people. In Guinea-Bissao, furthermore,
political and administrative conditions are ahead of those in
the liberated districts of any other Portuguese colony.

The nationalist movements receive aid from four main
sources, beginning with the countries round about. The PAIGC
can draw upon Guinea-Conakry, the GRAE on Congo-
Kinshasa; Congo-Brazzaville and Zambia supply the MPLA,
while Tanzania and Zambia assist the FRELIMO. And almost
all the African countries help, especially Algeria. Then there
are the organisations for African unity, such as the OAU itself,
founded at Addis Ababa in 1963, and the African Liberation
Committee. Soviet Russia, the people's republics, Cuba and
Red China help. So, too, do several organisations in the West,
and Western countries such as Sweden.[15]

Delgado, Niassa and Tete. In February of 1969 Eduardo Mondlane
its leader was assassinated in unexplained circumstances, although some
of the nationalist leaders have accused Chief Kavandame of having
been implicated.' David Martin, writing in the *Observer* of 6 February
1972, affirms that the killing was planned by the PIDE.

[13] See Pier Lombardo Vigorelli's *Il Monstro lusitano*, in the *Argo-
menti socialisti* pamphlets, Rome 1970.

[14] See David Andelman, 'Profile of Amilcar Cabral', in *Africa Report*
for May 1970; Gérard Chaliand, *Lutte armée en Afrique*, published
by Éditions Maspero, Paris 1967; and Basil Davidson, on 'Arms and
the Portuguese', also in *Africa Report* for May 1970.

[15] See Paul Whitaker's article previously referred to in which he
writes: 'The Swedish Foreign Minister, Torsten Nilson, promised the
congress of the Swedish Social-Democrat party to give financial aid
to the FRELIMO and the PAIGC. Later the parliament in Stockholm
voted unanimously in favour of granting 720,000 kronor to the
FRELIMO and a million to the PAIGC for the year 1970.' See
Africasia, Paris, December 1969.

In 1961, with a view to co-ordinating their diplomatic activities and allocating the international aid received, the PAIGC, the MPLA and the FRELIMO set up the Conference of Nationalist Organisations in the Portuguese Colonies, or CONCP, with permanent headquarters in Algiers. A world congress of support and solidarity was held in Rome in June 1970, the first meeting of its kind ever to take place in a NATO country.

It seems that the independence movements in the Portuguese colonies pursue a policy of non-alignment and have no ideological objections as to where the aid comes from.[16] Gestures of sympathy, and often increased assistance, pour in from trade unions, political parties, youth movements and religious organisations. At its conference in November 1969 the *Commission Justice et Paix* of the Church in Belgium, for example, resolved to lay before the Government and Parliament a motion that Belgium should :

(a) vote in the United Nations in favour of the independence of Guinea-Bissao, Angola and Mozambique;
(b) cease to supply arms to Portugal, even when supposedly for use in metropolitan Portugal only;
(c) do what she could within NATO to persuade the Western nations to make Portugal end the colonial war; and
(d) undertake to give economic aid to the new African states as soon as independence comes.

There are signs that similar action may be looked for from almost every European country. Successive condemnations of Portuguese policy have gained thumping majorities in the United Nations since 1962 and they are undoubtedly backed by a large body of opinion. In 1968 UNESCO, too, decided to deny aid of any kind to Portugal as long as she adhered to

[16] See *Le Monde*, 5–6 July 1970: 'During the Rome conference the nationalist leaders made no secret of their wish to cut free from the influence of the Eastern countries. It is hardly surprising that Paul VI, who refused to receive a deputation of Portuguese priests while he was in Uganda, desires to encourage this development.'

her 'policy of colonial domination and racial discrimination, while promising it, in co-operation with the OAU, to the nationalist liberation movements.[17]

The PAIGC, the FRELIMO and MPLA have created in their territories democratic committees to run schools, farming co-operatives, shops, hospitals and even courts of law.[18] In this way they are obviously building up a revolutionary fabric that will lead to the *de jure* creation of actual states. Most of the United Nations would surely agree with this and it would place Portugal in a most difficult position. In another department, of course, she is in a difficult position already : over 3,000 soldiers were killed in the colonies between 1964 and 1969, proportionately as great a loss as that of the 60,000 Americans who died in Vietnam in the same space of time. Also to be taken into account are the numerous desertions, especially of younger men, many of whom refuse to complete their military service rather than take part in a war.

There being no arms industry in Portugal, or only a very minor one, it is instructive to know who supplies her. The NATO countries who let her have arms as a fellow-member of the Atlantic Alliance, have stipulated that these should not be used in Africa, but in fact no check has ever been made. According to Basil Davidson her two chief sources of supply since 1961 have been France and Federal Germany. France furnished twenty Nord-Atlas transport aircraft and fifty-four Alouette III helicopters with no proviso as to what she did with them. Western Germany also sold her forty Fiat G-1961 fighter planes (not to be used in Africa), with anti-guerilla modifications. And from the United States the Portuguese Air Force has taken delivery of fifty F-84 C Thunderjets, thirty Cessna T-37 C trainers, a large consignment of Harvard trainers, eighteen Lockheed PV-2 bombers, twelve Lockheed

[17] See *Lutte de libération dans les colonies portugaises*, Paris 1969. Other international bodies as well as UNESCO took the same stand; they include the ILO, the World Health Organisation, the Food and Agriculture Organisation, etc.

[18] See Marcelino dos Santos, op cit., on the Rome conference of June 1970.

Neptune PV-2's and twenty B-26 bombers. More recently, despite the embargo, America has authorised the purchase by Portugal of two Boeings for use as troop-carriers. Bombs and napalm come from sundry European sources.

Portugal has also had shipping from Great Britain, Western Germany and France. Two former frigates, entirely refitted, were sent from Britain in 1961 and are now patrolling the coast of Angola and the Congo estuary. In 1967 and 1969 France sold her four frigates and as many submarines for 100 million dollars, payable in instalments.[19] Six warships of 14,000 tons each were delivered in 1970, built in Hamburg in Federal Germany, and in Spain. Clearly this is not all, but it is enough to indicate the assistance given by some of the Western powers.

Two questions have to be asked about this war :

(1) has the Portuguese Government any reasonable prospect of putting down the nationalist movements by force?
(2) if she has no such prospect, then what are her real reasons for carrying on with a policy that puts her beyond the pale of the civilised world?

A few frenzied statements apart, there has never been any forecast from any member of the Government or senior commander as to whether, when or how the war is going to end.[20] The implication seems to be that it could well go on for ever. Salazar, remember, was wont to call for a girding of loins and a gritting of teeth and to declare that the battle would be long

[19] See 'Arms and the Portuguese', the article by Basil Davidson already cited.

[20] Recently—see in particular *L'Express* for 11–17 October 1971—General Kaúlza de Arriaga, C-in-C of the Portuguese forces in Mozambique, has been cheerfully anticipating victory and said so more than once since the opening of his offensive, Gordian Knot. But Operation Gordian Knot, despite some successes, is far from having halted the guerrilla activities of the FRELIMO in the north and the Portuguese have sustained heavy casualties.

but the country could endure indefinitely; 'proudly alone' if she had to. And who can doubt it, when America, hovering between two stools, continues publicly to proclaim her anti-colonialist creed yet fails to vote against Portugal in the Security Council and the General Assembly of the United Nations? The war could, indeed, go on for ever.

Lisbon has always protested against the scandal of international aid to the nationalist movements and always, therefore, the Portuguese establishment has supported the most reactionary organisations in Africa and taken all possible advantage of geographical differences, inter-tribal jealousies and disputes of every kind. As a result of these tactics the Government has found itself in more than one most delicate situation. It is common knowledge that it upheld the Katanga secessionists and sent aid to Biafra some years later from São Tomé; latterly Portugal has been accused in the United Nations of having borne a positive part in the invasion of the Republic of Guinea. As far as Katanga is concerned, the international press revealed at the time, after the fall of Tshombe, that mercenary bases existed in Portuguese territory. Lisbon tried in vain to deny that this was so, but Salazar admired Tshombe and never pretended otherwise. In 1964 he told a reporter from *L'Aurore*, 'White men, they say, can be entirely replaced by blacks, but that is not true. The whites are the only people capable of planning and organisation, and Tshombe knew it.'

In April 1963 the Foreign Minister, Franco Nogueira, proposed to open negotiations for a non-aggression pact with the countries bordering on Angola. The only African country to accept was Malawi—a glance at the map and one sees why—but this disappointment for the Government was apparently offset by rifts among the nationalists. There were two important defections in 1969, those of Lazaro Kavandame in Mozambique and Rafael Barboza in Guinea-Bissao. In any case, the Government had always kept up some contacts among the nationalists.

And yet, despite all it can do, the regime is weaving Penelope's web in Africa. The war has become an evident fact of life in the colonies and can only spread and grow fiercer as time goes on.[21] Mere fighting will never solve the problem.

What has impelled the Portuguese Government to adopt a policy of such complete intransigence? Or, to put it another way, if the country keeps the colonies, what has she to gain? There is no doubt that the exploitation of Africa suits the interests of dominant business cliques, but it is by no means certain that the end of Empire would inevitably impoverish the people of Portugal; and this, ultimately, is the angle from which we must look at the question.

Angola and Mozambique offer sure commercial advantages within a society whose framework is that of Portugal. Both are producers of raw materials, both are outlets, preferential still, if less so than formerly, for Portuguese goods. But is this enough to warrant the sacrifices that have been made to carry on the war? The Government likes to underline the economic integration of the motherland and the *Ultramar*, but this integration is a myth. There is no means, even, of moving money to and fro between them, nor of free convertibility. The Angolan and Portuguese escudo still differ in value by some fifteen or twenty per cent and there is frequent dealing on the *marché parallèle*.[22]

Certain sections of the whites in Angola and Mozambique have voiced their impatience and irritation with the centralising Government of Lisbon; and when Marcello Caetano, speaking in Africa, and in Mozambique particularly, held out prospects of increased autonomy, these were the complaints he sought to allay. It was, indeed, a slightly new note to strike, but the autonomy he was talking about aims at an absolute predominance of white minorities.

It is also true that the colonies are not attracting any overflow of population, as would normally be the case, and this

[21] See the series of articles, *Une guerre sans fin*, published daily in *Le Monde* between 4 and 7 June 1972, and *Le Portugal malade de l'Afrique*, during March of the same year.

[22] Measures taken since the beginning of 1972 to regularise this situation have caused considerable discontent both at home and in the colonies.

for two reasons. First is the very small rate of population-increase in Portugal, where the labour shortage is at the moment serious; and secondly the Portuguese worker, who has the lowest living-standard in Europe and no immediate prospect of improvement, and who sees emigration as the best way out of the daily problems that beset him, emigrates to the industrialised countries which pay him better wages. He goes to France and Western Germany. From 1951 to 1960 only a fifth of the 600,000 emigrants chose Africa.[23] Emigration has increased since then and probably 160,000 people now leave the country every year, legally or otherwise. Of these, 8 per cent at the very most go to the colonies.[24]

Despite much official propaganda the plan for settling soldiers in the colonies at the end of their military service has also been less successful than was hoped. One large centre was to have been Cabora Bassa in Mozambique, while a million whites were to be established in part of the country made habitable as a result of the Zambesi river scheme. Economic reasons apart, the object was obviously to rear a veritable human barrier in defence of southern Africa. But Portugal alone cannot furnish so many men in reasonable time and will have to call upon white immigrants from the poorer European countries. The purpose of the project, in other words, is to reinforce South African apartheid, a system unrenowned, to say the least, as a producer of multi-racial societies.

The colonies are undeniably advantageous to certain business interests of metropolitan Portugal, but it is equally true, and in total contradiction of all that officialdom has to say, that their exploitation will tend to increase under the political and administrative yoke of Lisbon. Internal payments in the escudo zone are made in the national currency through the Bank of Portugal and export profits, in gold or foreign currency, thus go to the mother-country first. Angola coffee sold in the United States, iron-ore exported to Japan and Federal Germany, petroleum for trans-Atlantic countries and South

---

[23] See *Dossiers sur les colonies*, op. cit.
[24] South Africa, alone in the African continent, has any large intake of immigrants from Portugal.

G

Africa, the South African gold that pays the negro miners from Mozambique, the dues and revenues from the international railroads and the port facilities—they all produce foreign currency in large amounts, and all for the benefit of mainland Portugal. With it, and it alone, she regulates her balance of payments. It partly explains how she has managed to increase her monetary reserves.

Cash sent home by Portuguese emigrants in Europe is of course another and not unimportant item. In 1970, for instance, more than 14,000 million escudos came, or over 490 million dollars. But still it is natural to inquire whether all this colonial exploitation, enriching as it certainly does financial and industrial concerns at home, can, on strictly economic grounds, balance the expense of the armed forces and the national effort by which we hold the colonies. Every economist nowadays says no. The very existence of the colonies has, in these last years, hindered the development of metropolitan Portugal and prevented any change in its traditional economic structure. Nor can anyone deny that the country is at present passing through a grave crisis whose economic aspect has worsened since 1966 and which is basically due to the Government's colonial policy. The cost of the war is a colossal mortgage, weighing down the future. If Portugal wants to stimulate her economy and raise the living-standards of her people she must connect up with Europe in spite of capitalism and its drawbacks. And to be a part of Europe she needs a modern and progressive outlook, one entirely opposed to 'colonial warfare' and all the cherished traditional values and anachronistic exploitation that that implies. In time some sections which support the Government will come to understand this conflict of ideas, for they do seem to realise what fatal dissensions are engendered in the country by official policies.

When the Government opened the door to foreign capital in 1961 it showed itself prepared, for the sake of continued domination in Africa, to allow the big companies to treat Portugal herself as a colony. Quietly, with the minimum of publicity, Salazar began from that date onwards to internationalise his Empire, economically speaking. As the Hamburg paper *Die Zeit* very neatly put it on 24 March 1961, he turned to the Americans, the Germans and the Japanese to develop his African possessions for him. Without doubt, foreign investment has been encouraged in the last few years. Encouraged with ten years' tax exemption, with guarantees as to the repatriation of capital, dividends and profits (which are higher than they would be in Portugal); with tax-free machinery, essential materials and so on.[25] Naturally in the circumstances the foreign investor has not had to be asked twice. But neither has he gone into Africa to develop the Portuguese colonies or improve the lot of the local populations. He is there first and foremost for the enormous profits to be made under the protective shadow of South Africa.

It is safe to say that the main economic interests in the colonies today are concentrated in the hands of foreign enterprise or of Portuguese companies in which foreigners hold most of the shares. The list is long and we shall take a few examples only. The Angolan Agricultural Company, or CADA, is dominated by Rallet and Co., the French bankers, and controls much of the coffee-growing. The Angola Cotton Company, COTOMANG, is connected with the Société Générale de Belgique and has one of the largest cotton concessions. British interests are prevalent in the Benguela railway. The Lobito Mining Company, Companhia Mineira do Lobito, working the iron of Cassinga, belongs to a consortium directed by Krupp. DIAMANG, the Angola Diamond Company, belongs mostly to the De Beers group of South Africa, though Morgan's Bank, the Société Générale de Belgique and the Ryan Guggenheim group of America are also involved and only 11·5 per cent of the capital is Portuguese. 70 per cent of the Lobito Fuel Oil Company, CARBORANG, belongs to Petrofina, a subsidiary of the Compagnie Financière Belge du Pétrole, which also holds the capital of Petrangol, the petroleum products company. Gulf Oil, with the petroleum concession in

[25] See the report of the Mozambique, Angola and Guinea Liberation Commission, presented to the Rome conference in 1970. Also Eduardo de Sousa Ferreira, op cit.

Mozambique, and Cabinda Gulf Oil, are both American. The Mozambique Coal Company is controlled by the Belgian Société Minière et Géologique. Angolan Manganese belongs to Bethlehem Steel of America; Sean Sugar in Mozambique is Anglo-American; and so it goes on. I am omitting here such giant Portuguese concerns as the Companhia União Fabril, almost all of them associated with foreign capital and foreign banks.

Obviously foreign capital does not come in like this without conditions, and the fact that so much of it is South African is another uneasy aspect of the situation. Here the most striking instance is the Cabora Bassa project.

One of South Africa's handicaps, let us not forget, is a shortage of energy. This accounts for her renewed interest in plans for using the resources of Angola and Mozambique and her consequent assurances of agreement and co-operation. There is nothing fortuitous about this policy; it is all laid down in the programme of the new Pretoria-Salisbury axis.

What, then, is the Cabora Bassa project? It is a dam, to be built 150 kilometres north of Tete in one of the richest farming and mining districts of Mozambique; 33 metres long and 170 high, it will regulate the waters of the Zambesi by means of a twenty-kilometre-wide reservoir, 200 kilometres long. A million and a half hectares of land will thus come under cultivation and the hydro-electrical centre will provide energy on continuous current to places as far away as Johannesburg, which is 1,400 kilometres—well over a thousand miles—distant.[26] On so long a journey that current will be vulnerable and South Africa will therefore maintain troops in Mozambique to guard against acts of sabotage.[27]

Work began in October 1969. The first phase should be finished in March 1975, the second in January 1977 and the third in January two years after that. The whole thing will cost 9,000 million escudos, or 315 million dollars.

The builders at Cabora Bassa are ZAMCO (Zambesia Consôrcio Hidro-elétrico), a consortium dominated by the

[26] See Eduardo Sousa Ferreira, op. cit.
[27] Op. cit. and see *Seara Nova* for March 1970.

Anglo-American Corporation of South Africa. Construction costs are guaranteed by the Banque de Paris et des Pays-Bas, by the Union of Acceptance Bank of Johannesburg, the Deutsche Bank and the Banca Comerciale Italiana. Several auxiliary projects are covered by Portuguese banks, the total Portuguese stake in the affair amounting to something like 1,700 million escudos, or fifty-nine million dollars.

The Swedish electrical company ASEA, which owns exclusive rights to a new method of conveying continuous current, has pulled out under Government pressure in Stockholm. In Rome the Government has also announced its refusal to allow credit guarantees to any Italian firm taking part in the construction of the dam. Similarly, President Kaunda of Zambia went to Europe in the attempt to persuade the French and West Germans of the risky nature of the enterprise. Cabora Bassa is indeed a venture on an unusual scale for Portugal, and manifestly based on politics. Not surprisingly, it has aroused opposition on all sides and people fear that it will encourage South Africa in her expansionist policy : the *Johannesburg Star* has said that Cabora Bassa, with its attendant understandings and agreements, spells the beginning of an economic community in the southern part of the continent.

And Cabora Bassa in Mozambique, like the Cunene Basin scheme in Angola, will go far to alter the geo-political conditions of southern Africa. As Eduardo Mondlane, the FRELIMO leader, said, 'If we do not destroy the dam it will destroy us and white, racist Africa will have won.'

As interests so much more powerful than she is make themselves felt, so Portugal sees every initiative steadily slipping away from her in Africa, and thus her colonial problem forms part of a dangerous international situation. The tacit alliance between Lisbon, Salisbury and Pretoria will lead inevitably to the emergence of a new Rhodesia in Angola and Mozambique. The war-effort in Guinea-Bissao grows daily more costly, to make that colony daily less profitable to the ruling class. It will be enormously difficult for Portugal to hang on there. The trend of world politics must decide the fate of Macao and Timor. That leaves the archipelagoes of Cape Verde and São Tomé, and if the mother-country tries to apply her official African programme there, nothing but trouble will follow.

But are there no other possibilities? Have we time to deflect the Salazarist policy now being pursued by Marcello Caetano? These two questions constitute the great future challenge to the opposition in Portugal. Only a democratic Government can have the means and enough authority to end the warfare without delay by opening negotiations with the African nationalist parties and so set the colonies on the road to independence. The problem is one of readaptation. It calls for breadth of mind, imagination and resolution; all the more so since there is no universal remedy and each case requires a separate answer.

Nor should it be forgotten that the concerns of the Portuguese and African peoples are basically the same. Therefore the colonial problem must be solved by discussion in a spirit of brotherhood, it being admitted that the independent states of the future will be governed by black majorities who will respect the legitimate interests of the white inhabitants. Politics apart, the main battle is really against under-development. Both Portugal and the colonies must be released from the strangle-hold of the big multi-national exploiting companies.

In February 1970 there appeared in *Révolution Africaine* an article by Agostinho Neto which he called 'Tasks for the Year'. In it he explained, 'When the colonial war is over right relations can be established between the two peoples (Portuguese and Angolan) with a proper respect for freedom and equality. We may accept, and congratulate ourselves upon, the fact that the democrats of Portugal oppose Fascism and the colonial war. We may look upon them, with their courage to fight for freedom and their desire to end the war, as friends and allies, with whom good relations will be possible.'

The Lisbon Government will naturally read these words, coming from such a source, as proof positive that Portuguese democrats are traitors to their country. It doesn't matter much.

The taboos of the regime make moral and political nonsense and we must ignore them. For the democratic opposition can never regard the struggling people of Angola, of Mozambique and Guinea-Bissao as their enemies and in time it will be honoured for that fact. By keeping alive the possibility of debate, a debate between brothers, it will not merely show the world a different Portugal, humanist, tolerant and progressive; it will be paving the way for a great revival of the whole nation.

Chapter Ten

Increased Severity

The last years under Salazar were drab and difficult. While the regime was in arms in Africa, the current of world opinion set powerfully against colonialism. Expelled from several of the international organisations and condemned in the United Nations, the dictator tried, with no marked success, to rally public feeling to him. He made sure of foreign support by encouraging investment from abroad, but imposed stricter government at home and reduced every dissident voice to silence.

For, after the long static period, Portuguese society now began to stir. A new dynamism had followed the brisker business conditions brought about by the colonial war and at first some people even thought they detected a slight forward tendency. Western Europe made rapid strides in the sixties and Portugal saw considerable changes as a result, together with a measure of economic expansion from sheer force of circumstance. The heavily industrialised countries, needing workers, drew many more emigrants away, and this in turn seriously affected internal conditions, for the rural districts were being deserted. By the end of the decade emigration figures were alarming. Land and manufactures were left to take care of themselves; even intellectuals and technical staff, too closely restricted in Portugal, packed their bags and went. And though this movement abroad laid a heavy mortgage on the nation's future it did, of course, serve indirectly to solve a few immediate problems. With labour hard to get and wages up, social tension was reduced, and the money sent back to the emigrants' families was a main source of foreign currency to the state.

The period of army service was extended to four years as a

matter of military necessity, and so the young men, especially the students, grew restive. Government propaganda tried hard to persuade the nation that hostilities had been pressed upon it by others, but still people saw the war as something that was happening elsewhere, outside their own country and not immediately to do with them. The Church herself, for so long the ideological mainstay of the regime, began to waver a little, above all on the question of colonial policy.

The whole social structure of Portugal started to react, jogged, as it were, by the poverty-stricken workers. The country's economic position grew worse, particularly after 1966, when the effects of the war really began to tell. Today the income per head of the population is little more than half what it is in Spain; only some years ago it was the other way round.[1]

In the absence of trade unions, however, no political profit could be made from the situation, and this goes far to explain why the masses seemed so uninterested and relatively inert. Yet whenever there was any chance of showing what they felt they made their dissatisfaction very plain. In those last few years small manifestations by the thousand took place all over Portugal, but their political impact was nil because of Government repression and the censorship. The parties of the oppposition, with normal channels of communication barred to them and ruthlessly persecuted as they were, were unable to harness this potential force.

Political intimidation at that time was more severe than ever, for the Government was determined to keep its power at any price, even if that meant denying some of its former principles.

Salazar was a disciple of Charles Maurras. Power appealed to him for its own sake and he used it for the benefit of a privileged caste entrenched at all the vital economic and social points of the country. This new class, in Djillas' sense of the term, grew up in the dictator's shadow and still keeps the main

---

[1] The OECD's *Observateur* No. 50, for February 1971, gives the national gross product for Spain as 870 dollars per head, as against 600 for Portugal.

wheels of the system turning after he is gone—a financial and political élite paramount in the recent life of Portugal. Their interests were the deciding factor in basic issues that affect the whole nation's future.

The rule of Salazar finished in an atmosphere of commercialism and sordid lack of idealism among those at the top. So much is evident in the appointments he made. Mediocrities held the chief posts in public life; no plan was ever put forward that could possibly rouse the universal interest; and repression was heavier and heavier.

There is no doubt that for the vast majority of responsible people the regime meant nothing and promised nothing. It was a mere antiquated survival. The aged dictator himself was the very type of a tired old man, doing no more than utter his apocalyptic threats and forecasts. He had passed his life in seclusion, away from the mob and almost as a recluse; he had never been loved or even understood by the generality. In the entire history of Portugal there had been nothing like the deep channel that divided him from the people.

But not all his unpopularity, nor the steady lessening of support for the dictatorship, enabled the other side to do anything. Since every legal way was blocked, a revolutionary solution would have to be contrived, yet any revolutionary attempt was found to fail. More or less resignedly, the Portuguese had to put up with Salazar to the bitter end.

About the middle of 1962, on Students' Day—a celebration which had been forbidden on the grounds that it was subversive—a student strike was declared at Lisbon and spread rapidly to both other universities. Suddenly, after years and years of apathy, the students went into action, and in crowded meetings protested against the obscurantism and Government oppression in the university. The climate of hope and unity they engendered was felt beyond the student cadres in the capital and many of the professors who had not been completely corrupted joined in the great protest movement. This was the hour cleverly chosen by Marcello Caetano to resign his rectorship and so manage to be seen standing slightly aloof from the regime he had constantly served without actually having to declare sympathy with the student strikers.

From then onwards, and long before the events of May 1968 in France, the university problem was permanently with us, and in struggles almost everywhere student power was ranged against the Government. Persistently the students fought the regime on specifically national questions arising from Fascism and the colonial war. They have never ceased to demand autonomy for the universities and the right to create student bodies as they please, while of late all the usual elements of student protest have been adopted along with their own purely Portuguese problems. The Government has maintained that this student crisis stemmed from a universal movement, but it has in fact certain special aspects.

Students had protested against the Government before 1962, but there had been nothing comparable to that year's great upheaval; 1962 made clear just how much discontent existed in the universities. Since then hundreds of students have been arrested and many of them tortured by the PIDE. As a result there are Portuguese students scattered over Europe who have left their country, either to escape persecution or to avoid having to fight in Africa; more and more of them, all the time. All these young men, forced to quit Portugal, are studying and working abroad, often under enormous difficulties, but at least with the chance of a better political education than their fathers had.

Another marked feature of Salazar's last years was the conflict of the regime with an important sector of the Catholic Church, for after Vatican II a great many of the clergy—especially priests under the age of fifty—and various lay organisations began to raise their voices in opposition.

As we have seen, the Bishop of Oporto was driven into exile for ten years in 1959, and Catholic intellectuals in increasing numbers proclaimed their disagreement with the Government. The process was hastened by the colonial war, of which the Vatican could not approve, and the arrest and deportation of several coloured priests, notably Father Joaquim Pinto de Andrade, who is still in prison, did even more. Many

Catholics joined the democratic opposition and what happened to the Catholic group known as *Pragma* shows how undecided was the official attitude. It was banned by a Catholic Minister, more than once proceeded against by the PIDE, who arrested some of the leading lights, and finally allowed to operate under close surveillance.

An attempt was made to create a party nucleus with the Christian Movement of Democratic Action, but this never came to very much. More successful was the work done by Catholics among trade unions through the Workers' Cultural Centre which, in spite of all obstructions, helped to train democratically minded trades union officials.

The intellectuals, too, were sorely tried during those final years of Salazar. Fascism proverbially hates intellectuals and its most contemptible measure against them was the suppression of the Authors' Society. It had been appallingly difficult to get permission to found such a society in the first place and authority viewed it with mistrust from the very beginning, in the fifties. Understandably, for the vast majority of Portuguese writers are anti-Fascist and every leading literary figure, without exception, has come out against the regime. Some of the society's presidents, men like Aquilino Ribeiro, Jaime Cortesão or Ferreira de Castro, have happened to be prominent in the democratic opposition too. The Portuguese Authors' Society in the years of its existence won international renown and established relations with intellectual circles abroad. Then the Government began a frightful campaign against it, culminating in the suppression of the society and the arrest of members of the panel which had awarded a literary prize to the Angolan writer Luandino Vieíra. The club premises were attacked and the contents, not excepting the library, archives and pictures, were destroyed.

In 1965, elections were held to the National Assembly. The atmosphere in the country was gloomier than ever. Under the constitutional amendment of 1959 Admiral Américo Thomaz had been re-elected some months previously as President of the Republic for a further seven years, an event which evoked not the faintest shadow of public interest. The Admiral was in fact appointed by the 'élite' of the regime; that is, by an electoral college consisting of members of the National Assembly, all of whom naturally belonged to the one and only party; of members of the Câmera Corporativa; and of delegates from the municipal and legislative councils of each province, including those of the *Ultramar* : all of course Government men. The sole discordant note in the so-called election was struck by Professor Francisco Pereira de Moura, an economist of repute who sat in the Câmera Corporativa. He wrote an open letter casting doubts upon the validity of the procedure.

The domestic situation in 1965 being what it was, many of the opposition advocated abstention from the poll. Not a single condition had been met that would allow us any real voice in the conduct of affairs, and fear and indifference were only too profound and obvious on every side. In spite of all this, however, the Communists were in favour of taking part.

In 1964 there had been an anti-revisionist, pro-Chinese split among the Communists, which gave rise to the Portuguese Marxist-Leninist Committee and the Popular Action Front, or FAP. Francisco Martins Rodrigues, João Pulido Valente and Ruy d'Espinay, who had led the splinter movement, were eventually arrested. The two revolutionary groups were against 'electoralist' action and criticised the legal struggle recommended by the Communist Party and other political forces, including the Socialists. Unlike the orthodox brethren, they were for violence as the prelude to armed conflict. Peaceful co-existence, within or without, was not for them.

Rent by internal schism and kept severely in order by the police, the Communist Party was thus in no state to mobilise the masses in 1965. Moreover, there were increasing signs that it was losing working-class support. Defections from within the party itself—of Rolando Verdial, for instance, a member of its Central Committee, or Nuno Alvares Pereira, an official of the student section—had unmasked many militants and almost paralysed it for political action.

The Socialists and the Liberal Republicans, still attached to the Democratic-Social Directive of Professor Azevedo Gomes, were unsure what they should do. The Catholics too were doubtful, divided as they were over whether or not the time were ripe to start an underground movement of Christian-Democrat complexion. Other more recently founded groups, with no very definite party lines, seemed ready to seize what advantage they could from the elections, provided that certain guarantees were forthcoming.

In the end the democratic opposition combined to present lists of candidates in five electoral divisions—Lisbon, Oporto, Leira, Viseu and Braga. At the last moment the Catholics decided not to put any candidates forward on the general opposition list.

The democrats of Braga, totally convinced that circumstances there were unusually favourable, resolved to conduct a separate campaign, but candidates in the other divisions signed a collective 'Manifesto to the Nation', drawn up by me at their request. This was a detailed presentation of the chief political and economic aspects of life in Portugal, and ended with a kind of ultimatum to the Government. Briefly, they demanded freedom to pursue electioneering activities and to hold meetings during the campaign and the unrestricted right to check the ballot. Without these concessions they would withdraw from the election.

For international reasons the Government was anxious that they should do nothing of the kind, but neither was it eager to grant conditions that would make its own victory less than complete and so start a process of liberalisation. It solved things by authorising publication of the entire manifesto while launching at the same time a 'patriotic' drive, in the colonies as well as at home, against what the manifesto had to say on behalf of self-determination in Africa. All our candidates were branded as traitors to their country and threatened with the consequences. This at least forced the Catholics out into the open; they circulated a signed memorandum in which dozens of them, including members of the old traditionalist families, rallied to the opposition.

This bold declaration added fuel to the flames. The Catholic fellow-traveller joined the traitor democrat as prime target of the 'ultras' of the regime. The minimal demands were not met and the opposition withdrew its candidates, but the 1965 campaign was not quite wasted after all. Courage had been found to speak out against the colonial wars and the opposition had made use of this to outline a possible solution of the conflict.

I worked actively for the opposition during this campaign. The fact of having presented the manifesto as a candidate for Lisbon had put me in the limelight and I became the favourite object of official attack. Also, of course, I was recently out of gaol and had seen to it that the assassination of Delgado was made a central issue—one that was clearly embarrassing in Salazarist circles.

Unhappily, Professor Azevedo Gomes died in a motor accident at the end of the year and with his death there disappeared from the political scene the most respected figure, after those of Jaime Cortesão and António Sérgio, of the opposition. Within the Social-Democrat group profound differences had already arisen between the Liberal-Republican wing, which included some moderate Social-Democrats, and the Socialists themselves. They had united over the colonial question : a common if precarious platform, for it did not take them beyond generalities, although the former Prime Minister Cunha Leal was a convert to self-determination. But apart from this most important subject there was disagreement on sundry national problems, and especially as to the right time and the right way of tackling them. And all this rose to the surface and became serious when Azevedo Gomes was dead.

The Democratic-Social Directive, tolerated by the Government at any given moment, gave the Socialist group I represented the political cover we needed to make our exertions legal. At the cost of frequent sacrifices we managed to initiate a great deal of opposition activity from 1955 to 1965.

But pragmatism in politics is an expensive luxury. Because we tried to be moderate many young people, particularly after the student troubles of 1962, began to take literally every word we said. Often they were unable to distinguish between some tactical concession on our part and the defence of a principle.

Matters were further complicated by the Catholics who, as
one-time collaborators with the regime, now had impulses
quite opposite from ours and felt they should preach a left-wing
gospel to outstrip our own. This was when the campaign
against Social Democracy was set on foot, deliberately identify-
ing it with Socialism. An attempt, based on our ideological
differences, was made to confuse us with the Liberal Republicans and make us appear as a 'right-wing' opposition.

The complexity of our national problems was giving rise to
more and more variations of opinion within the opposition.
Simple anti-Fascism was no longer enough. Speeches made on
the death of Azevedo Gomes, notably those of Cunha Leal
and António Macedo, and my own, prove that two languages,
two distinct styles, were to be found within the Directive. Having coalesced into an autonomous movement, the Socialists considered the moment had now come to follow their own path.

Socialist tradition has never been very strong in Portugal.
The founders of the Socialist Party in the latter half of the
nineteenth century were men of high intellectual and moral
standing, such as Antero de Quental, the great poet, and José
Fontana, the working man, but it was not a movement for
the masses. It never took up a very decided attitude towards
the Monarchy, seeming not to mind overmuch what form of
Government there was. It was the Republicans, politically
radical and anti-clerical for all their typically petit-bourgeois
aims, who personified the opposition and were the great popular
party of the time.

From 1910 to 1926, during the First Republic, the Socialist
Party played a minor role; also, in the early decades of this
century, the working classes came increasingly under the
influence of anarcho-syndicalism, which was especially powerful in the CGT. When the dictatorship dissolved political
parties the Socialists fell into a slow and irreversible decline.
They never took kindly to a life of clandestine activity and
never matched the Socialist Party or the UGT (General
Workers' Union) in Spain, which became decisive forces among
the organisations of the left.

There were sundry efforts in the thirties, forties and even

so late as the 1950s, to create some sort of Socialist underground, but nothing much came of them and the bulk of the people did not respond at all. There was the Republican and Socialist Alliance of 1932–34, the Action and Socialist Indoctrination Group of 1942–44, the Socialist Union of 1944–50, the Workers' Party in 1947, the Socialist Front of 1950–54 and the Republican and Socialist Resistance of 1955–64. The Fascists tolerated no opposition party save that of the Monarchists and by thus driving any others underground effectively prevented the rise of new political organisations. The Communists alone, thanks to their peculiar party structure, were adapted to fight on in these conditions.

But there were signs of a revival of democratic Socialism nevertheless, even apart from the way the Communist image was worsening in the shadow of Stalinism; such were the Socialist ideas of the *Seara Nova* group, for example, and the co-operative doctrines of António Sérgio. Unquestionably there was, and still is, room for a Socialist Party in Portugal. Room among large sections of the workers and peasants, of the younger generation and the intellectuals; even in the liberal professions, public officials and middle ranks who constitute the lesser bourgeoisie; room for a Socialist Party to stand somewhere between the Communists on the one side and the Republican, Liberal or Christian Democrat formations on the other.

Certain moves were in fact made, chiefly among Portuguese exiles, towards establishing a party on Socialist lines (the ASP, or Portuguese Socialist Action group, was a case in point), but, quite simply, freedom was lacking in 1965 to set up what would have had to be a clandestine organisation. At most some sort of Socialist movement might have been founded, with no organic party structure; and to achieve even so much, struggling full-time with the police and unable to proclaim a definite set of beliefs, all comers must have been welcomed, from moderate Socialists on the European Social-Democratic pattern to those of Marxist persuasion, such as are found among the PSU in France, to say nothing of former Communists disillusioned with Stalinism and ready to embrace democratic pluralism. The attempt was made, but the results were not always very encouraging.

One should add, of course, that the creation of any powerful Socialist movement needs the effective support of the working class, and Government repression makes it extraordinarily difficult to get such a movement going in Portugal. Also, the Communist Party, having been for so long, and to its enduring honour, the only underground organisation active among the workers, has occupied positions which it often keeps merely because no one has bothered to dislodge it.

For another thing, the working class had not shown itself exactly audacious during the last years of Salazar, and with good reason. The official, vertical trade unions, dead things under strict official control, were hardly a promising field of action, while the formation of clandestine unions had again and again been proved impracticable and led only to sterner reprisals against the worker.

One more obstacle in the path of a meaningful Socialist Party was the impossibility of uniting Catholics and non-Catholics in one Socialist-orientated group. Too many old prejudices existed on both sides. Yet in a land with so strong a Catholic tradition any attempt was doomed to partial failure unless such a union could be brought about.

From 1966 onwards we made great efforts to do just this—to gather the non-Communist left into a movement sufficiently flexible to allow the various brands of Socialist to live side by side, with Catholics and non-Catholics especially in mind. There was nothing specifically anti-Communist in the idea. On the contrary the intention was to maintain relations with a party which, considering the power it represents, must certainly take its share in the eventual reconstruction of the country—providing, of course, that Portuguese Communists, like those of Italy, Spain and even France, show themselves willing to respect the ways of democracy, both now and in the future.

There must be an autonomous, powerful Socialist Party. It is one of the elements we need if we are to sort the situation out and arrive at a democratic solution in Portugal. Nor, I think, can we do without Christian-Democrat and Liberal-

Republican organisations capable of mobilising moderate opinion. The existence of Social Democracy might also do much to make the Communist Party less ready to push into the lead, less dogmatic and less eager to adopt every notion that proceeds out of the Soviet Union.

Many people concurred in this appraisal of the situation in Portugal at the end of 1965, and so there was some chance of success. The review *O Tempo e o Modo*, then in its first, less ultra-left phase, helped to forge bonds of brotherhood and political agreement between Marxist and Catholic Socialists. The whole experiment was something very new in Portugal and, though greeted by outspoken criticism from the left, turned out to be most fruitful. It led to exchanges of opinion and to personal contacts that seemed full of promise though, as always, there were the difficulties of police restraint and censorship. But all the possibilities are by no means exhausted. Since the events of May 1968 in France a multitude of small left-wing groups have made their appearance in Portugal, so that we should in some measure re-think the problem of fresh organisation among the constituent forces of the left.

These notes have been necessary in order to illuminate my own political conduct during the dictator's last years, when I had one purpose and one only—to do all I could against Salazarism and for the coming of a democratic order.

I was having to go abroad quite often at the time in connection with the Delgado affair, and so had the opportunity to meet leading Socialists from other parts of Europe and members of other democratic parties. My political horizon was enlarged as I began to see new possibilities of action.

I have always thought that Salazarism lasted so long partly because of the way in which our democrats were cut off from the rest of the world. Isolated from Europe first by the Spanish War, then by the Second World War, the democratic opposition was immured until recently in a sort of political ghetto. Who, at that period, could know what was actually going on in Portugal?

One thing may be said for the colonial wars: from the

moment they started they awoke a general curiosity about us which increased with the integration of Western Europe, since we are, after all, as much a part of Europe as are Spain and Greece and Turkey, the poorest members of the family.

The only political links between our opposition and progressive circles elsewhere were, in fact, made through Communist or para-Communist channels. Salazar's favourite thesis, the claim that really earned him foreign support and approval, was precisely that if his regime went, Communism or chaos would ensue; and now, somewhat paradoxically, the absence of any sign of life from an independent opposition seemed indirectly to prove that he was right. Europe was unaware that there *was* any democratic alternative to Salazar, and its embassies in Lisbon, snowed under by official propaganda, systematically minimised the influence of the non-Communist opposition.

In Spain, a Liberal, Socialist and Catholic opposition began to emerge and spread about the mid-fifties, but in Portugal the political opinions of the parties that were governing Europe, from Socialist to Liberal-Conservative, were seldom even heard of. Now the moment had come to change all this, to underline the fact that there was indeed a democratic solution, and the scheme we issued in 1961 for the democratisation of the Republic was an important item in our programme.

Something on this scale called for a large team rather than a handful of planners, but unhappily many of the opposition leaders were limited and provincial in outlook. They cherished mistaken scruples about washing dirty linen in public, they were terrified of the police, and the experiment failed. In those last years of Salazar's lifetime everybody was apparently waiting for the clouds to roll away of their own accord.

I myself, as a Socialist, have tried to increase our contacts with every such movement in Europe. I thought, and I still think, that Socialism in Portugal must follow a path of its own. We should not model ourselves on anyone else, but that does not relieve us of the moral duty to study and learn from what happens in other countries. Through Portuguese fellow-Socialists in exile—men such as Tito de Morais and Francisco

Ramos da Costa, who have laboured like giants in the cause—
I was able to meet many distinguished European Socialists with
whom my bonds of friendship and brotherhood were deeper
than those of ideology alone.

But because of all this my personal position grew steadily
more difficult. I was taking a calculated risk. By openly avowing
myself a Socialist, and by being in open communication with
like-minded circles abroad, I created awful problems for the
Government at home, and these increased as I became a sort
of magnetic pole in domestic politics, exposed to attack from
the right and from one section of the left as well. My professional appearance at a string of trials intensified the situation,
for political trials offered the only opportunity there then was
publicly to criticise the regime with some hope of being heard.
I was also getting a name in the outside world and there were
political parties and foreign governments, diplomats and people
from leading international newspapers who took progressively
more notice of me.

The authorities felt hampered as a result in attacking me
with their customary violence and for a time they hesitated
visibly. How could I best be dealt with? The successive gaol-
sentences I received from 1965 onwards aroused repeated
protests from international lawyers and in the press, and more
than once the accusations were so flimsy that the Law Society
of Portugal intervened on my behalf.

But I had earned international recognition as a Socialist
and it was harder for the Government to molest me. This was
not only because of my friendly contacts with those European
administrations which included Socialists; it was also because
those friendly contacts of mine bore inconvenient and implicit
witness to the presence in Portugal of left-wing, non-
Communist groups in active opposition to the regime. And
then, from another point of view, what if the Catholics were
to adopt my dangerous example? It was a challenge Salazar
could not ignore, and therein lay my calculated risk.

In 1966 the Socialist International sent its Secretary-General,
Albert Carthy, to Portugal. His mission was to end the isolation
of decades by getting in touch with Portuguese Socialists, and

the day he left we had a press conference of which the authorities knew nothing until he was already on his way to London. That visit began a series of fruitful contacts which were to link us closely with Socialist parties all over the world and which have increased in both directions. I was officially received by Pietro Nenni when he was Foreign Minister in the Italian Government of the centre-left, and by de Martino, who was Vice-President at the same time. I had official interviews with several of the British Labour Ministers and with leaders of the Social-Democrat Party of Western Germany. In Sweden I talked with the Prime Minister, Tag Erlander, and his Minister of Education, Olaf Palm, who was to succeed him. I have had friendly meetings with Socialist leaders from Latin America and the third world. On the same errand I have been to Cuba and Yugoslavia and have learned a great deal from the study at close quarters of their differing Socialist experiments. And all these perfectly normal occasions, which one would never mention twice save in connection with my own country, irritated the Government past bearing. Only those who lived in Portugal in that last stretch of Salazar's rule can imagine how scandalous such activities appeared to the eye of authority in Lisbon.

From 1965 onwards I was the object of suffocating vigilance from the police. My telephone-calls, my post and all my comings and goings were checked the whole time. I had to have a special permit from the PIDE before I could leave the country, and this was more than once refused. I had to let them know the exact date of my intended journey and at which frontier-post they could expect me. Plain-clothes men dogged me day and night, outside the front door and outside the office. Under pressure from the Foreign Minister, the American ambassador forbade one of his staff to come to my house, so I had to meet him in a Lisbon park. The whole thing got to such a pitch that when I invited some Swedes and Danes of the diplomatic corps to a summer luncheon-party at my house at Sintra, not far from Lisbon, the PIDE equipped themselves with a long-distance camera, surrounded the garden and filmed us all at table.

Little by little the police tightened their supervision and my friends agreed with me that the Government was looking for any pretext to put me permanently out of action. I was many times advised either to seek the shelter of a foreign embassy or to guard against actual physical attack, though this in fact was never used.

They found what they wanted at the end of 1967, when the Ballets Roses scandal broke out. Several well-known Portuguese financiers and socialites were involved in this, including, so it was said, three members of the Government. Joaquim Pires de Lima, a fellow-lawyer who was keen to work for the opposition among the Catholics, told me as much as he had gathered, adding that the Judicial Police wanted to go on with the case and that Antunes Varela, then Minister of Justice, supported them. There I had to disillusion him : those implicated were so very well known that the Government would certainly have hushed it all up as quickly as possible. However, by now an article had come out in the magazine *Jeune Afrique* which lifted a corner of the veil; this, my friend thought, would make hushing it up very difficult and we should see one of the most sensational trials ever held in Portugal.

By mere chance, in court a few days afterwards, I happened to look into one of the dossiers on the case. These files passed from hand to hand and were widely discussed by lawyers, judges and legal officials, all of them undisguisedly curious. The politicians and diplomats of Lisbon knew of the affair already and had plenty to say about the in-fighting for power among members of the regime, for the scandal was generally assumed to be somehow connected with the question of Salazar's successor. The by now ex-Minister of Justice was supposed to be in line and to have given the go-ahead for a full inquiry because this would implicate other Ministers, very near to Salazar.

At this point an English journalist named O'Brien arrived in Lisbon to report on the Ballets Roses business for the *Sunday Telegraph* and in due course turned up at my office. He told me he had been in Portugal for several days and had not yet managed to see Professor Antunes Varela at Coimbra. Knowing nothing special about the Ballets Roses, I suggested he should go along to Pires de Lima, who had one of the files. There and then O'Brien telephoned to Pires de Lima's house, or rather to the house of his father with whom he lived, and who was Director-General of Political and Civil Administration at the time.

Much later on I learned what happened next. The English journalist never spoke to Pires de Lima the lawyer but only to his father, who led him to believe they were one and the same person and refused, for what he called 'patriotic reasons', to give details of the scandal. Then, realising what O'Brien meant to write and wishing to spare his son any unpleasantness, the elder man thought the easiest thing to do was to blame me for the whole 'misunderstanding'. And this I in turn realised very soon afterwards, when the PIDE interrogated me at their headquarters.

Back in London O'Brien published an article based on the rumours in *Jeune Afrique*, but stating that he had made inquiries at Coimbra and in Lisbon. The article contained nothing that was not already known among newspapermen and diplomats in the Portuguese capital, but the next afternoon I was arrested at the office—without a warrant, as ever. The questioning soon revealed that I was accused of disseminating false news to foreigners, of a kind likely to damage the national reputation.

'And this time,' Sachetti informed me, 'you've brought the Prime Minister into it; personally.'

I naturally denied any such charge and some days later the *Sunday Telegraph* man also categorically denied that I had been his source of information. All the same, they kept me in gaol for three months, during which time I was allowed to see my wife, and no one else, for fifteen minutes every week. For the final fortnight I was moved in with the civil offenders and when the president of the Law Society protested he was told it was too great a risk to have me in a cell with political detainees. Being a lawyer, I might have furnished them with good legal arguments detrimental to the police!

My arrest put a new complexion on the case of the Ballets

Roses, for indirectly it confirmed that the Government had something to hide. There was, too, a distinct impression that the PIDE, interposing in the matter of Salazar's successor, were wanting the affair to receive a great deal of publicity abroad. Journalists from all over the world came dashing to Lisbon, where the chaste dictator was apparently prepared to defend certain of his Ministers from charges involving the corruption of twelve-year-old children. Special correspondents from the *New York Times* and *Time* magazine were turned back at the frontier.

Twisted echoes of all this reached me, cut off in my cell, via the PIDE questioning and the fulminations of Sachetti. When nothing incriminating could be produced against me the Government changed its tack and six weeks later arrested an associate of mine, the lawyer Francisco Sousa Tavares, and the write Urbano Tavares Rodrigues. The object was evidently to find some grounds for arraigning the three of us, but the police got no further with this manœuvre than they did with my imprisonment.

When at the end of three months I was still in custody awaiting trial my own lawyer invoked *habeas corpus* on 29 February 1968 and on 1 April they released me, on an order dated the previous day. A mistake, Sachetti solemnly pointed out; I really ought to have been home twenty-four hours earlier.

But this was not the end of my problems. Once again the PIDE had shown itself incapable of bringing a case strong enough to put me inside for a long term, and revenge was not delayed.

Three very cold winter months in a cell like an ice-house had made a restful holiday in the Algarve seem a very good idea. My wife thought another car was tailing us as we drove down there, but that was nothing new and I took no notice. In the days that followed, however, the vigilance became so obvious as to be a positive nuisance. Instead of one car we acquired an escort of two, in radio communication, and a total observation force of five men and a woman.

My wife, warned by various hotel-managers that all this was not exactly welcome, began to think that something nasty was being planned for me—a road-accident, perhaps. We were in a part of the country which, normally thronged with tourists, was at this season very quiet and the fate of Delgado was, I must admit, in both our minds. We decided to get back to Lisbon.

This we did and the very next afternoon the police came to my office and arrested me with no explanation at all and without showing a warrant. I was not in fact under arrest, they said, but the Prime Minister had ruled a few hours previously that I was to be deported next day to São Tomé, in the Gulf of Guinea, there to remain, under surveillance, for an indefinite period.

With no time even to change my clothes, and nothing but some linen in a small suitcase, I left my family, my friends, companions and profession. I was not allowed to use the main gate at the airport. From the plane I looked back at the lighted building, and there on the roof were a crowd of people, with handkerchiefs waving. They were my friends and my companions, students, workers, intellectuals. I don't know who had told them, but they had come to say goodbye. I saw them attacked, suddenly and savagely, by the police and afterwards learned that my wife and daughter had been hit, as were some of our friends, as well as ordinary passengers and others who were there by chance and had no notion of what it was all about. That was the picture I carried away with me on a March night of 1968.

By the time I reached São Tomé the foreign radio stations— Radio Brazzaville for one and of course the BBC—had given news of my deportation in their Portuguese-language programmes, so that I was awaited with mingled apprehension and interest by the whole population.

São Tomé itself is a small and drowsy equatorial town with an oppressive climate. The vegetation is lush, the landscape incredibly beautiful. The coloured inhabitants, most of them imported, unwillingly, from the mainland of Africa some generations ago, number not more than 60,000. They speak a dialect of Portuguese and have, I am afraid, no say in the social and economic life of the place. The real lords of the island are the whites, perhaps 3,000 of them, who regulate their entire lives by metropolitan Portugal and think only of going back there to settle down once they have amassed a little money. Between the two communities there exists an almost complete mistrust that has grown worse in recent years. The wealth of the island lies in cocoa, coffee and coconuts and practically all of it belongs to Portuguese companies whose powers are exercised by managers known as *roceiros*. Not so very long ago these men could do whatever they liked here and even Government officials who refused to conform were marched by force on board their ships for home.

On my arrival I was inspected, I remember, as though I were some rare bird; an inspection the more minute since there was only one plane a week and all São Tomé turned out to see it land.

Again I heard that I was not under arrest, properly speaking. I was 'living under surveillance', could stay where I wished and pursue my profession if I wanted to. I took a room in one of the town's two *pensions*, resoundingly entitled Pousada de São Jerónimo.

The local PIDE chief, Nogueira Branco, was menacing and mild-spoken. One's immediate impression was that he didn't want problems. He had been out here for several years, had put his savings into farming and seemed to be doing nicely. All the same, he had expected to be doing better. The war in Biafra had given him a lot of extra work, for most of the military aid to the secessionists came through the airport at São Tomé. Planes landed there from many countries, from South Africa as well as Sweden, and the whole island was crammed full of mercenaries and missionaries, near-missionaries and journalists. My arrival in his midst, heralded as it had been in the world press, was not exactly calculated to soothe the poor man's nerves and he surrounded me with such an atmosphere of suspicion and spy-mania that he made himself quite unbearable and absurd.

Obsessed by the fear that I might escape, he set twelve of his police to watch me. I could not stir a step without them and in a place where everybody knew everybody else and there were fifty kilometres at most of surfaced roads, this verged on the ridiculous. One rash businessman from Portugal who invited me to go for a drive did not even succeed in staying the night : the army flew him out the same day. After that I was forbidden to leave the town without first obtaining a police permit. As it was hot, I bought an old Volkswagen for getting about in the daytime when it was exhausting to walk. They all went mad. Each of the twelve policemen put in for a motorcar of his own and one, especially zealous, managed to cause an accident.

But it was not enough for the PIDE chief to have me shadowed for twenty-four hours out of the twenty-four. He worried dreadfully in case I should infect the populace with my subversive notions, and devised a regular quarantine system for keeping me apart. Anyone with whom I exchanged a single word was hauled in by the PIDE and questioned as to what had been said. Nogueira Branco next abandoned gentle hints and started to use threats. The Town Clerk, a man I had been at school with, was told he would be on the next flight to Portugal if he spoke to me; his children, who were coming to me for lessons in philosophy, were similarly warned off. In short, the scheme worked like a charm and I felt more and more isolated. Four or five brave souls, and only four or five, stood by me.

It was the Governor who more than anyone found the situation galling. Lt.-Colonel Silva Sebastião was a man of liberal tendencies who had spent his whole life in the African service, and home politics were a closed book to him. It was his dearest wish to make something of São Tomé and my deportation amounted to a slur. He also, and with reason, failed to see why Lisbon should have chosen this moment to attract the world's attention by deporting me there at all when he had his hands full with the highly secret and delicate Biafran Aid operation. Thinking of these things, he assured me finally,

'We shan't both be on this island for more than three months, and that's certain.'

But he was speedily summoned to Lisbon, where Salazar told him to stop bothering his head about me and leave the PIDE to get on with their own job. He obeyed these orders and things were appreciably worse for me thereafter.

In theory, I had permission to exercise my calling. There were then three lawyers on São Tomé, but since one had been suspended as a disciplinary measure, one was also the notary and badly pushed for time and the third was on the point of retirement, I could presumably look forward to plenty of work.

I had been there a fortnight or so when I was asked to become legal adviser to Agua-Izé, a subsidiary of the CUF group (Companhia União Fabril), in Portugal, and the biggest agricultural land-holders on the island. The suggestion came from one of their top men, Jorge de Melo, for whose sister I had once acted in a family matter. Because of this, and since she was herself a shareholder, I decided to consult her before accepting. I made the mistake of sending my letter through the mail. It was opened and photostated by the PIDE and shown to Salazar, who had a personal word to say to CUF. As a result I heard from my former client by return of post how delighted she was that I should be representing her company, while the local manager heard from Jorge de Melo that he had better find somebody else.

That is all quite typical of the attitude of big business when confronted by the powers that be and, had the police not taken care to spread the story to the four corners of São Tomé, would have been unimportant. As it was, the effect was soon apparent. If the foremost company, not only here but in all Portugal, declined, under official pressure, to use my professional services, then who was going to summon up courage to do so?

My post was tampered with again when Martin Luther King was assassinated and I sent my condolences to the American ambassador in Lisbon. The PIDE called me in and brazenly informed me that my letter could not possibly go, as I had been forbidden to indulge in political activity on the island. Such candour, even from them, surprised me and I said, 'Do you realise what that means? You are telling me that you are interfering with my letters. That is against the Constitution. It's a very serious thing.'

'Well, don't let it worry you,' was the curt reply. 'That's our look-out.'

In spite of pressures of this kind, however, I did undertake the defence of a poor customs employee on a charge of theft. It was a minor case, but the repercussions were tremendous. The prosecution was relying entirely on a forced confession, but on my advice the man retracted this in court and gave details of how he had been treated. This caused a furore. The hearing went on for several days and the public, African for the most part, crowded in to listen silently to the interpleading. My PIDE inspector saw the whole affair as political from the start. What threats were used against the Indian judge I do not know, but they had obviously been made. He was jumpy and domineering and his ill-placed remarks more than once led to disturbances in court. My speech for the defence lasted nearly two hours and as it managed to demolish all the prosecution's evidence, everyone thought my client would get off or receive a token sentence only. The sentence, when it came, after an interval of a week, was to thirteen years and some months' imprisonment.

The accused man's wife was a remarkable woman. 'This isn't meant for my husband, it's meant for you,' she told me. 'They don't want you setting up as the poor man's lawyer in São Tomé.'

The sentence was later quashed, but it was indeed a warning to me. From that time on I saw that I should only harm my clients when I had any, and I lost the desire for professional work. I thought of teaching at the local secondary school but here, too, I ran up against insurmountable obstacles. My wife, who had by now arrived to join me, was looking for the same sort of job. She had all the right aptitudes and teachers were needed, but when she put in for a post the Governor sent for me. Would I please see that she dropped the idea? Orders had come from higher up and he had to refuse her application.

On 8 September I was at the barber's—the barber doubled as our only bookseller—when a neutral voice came over the radio announcing that the Prime Minister had been operated on the night before for a brain haemorrhage. The news was like a thunderbolt. Instead of passing the expected years on São Tomé I saw myself half-way home already. And from that day on I felt convinced that people were looking at me differently. Even the PIDE seemed more reasonable somehow. Almost human.

Chapter Eleven

After Salazar

The fortieth anniversary of the dictatorship was celebrated in May 1966. In that year Salazar at the age of 77 went up in an aeroplane for the first time in his life and flew to Braga to unveil a statue of Gomes da Costa, military leader of the coup of 28 May; the military leader dismissed and sent to the Azores so soon afterwards, then solemnly presented with a marshal's baton.

Salazar chose to end his speech on this occasion with a dash of black humour. 'Now,' he said, 'as we celebrate this fortieth anniversary of 28 May, comes the ideal moment at which to end the rule of thirty-eight years, with all its bitterness.'[1] He paused and threw a cold glance at the audience. His henchmen, taken unawares, reacted in various ways. Some made deprecatory noises, others clapped. Confusion spread for several seconds as the old man gazed upon them. He then restored silence and went imperturbably on.

'I do not intend to retire, for in the mad state of the world today such an intention would be read as a sign of changing policy and might damage the achievement of thousands of nameless heroes fighting overseas. It is only right and proper that we keep them in mind and offer them our homage.'

The spell was broken. Salazar, after all, remained. But he knew that in conjuring up before his stupefied adherents the spectacle of his retirement one of these days he was raising the problem of who came next. He knew that the man in the street, like the man in the corridors of power, would now be having little talks and making guarded guesses.

[1] *Discursos e Notas Políticas* of Oliveira Salazar, published at Coimbra, 1967. See vol. VI, page 437.

The problem first became acute in 1958 when Delgado was a candidate for the Presidency and it was clear just how unpopular the Government really was. We have seen how, when Salazar sacked President Craveiro Lopes for having dared to display some gleams of independence, his future successor, Marcello Caetano, then Minister of the Presidency, upheld the theory that the Prime Minister himself was the right official choice. That, of course, would entail the appointment of a new Prime Minister and automatically indicate his successor.

But Salazar didn't see it like that. As long as he could, he made use of the rifts and rivalries among his prospective heirs. 'Divide and Conquer' was his motto. Moreover, the last thing he wanted was the Presidency, with all its attendant ceremonial obligations. But there was a further reason for his attitude, one he referred to in an interview with *Figaro* on 5 November 1966 : his death in office as President of the Republic would mean electoral campaigns and a testing-time for the whole dispensation. And Salazar had no illusions on this subject. He knew that the political structures of the regime amounted to no more than a few simple rules of thumb, without cohesion, and he wished to avoid what he called a 'constitutional *coup d'état*'—in other words a change of system by legal methods, from within. By appointing a President he could personally trust he ensured that when the moment came the chosen Prime Minister would be someone he had himself previously designated. All would be smooth as under an absolute monarchy.

Certainly he was not going to leave the delicate choice to the President's unaided inspiration, and took good care to make it in his own lifetime. To avert intrigue a few of his close supporters were let into the secret, but a secret it remained to the very end. The hesitations which then arose were due to the special circumstances of his illness. He lived on for months, unable to fulfil his role, but events took place as provided for in the Constitution and public opinion was not consulted. When the President of the Republic installed Marcello Caetano

H

he did so, in all likelihood, at the express wish of Salazar. One day we may know just what happened.

The question naturally arises, why Marcello Caetano? The answer is that he was the best placed of all possible candidates. It was a logical, almost an inescapable, appointment. No other figure of the regime had had a career that taught him more about the problems of Portuguese administration, nobody had become more part and parcel of the system.

Caetano's youthful background was one of *integrista* Catholicism and he was originally a Monarchist. As a fierce critic of democracy and parliamentary Government he was peculiarly well fitted to appreciate, comprehend and approve the military dictatorship, and this is exactly what he did. From the moment that Salazar came to power the other followed his career with admiring interest.

When his law studies were finished he went as legal adviser to the Ministry of Finance when Salazar was in charge there, and later did a great deal of work on the Administrative Code which was to give a more markedly authoritarian cast to the whole structure of local and provincial Government.

A political empiricist, Caetano developed under Fascist influence in the 1930s and, partly as a result of a visit to Italy which attracted some attention at the time, emerged as a leading advocate of the New Corporative State on the Mussolini model. He thus gradually moved away from the traditionalist *Integralismo Lusitano* school of thought to which he had subscribed as a young man.

From 1940 to 1944 he was National Commissioner of the *Mocidade Portuguesa* and photographs from those years show him standing at attention, smartly belted into his brown uniform, arm raised in a Roman salute. Then he was Colonial Minister until 1947 and a devoted Portuguese Empire-builder. In 1947, as president of the Executive Committee of the National Union Party, he campaigned for the Government against General Norton de Mattos and sought to continue within that sole authorised party the training-system for political personnel he had introduced in the youth movement.

He decided finally to forsake the Monarchists at the third National Union Congress at Coimbra in 1951.

When, in 1950, he was chosen as president of the Corporative Chamber, Marcello Caetano became fourth in the official hierarchy—the fourth most important man in the state. In 1952 he was made a life member of the Council of State. By 1955 his dazzling progress had brought him to the post of Minister of the Presidency and, for the first time, to close collaboration with Salazar. Henceforward nobody could fail to recognise that he was a possible, if not the most probable, successor.

At this time, General Santos Costa, an old co-worker of Salazar and his chief liaison with the armed forces, was trying to lead the regime towards the Monarchy. It was not long before rivalry sprang up between him and Caetano, and manœuvring and debate ensued within the Government. Partisans of the two 'claimants' were divided, not only over the question of Monarchy or Republic, but also over how Portugal was to become a part of the democratic post-war world. Santos Costa was an impenitent Germanophile with a reputation for intransigence. Caetano, suppler and more openminded, was looked upon as the evolutionist, anxious to liberalise the regime. As ever, Salazar settled an argument the nation at large knew nothing about, and got rid of both men in the Cabinet reshuffle that followed Delgado's presidential campaign. In 1958 Marcello Caetano began his long sojourn in the wilderness.

He went back to Lisbon University, to his former job as Professor of Administrative Law, and was Rector at the time of the student troubles in 1962. When he resigned, and made good tactical use of his resignation, it was officially for reasons of health, but actually over differences with the Minister of National Education. He had been able enough as a professor, though difficult of approach and distant with those he taught, but from 1962 onwards he cultivated a new and liberal reputation. In university and public life he now presented a strikingly different image.

The problems of the regime meanwhile had grown worse

and were causing the gravest disquiet. The country was slowly foundering in a colonial war that put any possibility of change out of the question. Marcello Caetano, prudently saying nothing, appeared to many of his supporters as a silent critic of official policy.

In the course of the year 1962 a report, rumoured and never denied to be by Caetano, was circulated among people close to the centre of things. It was sent to the Colonial Minister and dealt with the eventual modification of our system of government overseas. The initial basic argument was : 'Any solution of the problem must, in present circumstances, fulfil three conditions. Firstly, it has to give good grounds for the improvement of our international diplomatic relations, especially with friendly countries; secondly, it must endanger neither our national interests nor, above all, Portuguese lives and property in Africa; and thirdly, it should provide a workable administration.'

'The only constitutional modification to be considered', it went on, 'is that of transforming the present unitarian state into a federal one.

'The community of Portugal would then consist of three Federated States : Portugal itself, Angola and Mozambique (to which Portuguese India might be added as a point of principle), and the provinces of Guinea-Bissao, São Tomé, Macao and Timor. The Cape Verde archipelago would go in with the neighbouring islands.'

In the world of 1962, when General de Gaulle was preparing to grant Algerian independence, Caetano believed that this programme was the only card to play and justified it in these terms :

'Because (1) it is a big step towards self-government for the two provinces; (2) it gives responsibility to the settlers by allowing them more voice in the administration; (3) it proves to the rest of the world that we desire progress; (4) it meets both the desire for self-determination on the part of the provinces (together with foreign demands that they be given autonomy), and the necessity for keeping them under Portuguese influence and upholding them in every way possible; and (5) it means that they will have greater financial freedom under the Federal Constitution, and could raise foreign loans with no other sanction than that of the Federal Council.'

These proposals were never publicly aired, nor were they taken seriously by the political and economic leaders of the country. Salazar rejected the plan outright. Had any member of the opposition produced any such scheme he would have been accused of treason and dragged into court for offences against the security of the state.

But in 1970, when Caetano had become Prime Minister, the programme for constitutional revision and colonial autonomy laid by the Government before the National Assembly fell far short of what had been thus outlined in 1962. Did the facts of power prevent him from making a progressive move, or had he himself gone backwards?

It was not only the public offices he held within the regime which made Caetano the ideal successor to Salazar. Church and hierarchy trusted him as fully as they did the old dictator and he was always close to them. But in contrast to his predecessor he was abreast of developments in Catholic thought and in touch with certain politico-religious experiments, as witness his friendly relations with the Opus Dei potentates in Spain, Lopez Rodó prominent among them. Content that the Church should keep most of what it had acquired in the way of prerogatives and property over the last decades, he was equally ready to attempt the reclamation of sundry so-called 'advanced' sectors of Catholic opinion.

For another thing he had, as legal adviser and director of some of the largest companies in Portugal, built up enough goodwill and gained enough experience to emerge as the favoured candidate of big business. Big business was not waiting for Salazar to die before making its preference clear, and he could not ignore its pressure. Caetano as Prime Minister was, in this regard, just what the regime wanted, a perfect choice.

Seventeen years before the event, speaking of the succession at the third National Union Congress, Caetano had said, on 23 November 1951, 'The continuation of the Estado Novo after Salazar presents no problem precisely because his doctrine and his work exist. . . . And when the day comes that God in His wisdom requires another to step into his place I have every hope that the Estado Novo will keep easily on its appointed way, provided that Portuguese patriots are able, personally and politically, to exercise the three virtues of unity, calm and reason at that necessarily critical time.' The problem, therefore, had been foreseen and thought about. As early as 1951 a man was offering his services for the critical juncture of the dictator's death, and that man was Marcello Caetano, with seventeen years of calm and reasonable expectation still to go.

According to the Constitution the choice of a Prime Minister lies solely with the President of the Republic. The Government is not controlled by the National Assembly, being answerable to the Head of State alone. It follows therefore that the Prime Minister is appointed and dismissed by the President, as are the Ministers he as Prime Minister may nominate. As the President is now elected by a limited body, the regime has had no claim to political legitimacy ever since the will of the people was excluded from the process. It is the President to whom the Government is responsible and he is in fact independent of the people. In other words, the Salazarist Constitution is a vicious circle that cannot be broken legally and which offers no possibility, in the normal course of events, of any change in the administration.[2]

Thus the retirement of Salazar and the appointment of a new Prime Minister rested with the President of the Republic alone, since the Constitution made them his affair. The country was at no time consulted, nor was there any reason why it should have been since there was constitutionally no means of consulting it. The vital forces of the Portuguese nation, and

[2] See the paper which I presented at the second Republican Congress at Aveiro in May 1969, *A Constituicão de 1933 e a evolucão democrática do país. (The Constitution of 1933 and the Democratic Evolution of the Country)* published by *Seara Nova*, in vol. II of its *Transactions* of this Congress.

its public opinion in general, had no legal way of making themselves heard and even less chance of participation. Everything was done according to one man's will.

Any regime, even when founded on personal power, is the result of some balance between forces and Portugal is no exception to this rule. Of the three such forces which may be discerned, not one intervened directly over Caetano's nomination.

First is the group of large-scale profiteers, a caste which grew up under the wing of Salazarism and now holds the principal levers of economic power and some key-posts in the economic sphere. Yet it does not always speak for the dominant economic interests. Some of the big agriculturalists and industrialists, for example, have already come round to a new and European view-point. Also, the big combines exert pressure on the Government, fight with it occasionally, and subject as they are to the laws of competition, make alliances and change partners all the time. They are not to be confounded with the politico-economic 'barons' whose commercial power is new and the fruit of their political careers. These people are fully aware that their own existence depends on that of the regime and are wedded to it firmly. With them should be included the officials of repression—the PIDE and the censorship, the National Republican Guard and so on—and a certain type of highly placed civil servant within the corporative system.

The army is, of necessity, the second force, or pillar of the regime, although generally speaking the armed services support it only in so far as they do nothing to destroy it. This however does not apply to senior officers, who almost always owe their appointments to governmental favour. And these latter years of the colonial war have seen a considerable awakening within the Portuguese army. As a profession it certainly means more than it did, with better prospects of quick promotion, but there is a great deal of anti-Government feeling all the same. Nevertheless, this is not easy to organise, owing to military supervision and the fact that officers of middle rank are liable to frequent posting.

The old dictator took advantage of professional jealousies

in the army to give the most important commands to weak or mediocre men. He always mistrusted up-and-coming senior officers as a threat to the regime, and for this reason no Portuguese Generals count for much politically or have become great national figures. Yet as the war goes on, and with the unsettled nature of politics since Salazar's death, the armed forces may well play a significant part before so very long.

And lastly there is the Church, or rather the Catholic hierarchy which has constantly shown itself in favour of the dictatorship. It has begun to draw away, as we have seen, since 1958, and especially since the Bishop of Oporto went to his enforced exile, though its links with the regime forbade its making any very vigorous protest at the time. There is pressure from some sections of the clergy, and from younger priests in particular, but the hierarchy continues to give support at vital moments while maintaining a guise of neutrality. And if anyone did consult the Church over the succession, we may be pretty sure that it championed Caetano.

The delay between Salazar's operation on 7 September 1968, his relapse on the 16th with a burst blood-vessel, and the naming of the new Prime Minister on the 28th, was not due to any hesitation as to who that Prime Minister would be. What made the President of the Republic pause was the thought of having to dismiss the dying old dictator. Immobilised by fear and respect, he could bring himself to do it only when the machinery of state was obviously grinding to a halt. During the waiting period allied Governments knew that Marcello Caetano was the appointed heir, and leading foreign newspapers openly supported him because informed circles realised that the whole thing was settled in advance.

Of the other possible candidates—Antunes Varela, the former Minister of Justice, Adriano Moreira, former Colonial Minister, Franco Nogueira, who was currently at the Foreign Office, and General Kaúlza de Arriaga, a former Under-Secretary for Air—none had sufficient weight or interest to ensure his own appointment. Caetano himself could not have forced the President to name him had the choice not been made already. Only the army might have forced the President's hand, but it was not united enough to state its case and save the situation. Even from his deathbed Salazar managed to impose his will without reference to the nation.

Following events as well as I could on the radio in São Tomé, I found the listless public attitude quite incredible. I remember the stirring appeals that came from the *Voz da Liberdade*, the 'Voice of Freedom', on the programmes broadcast by the Patriotic Front for National Liberation in Algiers, and how they were met with nothing but silence and indifference. There was striking disaccord between the language of the revolutionaries outside Portugal and the passivity of the Portuguese within. There, no spark was struck. The masses showed no slightest interest in what was happening, or at best a kind of sick curiosity. They speculated about the woman known as Senhora Maria : was she Salazar's legal wife or just his devoted housekeeper, like the good ladies who looked after aged village priests in time gone by? This and similar questions enthralled them more than the event itself. Even my most politically minded friends were off on their holidays, waiting undisturbed until the old man died.

The poet Afonso Lopes Vieira was absolutely right : he said that Salazar had taken a gelding-knife to Portugal.

Realistically viewed, however, things could not have been otherwise. The objective conditions required for a mass movement do not simply happen; and especially they do not 'happen' in a police state.

It must also be admitted that not one of the dissident parties had a plan ready to put into action as soon as the dictator died, and no definite call went out in those decisive days. News of Salazar's illness caught the opposition totally unprepared for several reasons, first and foremost being the lack of any overall anti-Government strategy. The fact is that it knew how to resist, and often resist heroically throughout the years of dictatorship, but it did no more than take advantage of circumstances as they came along and never had a master-plan for actually assuming power.

The revolutionary advocates of armed struggle—as distinct from the national anti-Fascist rising which the Communists have been preaching so doggedly for thirty years—have never clearly stated what its conditions are to be nor by what steps the Fascist order is to be destroyed. There are exhortations to violent but more or less unconnected proceedings which are somehow to create a climate of revolution, though no one seems to know exactly how; and this is probably why the revolution, so far as organisation goes, has not yet left the starting-post.

The clandestine League of Union and Revolutionary Action, the LUAR, was founded in about 1967 to launch a series of attacks upon the regime. The first move, aimed at obtaining funds for the future revolution, was the hold-up of the Figueira da Foz branch of the Bank of Portugal. I defended the ringleader, Herminio da Palma Inácio, when he came up for trial, and certainly the whole operation had been planned and executed with remarkable skill. They practically cleared out the Bank of Portugal, or 'recovered', as they put it, about 30 billion escudos, though new notes were issued and much of the loot could not be used. A second major effort, the occupation for some hours of the textile town of Covilhã, proved a fiasco. Palma Inácio was delayed on the way when his car broke down, recognised by members of the National Guard and arrested. He made a dashing and improbable escape from the PIDE cells at Oporto in 1969, but while he was in prison the movement he led fell almost completely apart.

As for the political groups who were urging revolutionary action, the Marxist-Leninists and the small bands of Trotsky-ites and disciples of Guevara, they did almost nothing. During this period the Communists, too, with all their talk of mass risings on a national scale, showed themselves incapable of mobilising the populace. Nor did the others, the Socialists in particular, do any better. Nothing really could be done as long as there was no master-plan and no central control of the diverse elements of opposition. The Republicans, Socialists and Catholics could, indeed, have indulged in para-legal action more easily than the others, but they too displayed an absolute lack of initiative and imagination. The few trained political groups among the opposition were scattered and ill-prepared and could not act fast enough. And yet the Government was in a state of paralysis for ten whole days.

And then there were all those who thought some change in the regime was inevitable after the dictator's death. So many people were saying 'Wait and see' that the establishment had all the time it needed to get back on an even keel. Once again, as at the end of the Second World War, the opposition missed the boat.

During the night of 26 September 1968 the President issued a communiqué announcing the appointment of Professor Marcello Caetano and next afternoon the new Prime Minister made what was perhaps the best short speech of his career at the São Bento palace in Lisbon. In a few words, without committing himself, he said enough to raise very high hopes of his Government and yet reassure the old guard that all would continue as before.

In thus pledging continuity while at the same time holding out some prospect of change, Caetano cleverly underlined the possible contrast with his predecessor. 'The country has been accustomed for many years to the direction of a man of genius. From now on it will have to get used to government by men who are as other men.'

Thousands of people in Portugal read this as irony, especially since he laid great emphasis on the herculean nature of the tasks awaiting him. But all in all, and despite conflicting interpretations, the speech contained a careful measure of welcome news for nearly everyone. Without too much regard for former assurances, Caetano made plain certain differences between himself and the old dictator. This shocked the dyed-in-the-wool Salazarists but he gave them casually to understand from the start that, while some easing-up was called for as a matter of tactics, they had basically nothing to worry about. Hence his pronouncement, 'The very sincere desire to establish a regime in which all Portuguese of good will may find a place is not to be confused with scepticism on the ideological plane, or any failure of purpose.'

Meanwhile, Salazar was hanging tenaciously on to life, and believing he was still Prime Minister, for the President had never quite summoned up courage to break the tidings of dismissal. As disclosed in *L'Express* on 21 April 1969, the Ministers had to gather round his bed from time to time and there receive and pretend to take note of his instructions. In the famous interview with *L'Aurore* on 6 September, which must have been the last he ever gave, he said that he regarded himself as being in office as before. Evidently, from the way he spoke, he knew nothing of Caetano's accession.

It was now that the Ultras made their appearance as a new factor on the political scene, all yearning for the Salazarism of yesteryear and thought to be more of a power than in fact they were. 'Ah!' people would sigh knowingly, 'if it wasn't for the Ultras. . . .' Caetano navigated the troubled waters with dexterity and firmness. With a finely calculated gesture to the left, the hint of a nod to the right, he manœuvred everybody in such a way as to strengthen his own position He used television as it had never been used in Portugal before and was not above a little well-organised mingling with the crowd. Intelligently and with splendid timing he anticipated the criticism that was beginning to raise its head : for already observant onlookers were asking themselves just where this dispensation differed from that of Salazar, and how far it would go.

He made his first visit to the south in October 1968 and, struck by the unwonted warmth of his welcome there, a reporter asked an old woman what she thought of it all. With refreshing peasant directness she hit the nail straight on the head.

'Oh,' she replied, 'this looks a much nicer Salazar than the other one was!'

Chapter Twelve

Disillusion

At his very first Cabinet meeting the new Prime Minister raised the question of my return to Portugal. To reverse my deportation outright would be a crude condemnation of Salazar and obviously unthinkable as long as he was alive, but Caetano was aware of the political and legal criticism that had been aroused and tried, indirectly, to find some way out. The sentence was accordingly reduced to one of twelve months only, to run from the date of my imprisonment in December 1967.

Here I may add that shortly before Salazar's collapse my solicitor, Dr Magalhães Godinho, had lodged an appeal in the Supreme Court against the Cabinet decision—a mere formality, needless to say, since this court was appointed by the Prime Minister and could not disagree with an official ruling. But the idea had occurred to me of asking Caetano for a professional opinion. He was a specialist in this department, I had been a student of his in Administrative Law and we had kept up friendly, if distant, relations. I therefore wrote to him from São Tomé, and received in reply a very polite refusal. Briefly, he said his opinion would have to be unfavourable, for he considered the decree under which I was deported to have been quite constitutional and not, as I maintained, illegal. He was sorry about what had happened; he hoped to see me soon restored to my family and practice. I didn't bother to argue, but in writing to thank him could not resist pointing out that such an interpretation of the law might well set a serious precedent which would perhaps affect the lawgivers themselves in time, for they could not last for ever. And within a few days Salazar had ceased to be the all-powerful dictator of Portugal.

When Marcello Caetano became Prime Minister Dr Pedro Pitta, president of the Law Society, requested an audience to tell him that a general meeting was to be called for the discussion of my case. The result, they thought, would be a unanimous protest against the Government's action and a unanimous demonstration on my behalf. Caetano did not even let him finish before announcing that the Cabinet had, on the previous evening, decided to allow me home. This was early in October 1968.

Away in São Tomé, I knew nothing of the reactions my deportation had produced in Portugal, but after Pedro Pitta's telegram brought me news of respite I began to see the Governor again. Much happier now, he sent for me several times and gradually revealed what authority meant to do about me.

Naturally—and one can quite see why—authority had found a solution that side-stepped all the principles at stake. The point at issue was whether the Government had the right to deport one of its citizens without trial, for an indefinite period, simply because that citizen was proving a political nuisance. Looked at from this angle, Caetano's decision was, to say the least, ambiguous, though it was widely interpreted as the first liberal gesture of a new chief evidently disposed to pacify the opposition. The world press treated it as such and, though the censorship still operated, the papers in Portugal commented in the same tone. What it was, of course, was a calculated political act, aimed at producing a given psychological effect. This being so, I never felt obliged to regard it as a personal favour but rather as the proper, and delayed, rectification of an injustice.

There were those who, accustomed to this typically Portuguese fashion of settlement by compromise, thought it odd that I offered no thanks to Marcello Caetano. But justice, in my opinion, does not call for thanks, even when it comes like a royal grace from the seats of the mighty. One merely makes a note of it.

The Governor asked if I might be allowed home a month early, and the suggestion was welcomed in Lisbon; public opinion was excited and there had been some fear of demonstrations. Also, my father's ninetieth birthday provided a convenient excuse. The Governor arranged my departure, in the utmost secrecy, on 9 November, carefully telling the PIDE nothing until the last minute. He thought it best to send me to Luanda, where I boarded an ordinary passenger flight. My family had not been told that I was coming. I reached the house at daybreak and let myself in with my own latchkey. I found the children fast asleep in bed.

After nearly a year away from active political life I could sense on my return a certain moderate hopefulness with regard to the new Government. Salazar was breathing, that was all, and the recently appointed Prime Minister had retained the Cabinet as before, with the exception of the Defence Minister and a few of the less important figures. One had the impression that he was wanting to gain time, consolidate his power and, so they said, embark upon a reforming policy as the only way of leading the country towards better days. Or that was the general conviction. And if he wasn't going faster, people added, it was because he was not yet strong enough to get his reforms through.

To make things a little easier after the last years of Salazar's rule he had slightly relaxed the censorship, promised a new press law in the near future and called for the collaboration of all men of good will. These measures were seen as an experimental slackening-off on the home front, intended evidently to assist Portuguese capitalism in its initial encounters with Europe.

But was this a sincere attempt to bring the country, step by step, back into the democratic company of Western nations? Or was it just a publicity stunt, designed at the same time to create a more favourable atmosphere and to disarm the opposition? In December, when I had been home a month, I made the following remarks on the subject to the *Diário de Lisboa,* in an interview which the censor slashed out of existence.

'Institutional changes mean a lot more than words; they

could give practical expression to the good intentions we hear about. So far we have seen nothing very much attempted in the way of any change that might allow citizens to take an active and normal part in the political life of the country, independently of official favours. We are still at the stage of promises or concessions. These may be timely; they are certainly adroit; but they have made no difference at all to the institutional *status quo*, which remains basically undemocratic.'

The reporter then asked, 'But do you not think it too soon for such changes yet?'

'The Government has not inherited an easy position and I am one of those who appreciate its herculean difficulties,' I replied, quoting the phrase of Caetano in his inaugural speech. 'I know we must not expect everything to be done in one fell swoop. There are objections to be overcome, interests and risks to be kept in view; it is not always simple to go against totalitarian notions and ingrained, unsatisfactory ways of doing things. But liberalisation is not a concession, an indulgence to be granted, a favour from on high. It is first and foremost a national necessity. We need it if we are to survive. The policy of the Ultras leads nowhere in the Europe of today. It would be a disaster for our economic development and bring us to a dead end. If our national energies are to be reawakened and the vital climate of confidence restored, our problems have to be attacked directly, urgently. The Portuguese must be presented with a programme that will kindle their spontaneous enthusiasm. Unless this happens there will be no lasting achievement and this Government will very soon encounter the same hostility as did its predecessors. Worse, it will be nothing but a reincarnation of those predecessors with a different cast.'

The suppression of this interview I took as a bad omen. It was becoming plain that Caetano's administration, like Salazar's, did not acknowledge the existence of a true, organised opposition, that it was still inimical to anyone who tried to discuss our national problems on a footing of independence and equality. It was the same old monologue over again.

Supporters of democratic freedom were cheered, nevertheless, by one or two timid innovations. Pressure from the police and the censorship lightened a little and a new syndical law modified the corporative management of the vertical trade unions. Moreover, under the Constitution, elections to the National Assembly (which was to be given constituent powers) were due in 1969 and the Government, mindful of this fact, embarked at once on its campaign. The executive of the sole authorised party was overhauled, its district committees were renewed and several Civil Governors changed. All these decisions were trumpeted far and wide by the powerful official propaganda machine.

The new head of the National Union was Melo e Castro, whose reputation as a leader of the most liberal section of the regime had caused his disgrace in Salazar's latter years. When Caetano took over the Government, Melo e Castro had sent him a telegram demanding the restoration of the essential liberties of political life, thus virtually declaring himself in favour of freedom of the press and of the establishment of parties or political groups such as might fight properly conducted elections on equal terms. The text of his telegram was passed from hand to hand, especially among the Catholics, and his appointment as chief of the National Union—which he immediately re-christened *Acção Nacional Popular* by way of marking off past from present—seemed particularly significant.

With the Government thus working towards the election, the opposition had to organise itself as quickly as possible, and this could best be done by each sector separately, according to its own ideas. Up to now the opposition had been a kind of mythical body, emerging occasionally into the light of day in what looked like an ideological chaos of sometimes contradictory opinions, then forced to vanish abruptly from the political stage, perhaps for years on end. Its members, doubtfully accepted or outlawed absolutely, were content simply to oppose, without bothering to define beliefs or party loyalties.

Now the right time seemed to have come for testing out the Government's liberal intentions. Each section of the opposition should, as it were, make a drive for legal standing, so that all together might win the right legally to take part in the political life of the country. I thought then, as I think today, that the existence of a number of autonomous strains, each with a creed of its own, does not preclude a united opposition. Rather, it fulfils one of the necessary conditions for giving that unity a solid and well-defined basis.

And so, in December 1968, I arranged a national demo-cratic Congress of Socialists which issued a National Mani-festo. This for all its deliberately moderate tone, was stopped by the censors, but it stated :

'*Political dialogue* is essential if we are to modernise the social structure of Portugal, and to achieve it the political forces which go to make up the nation must have *freedom* to organise and to act; the *single party* must no longer have a monopoly of power; and we must have a minimum of *security* against the arbitrary activities of the political police and of the censorship.'

From this starting-point the signatories of the document went on to demand certain *minimal conditions*. These were : a press law guaranteeing the constitutional principle of freedom of speech in all its various forms; a generous amnesty, to empty the prisons and bring home those who had emigrated for poli-tical reasons; the ending of the loathsome 'security measures' under which almost any opponent of Government could be kept in gaol for ever; and an electoral law that should meet the basic preliminary conditions for which the opposition had been agitating since 1945, beginning with an honest and properly checked poll.

It was almost impossible at that time to take the temper of the country. We had had the political crisis of the succession; the colonial war on three fronts was costing more in men and money every day and our colonial policy provoked in the Allied Powers an attitude that emphasised our isolation. Economic stagnation forced the Government to face the fact that it must call upon foreign loans if there were to be any consistent programme of productive investment. Economic and cultural under-development made our standard of living the lowest in Europe. Prices went soaring upwards, emigration had increased alarmingly and there was a fearful shortage of manpower. Large sections of the population were apathetic and confused. To crown all, the machinery of the state, and of the corporative system, was deteriorating. What the country really thought, after so many years of political non-expression, nobody could guess.

We had to struggle hard to change things. Here, it was thought, the legislative elections, by giving rise to extensive national debate, might speed up the process of making people politically minded and act at the same time as a gauge of the new Government's political good faith. Our manifesto had laid down that 'the undersigned definitely reject totalitarian Socialism, which is in any case no threat to Portugal under present circumstances. This they categorically affirm as a result of their own ideological position, with no thought of earning any diploma of good citizenship from the Government. None is needed, for as democrats and advocates of the multi-party system, they utterly deplore any such discrimination.'

This reference to 'totalitarian Socialism' provoked an outcry in quarters not exactly celebrated for scruple where others are concerned. They made it the excuse to mount a fierce campaign against the Socialists, who were taxed with anti-Communist activity or with wishing to isolate the Communist Party and negotiate with Fascists for 'preferential legality' at the expense of other political groups. All this baseless accusation did was divide and enfeeble the opposition and raise up misunderstanding and animosities that helped nobody but the common enemy and led to considerable discord later.

In this campaign against the Socialists or rather, as its instigators claimed, against Social Democracy—there was a special niche reserved for me. I was the favourite target of certain left-wing groups (not only of Communists, be it noted), and a principal scapegoat of all the woes and frustrations of the opposition. The attacks upon me increased and coincided oddly with the equally ferocious attentions I was then receiving from the extreme right.

I found it hard to credit that people with whom I had worked for so long could now be hurling such ridiculous charges at me without rhyme or reason, attributing to me things I never said, arraigning me as would-be collaborator with the regime. It was a murderous business and made sense only as a political necessity. Some real possibility of a democratic, alternative solution—and at that time it was a possibility—existed. It had to be destroyed. It centred round me and I was the man to get rid of.

Apart from malicious gossip and minor calumnies, the onslaught took the form of two related allegations. One was of opportunism, its worst insinuation being that I worked with the Government; the other that I was manœuvring to split the opposition in order to obtain 'preferential legality' for the Socialists. Both these charges, amply disproved by relevant facts and dates, were quite unthinkable. More, they were downright stupid, ignoring the realities of the situation and giving me no marks for my anti-Fascist past. Social Democracy was not in power in 1969. Fascism was. Some so-called progressives apparently had not grasped this truth, preferring us to believe that Fascism and anti-Fascism alike were done with, part of another era.

The hostility to me came out into the open at a commemoration held on 1 January 1969 at the Coliseu in Oporto. It was two months since my return from São Tomé and the first time I had spoken in public. Strategically placed in the upper rows were bunches of people a dozen or so strong who threw into the audience leaflets demanding unity and kept up a constant heckling.

While these youths shouted their repertoire of misconceived insults—'Opportunist!' 'Collaborator!' even 'Fascist!'—the first reaction of António Gonçalves Rapazote, the Minister of the Interior, as he listened to the direct police-relay, was to order my arrest the same night. The political sense of an adviser, however, over-rode his zeal and the campaign was allowed to continue, with much advantage to the Government.

And what had I said in this speech at Oporto to upset those of both extremes among my hearers? 'Our country is at the crossroads, as it was in 1891. We all know how desperate the position is, economically, politically and in the Overseas Territories; a position that springs from the monolithic obduracy of the regime and the stiff-necked spirit of those who control it. Today the men at the head of affairs know there is complete divorce between the Government and the nation. Hundreds of thousands of Portuguese leave their homeland every year in a terrifying wave of emigration unprecedented in our history.

'Liberalisation can be a valid measure, a step towards the easing of the problems that beset us, *if it is sincere and leads to the practical democratisation of our national life.* But if it is a bid to gain the approval of unobservant allies, or a political move to ensure that the same totalitarian structure stays in place, then we want nothing to do with it.

'A true dialogue presupposes freedom for political entities to say what they like and organise themselves as they please. It presupposes that our people need fear neither the police nor economic reprisals and that they may at last choose their own destiny. The prisoners must be set at liberty, the students and dismissed professors come back to their classrooms, the political exiles to their homes. We are within a month or two of elections which, unless they are unrestricted, will be meaningless. Though the opposition is made up of many strands of opinion, we shall surely be able to find a common and united platform; but nobody need expect us to bear a part in an electoral farce or to uphold any sort of hoax that makes a mockery of the people's will. We shall indulge in no secret negotiation. We shall not buy ourselves into the National Assembly by accepting shameful distinctions which, as democrats, we must reject.'

Unhappily for Portugal, however, the new elections could be no more than a repetition of those held under Salazar. The Socialists did what they said they would do. They drove no bargains for seats in the Assembly and repudiated all overtures made to them on that score. Excluded from politics for so long, they were excluded still, as, indeed, were other democrats—the Republicans, Liberals, Communists, left-wing supporters and Catholics. Only some Catholics who had ranged, if discreetly, with the opposition in the past managed, for what were given out as 'practical reasons', to gain seats after more or less private negotiations with the Government. They declared themselves independent but accepted the National Unionist label and have been known since as 'deputies of the parliamentary minority', in an attempt, so far unsuccessful, to change the system from within.

Throughout the early months of 1969 Marcello Caetano's Government went on actively preparing for the elections, modifying the various committees of the National Union in a blaze of publicity. The object was to attract the independents, or even erstwhile dissidents, to his side. The marriage of theory and practice, so one heard, would have to be postponed, and the administration in the meantime manipulated the franchise-rolls as it thought fit.

It was obvious that opposition requirements were to go unheeded. No means of organisation were made available to any of the anti-Government sectors who were planning to take part. Electioneering was more of a problem than ever, for the censor cut all interviews or articles whose tone was even cautiously critical. There was no sign of the new electoral law we wanted. In the end the count was made as usual, with no representatives of the opposition present.

Officialdom had worked out the figures in such a way that opposition opinion could have no effect at all. The number of registered voters was between 1,200,000 and 1,800,000 —scarcely 20 per cent of the population of metropolitan Portugal and the Atlantic islands, to say nothing of the thousands of people abroad who should have had a vote and have none to this day. Thousands, too, were struck off the roll on suspicion of liberal leanings, and in the colonies the franchise remained practically a white preserve. The percentage of qualified electors in the entire population is, moreover, so infinitesimal that it is kept a state secret.

As for the inequalities between the single party and the factions of the opposition whose existence is not even legally recognised, they are simply scandalous. The single party alone enjoys a proper political organisation. Through the Government, from which it is indistinguishable, it monopolises all the media; directly in the case of wireless and television, indirectly in that of the press and other means of communication. Almost all Portuguese newspapers these days are in the hands of high finance; the banks have either bought them on Government instigation or have a controlling interest thanks to the vast loans they furnish.

It was officially announced from the start of the campaign that the state TV and radio were not available for electioneering : opposition electioneering, that is. However, all candidates might use the commercial stations and no distinctions would be made. I therefore approached one of the main privately owned stations to buy time for a daily political broadcast, the script of which would naturally have to pass the censor first. Courteously the governor of its board of directors informed me that he had no time to offer; every free moment had been booked by this company and that company for their advertising in the months ahead. When I told him this presented no problem, since one of them had already agreed to let me have some of its time each day, he blenched a little and said,

'Then you force me to put my cards on the table. For a long time now I have been trying to get a permit for short-wave broadcasting. Before this statement about election stuff on the commercial stations came out, the Government warned me I could say goodbye to it if I let the opposition have any time at all. There's a fortune at stake, you understand.'

During the whole year of the pre-electoral period the National Union, thanks to the communications at its disposal, was thus free to pursue a colossal programme while we could do little or nothing. Counsels of non-participation began to be heard in some quarters. To check this tendency we organised electoral commissions in several districts not long before the elections were due, but they were considered illegal until the opening of the electoral period proper, twenty days before the actual date. In August 1969, with just two months to go, the Minister of the Interior was threatening to use the whole arsenal of official repression, including the infamous 'security measures', against all members of such commissions.

In Lisbon the Socialists had the idea of reviving the Franchise Promotion Committee that had done much good work for civic education some years before under António Sérgio. Various political bodies were consulted and a provisional combined committee set up which laid before the Government a series of demands for safeguards in the conduct of the elections, and above all in the counting of votes. Publication of these documents was forbidden, the demands were refused and the Government went further than Salazar had ever done, declaring the committee itself illegal.

As well as all this we were having to combat the deadly effects of the censorship which was curtailing some news-items, entirely disallowing others, and of the secret police, perpetually at their repressive work. Finally, there was the feeling of fear everywhere, a feeling the Government kept going to admiration. How, in such circumstances, can anyone talk of real elections, or claim that Caetano's administration and policy would be legitimised by them?

Logically we should have abstained, as the Liberals and the left wing advised, but politically speaking that was the least practical thing to do. Where all means of communication are blocked, as they are in Portugal, the opposition is condemned to total inaction if it fails to use what opportunities it has, restricted though they be. And abstention, in politics, usually amounts to a speedy death-sentence.

The better-organised sections of the opposition—the Socialists, Communists and Catholics—therefore agreed that they should take part, though without any great hopes as to the outcome. In a country that was politically asleep, the point was not so much to win as to wake it up.

A meeting at São Pedro de Muel on 15 June led, without too much difficulty, to the forging of a common programme. But it was harder to strike the balance between the different forces represented on the electoral commissions and make arrangements for co-ordination on a national scale.

With these commissions we came up against the question of base versus summit. Should the base choose its delegates at more or less representative meetings, or should the delegates be chosen by the summit—that is, at the political headquarters of the various groups? And a burning question it became, the subject of long and sometimes demagogic arguments and rancorous bickering.

All democrats must agree that the party caucus should have the largest possible say in the choice of its spokesmen. Even the centralising democrats admit as much, although they in fact are managed by bureaucracies who usurp the place of the general membership they claim to represent. With better reason the Socialists, too, agree, having always upheld decentralisation within their party, and with it the maximum of democracy at all levels, control of the leaders by the majority and normal tolerance of even minority tendencies, which are free to express their points of view.

But in the three or four months before the elections this was not the problem. Our sole concern was to choose the electoral commissions who would in turn pick our candidates for the National Assembly.

Had there been political clubs or parties in Portugal, then all could have been solved by multilateral agreement, as it is in other countries. However, since none existed save the Communist Party, the Socialists and the Democratic-Social Directive, and since the Catholics, like a great many of the younger people, were split into tiny factions, things were far more complicated. Regional differences, too, always a feature of legislative elections, assumed terrific importance. The right formula had to be found to harmonise the fragmented opposition, and this in an unfree land like ours. Should we hold special meetings, remembering that they would be under pressure from the police and afford no real opportunity for thorough discussion of essential points? In some districts this might of course be a splendid way of mobilising the different strata of the population, and so it proved in some of them, but there was nothing intrinsically democratic about it. The majority do not necessarily feel they are having their say because the active spirits manage to hold a meeting. It must also be realised that the Government was using its special agents to encourage divergencies among us and that many extremists gave them openings they were not slow to take.

To foment these divergencies was the particular job of the national press. One need recall only the insidious campaign in the weekly *Vida Mundial*, at a time when almost all its independent journalists were sacked. As it happened, I was myself the foremost target, but why, and in whose interest, was it launched?

Nevertheless, in all save three districts, the opposition did agree so far as to produce combined lists on which Socialists, Communists, Catholics and anti-Fascists of no definite party allegiance, were named together. The exceptions were Lisbon, Oporto and Braga, where two opposition lists were submitted, one by the CEUD (the United Democratic Electoral Commission) and the other by the CED, or CDE, the Democratic Electoral Commission. These two bodies spoke for different coalitions among the opposition, the CEUD consisting of Socialist and socialistically-inclined Catholics, and the Lisbon CDE of more pronouncedly left-wing Catholics, Communists and Progressives. But as they were condemned to a life of subterfuge, as were all political organisations in Portugal, they could not expound their actual variations of belief and the public therefore never fully grasped them. And as their programmes were virtually the same, electors inclined to one or the other list for what were essentially emotional reasons; friendship, perhaps, or expediency. Sometimes they even backed them both.

In the remaining districts, however, with their combined lists, things were different. Almost everywhere Socialists, Catholics, Communists, Republicans and independent anti-Fascists joined forces to offer themselves for election and in some cases the Socialists were adopted. The use of the initials CED by some of the Democratic Electoral Commissions in the provinces was, I think, a mistake, for the Government profited by the resultant confusion the better to attack the CEUD, which it regarded as the chief danger.

Several things account for the split in the opposition at Lisbon, Oporto and Braga. Had we had time to clarify our points of dispute and conformity we could have agreed on a platform and combined to produce a single list such as the vast majority of democrats desired to see. But in Lisbon especially we were too harassed by the Government to do so and it must be admitted that certain obstinate and protesting elements of the Lisbon CDE were quite as much to blame. The less glorious their anti-Fascist record of other days, the further left they tended now to be. A bad conscience about the past came out in the wildest radical talk.

The ill-informed public got the impression that the CEUD was a breakaway party, for the initials CDE and CED, to be seen all over the country, muddled everyone up and seemed to be those of the united opposition. Correspondence with the CDE of Lisbon amply proves that until the last moment the CEUD was offering a compromise. Union, in its opinion, should be generated from diversity, 'our differences accepted as a normal part of co-existence, without quarrelling for leadership'. By contrast the CDE leaders were 'impelled by their conception of democratic unity to keep their party on one line, in the manner of the National Union where diversity of opinion is held to imply a divisive attitude and is not allowed'.[1] This, basically, explains the internal differences of the opposition, at least in Lisbon, and why the CEUD was accused of heresy. All its olive-branches were rejected. In the end both CEUD and CDE invited the arbitration of a Commission of Union, which suggested a combined list from Lisbon, to be made up of six nominations from the CDE, five from the CEUD and one independent name which the commission would put forward. The CEUD accepted this solution, though unfavourable to itself, but the Lisbon CDE did not. As at Oporto and Braga it sent in a list of its own and faced us with a *fait accompli*.

Another difficulty was the official circulation of news-items designed to impede the opposition in its efforts to produce combined lists. Here the Government could count on its biased

[1] For more about this problem see *As Eleições de Outubro de 1969*, issued by Publicações Europa América, Lisbon 1970. Sources of the above quotations will be found at page 63 onwards.

communications media, on *agents provocateurs* who posed as
red-hot revolutionaries, and on the diffusion of vague rumour.

But although there were separate opposition lists in those
three districts, this did not have nearly the effect that authority
had hoped for. In spite of personal and political intrigue, and
even of attacks on the character of individuals, the lists were
not at variance; to a certain extent they were, indeed, com-
plementary. When the CDE of Lisbon was told that one of its
candidates, Firmino Martins, had been ruled ineligible and
disallowed by the Government, the CEUD refused to open
its own campaign until someone else was permitted to stand
in his place. I myself attended the inaugural press conference
of the CDE and even spoke in support of the chairman, Pereira
de Moura.

Several times we acted as one during that campaign. We
shared the few halls we managed to hire for meetings and at
the editorial conferences of the *Diário de Lisboa*, for instance,
it was plain to see how far candidates of both lists agreed.
Everywhere, in fact, the ordinary mass of anti-Government
believers joined hands in the struggle against the common
enemy.

Some democrats came to think that the existence of two
opposition lists was not so terribly important in the circumstances, since the election was rigged in any case and the waste
of votes did not matter very much. But I could not agree with
them. People had drifted away, frustrated, because we had
failed to sink our differences at a particular juncture and it
is at the popular level that unity brings a vast access of strength.
The high percentage of abstentions—51·9 per cent of the
voters in Lisbon, 42·5 per cent over the country as a whole—
was due to many causes, but the lack of unity among the
opposition was unquestionably one of the most important.

A book could be written about the illegalities of that campaign
and the handicaps entailed upon the opposition. The one
approved party had its proper machinery; it had been
reinforced the previous year with new cadres of management
and could draw on public funds. We, of course, were left to

use our imaginations, improvise and in the last resort to circumvent the stratagems of authority as best we could. Harried by the police and the censorship, we were expected to compile our nomination lists in the two short months before the polling-date, and to do so without permission to consult the registers for the names and addresses of the voters. The registers were available to the National Union, but the opposition was allowed to finish copying them only one week before the day of the election.

As the electoral law then stood, candidates were themselves responsible for providing voting-papers. The use of distinctive paper and print in many districts made the opposition papers recognisable from those of the National Union just by looking at them, and this, as one may easily imagine, frightened the would-be voter. The same law also forbade the distribution of papers at the actual polling-booths, so that we had a serious problem in distributing them at all, especially outside Lisbon. We naturally had to send them round by hand, since posting them meant guaranteed delivery a day too late.

For these and many other reasons it was hard for opposition candidates to get in touch with the electors, who very often could not even obtain our voting-papers. National Union papers, on the other hand, were automatically distributed by post, or by policemen in plain clothes who called at people's houses.

Nor should we overlook the anomalies of the electoral law. For one thing, it forbade any representation of minority groups and put the Government in charge of the campaign. This meant that the local Civil Governor had to give permission before meetings could be held or notices put up, and he was invariably someone whose job depended on the Minister of the Interior. For another, the registers were so composed that the electorate consisted of officials, professional soldiers, police officers, nuns and the richer members of the community, to the virtual exclusion of workers, small businessmen and all those who best represent the vital strength of Portugal. There were cases of well-known people, who had lived in the same place for years, being disqualified because they were not on the register. The writer Manuela de Azevedo, who edited the *Diário de Notícias*, shocked to find herself without a vote although fulfilling every legal requirement, tried to make the matter public. The censorship stepped in.

The opposition came up against a further difficulty with the supervision of the count, for only registered voters had the right to help with it and then only at their own local polling stations. This last condition, innocent though it seemed, made checking impossible in small places, where the police have always had the whip-hand and reprisals are easily inflicted. It explains how the abstention-rate in Lisbon, the most politically aware of Portuguese towns, could be 51·9 per cent whereas in some parts of the provinces over 80 per cent of the electorate duly turned up and voted.

Police pressure grew worse as the campaign went forward. The CDE office at Lisbon was attacked by persons who, if not PIDE themselves, evidently enjoyed the protection of the law. People leaving opposition meetings were met by a barrage of plain-clothes men bent on intimidation and incitement to disorder. Urbano Tavares Rodrigues, the author, a member of the CEUD standing for the opposition at Beja, was knocked about by plain-clothes police after a meeting at the Vasco Santana theatre in Lisbon; my wife, a CDE candidate at Santarem, was summoned to the PIDE headquarters and interrogated at length about her election address. Threats of persecution showered upon her until I protested by telegram to the Prime Minister.

The first opposition press conference I was supposed to take part in was interrupted by police in the presence of Portuguese and foreign journalists. Dr Magalhães Godinho, the chairman, refused to be stampeded, and thanks to his firmness the meeting was finally held, but the censorship suppressed most of what we said. Nobody heard of it save the few who saw the foreign papers.

The second bulletin of the Lisbon CEUD, some of whose contents had a political flavour, was seized by the police as it appeared, 36,000 copies in all. The same thing happened to the manifesto of the Lisbon CED, though when Professors

Pereira de Moura and Lindley Cintra intervened personally with Caetano, all copies of this were returned within a day or two.

In the teeth of official efforts to prevent our hiring private halls, we did manage to arrange meetings. The reports of these, however, were systematically distorted in print, and as they were held in improvised and usually tiny holes and corners, they made very little impact.

At this time, too, the police pounced upon several publications directly concerned with the campaign, including my own *Political Writings*. The printers doing some of the CEUD's election work were informed that if they continued to print anything political without Government permission they would be shut down and their machinery confiscated.

The young volunteers who distributed opposition literature, especially the bill-posters (and the text and lay-out of the bills had had to be passed, remember, by the Civil Governors), were victims of repeated clashes with the police. Not only were the posters and other materials frequently destroyed, but the workers would be arrested and beaten up in the cells. Needless to say, we protested constantly about this for the whole four weeks of the campaign.

In an attempt to break through the censored silence, I wrote challenging the National Union leader, Melo e Castro, to a live personal confrontation on television, and suggested that an independent Monarchist and one of the Lisbon CDE might also be invited, if he wished. This I did in a letter which the censorship refused to pass. I then appealed to him directly, by way of protest, in an open letter in the daily press. But the television interview was not authorised. The National Union and Marcello Caetano's Government followed the tried and true tradition of Salazar and set their faces against dialogue yet again.

Some shocking obstacles were placed by authority in the path of democratic electioneering. In particular, it impeded our use of the public services, especially of the post and telephone, and had we complained for ever it would have made no difference. The post, as I have said, regularly held back

notices of our meetings, timing delivery for the day after any
gathering or committee was due to take place, and negotiation
over the simple request for a telephone at the CEUD office
was incredibly prolonged. The instrument when we got it
was always going dead and never worked properly.

It may be asked, then, why the opposition took part in
such a fraud as these elections, and many sincere democrats
believed that all we did was help the Government in its attempt
to gain at last the coveted acceptance of the rest of the world.
But the results show why. The opposition, I repeat, never
contemplated victory, for victory was not possible in the political conditions of Portugal. Its great object was to cast a ray
of truth on the whole electoral process, and hasten the political
awakening of the mass of the people. One might claim that, if
we failed to win the elections, we won the electoral campaign.
Everywhere the Government fell back a little. Confronted with
concrete criticism it lost face, together with much of its
hold.

Many people had their first opportunity of participation in
any election since Delgado was a candidate in 1958. This
renewed their hopes, and sooner or later the opposition will
benefit. Furthermore, I do not agree that we could have with-
drawn at the last moment, as some of our supporters wished.
Once the electoral process was fairly under way, retirement on
the eve of the poll could have produced nothing but frustration.
Of all the election farces in Salazar's time, it was the Delgado
campaign, fought right through to the end, which did most
to brace the people's will to struggle on. They retained a clear
and generally held conviction of having been outraged and
bamboozled by authority, and no official propaganda could
shake them out of it. Democracy, moreover, comes through
democratic action, and we must expect our ups and downs.

The 1969 election figures gave Marcello Caetano a 100
per cent victory. As had always happened throughout the
forty-odd years of Salazar's dictatorship, not a single opposition candidate was returned. The whole National Assembly of
130 deputies had stood for the sole official party. Some supporters of the regime would in fact have liked to see a few

opposition members allowed in, and that would certainly have made a more intelligent showing; but all went on in the same old way. Caetano had been chairman of the National Union in 1949, when Norton de Mattos was in the field; he was Minister of the Presidency when Delgado ran in 1958. He had learned the form.

The majority of the Portuguese people, seeking some way out of the impasse of Salazarism, made their anti-Government sentiments abundantly clear in that short electoral period of 1969. The official results, contested in every case by every sector of the opposition, are therefore meaningless.

All impartial observers agree that the nation is tired of dictatorship. After nearly forty-five dismal years it can no longer understand to what end freedom has been sacrificed when the position of Portugal is unimproved and its standard of living still so low; and these are truths which a few of the regime's more open-minded adherents nowadays admit. The people will not be treated as children any longer. Indeed, why should they not share the liberty enjoyed all over Western Europe? The tourist trade and emigration have helped their growing awareness enormously. Democratic societies, whose prosperity is even more striking in view of the fact that Portugal was spared a devastating war and they were not, are so many unanswerable arguments against the hackneyed Salazarist doctrine. Looking at Europe now, nobody can possibly say, as Salazar and Caetano have declared so often, that the misery of nations arises chiefly from democracy, the party-system and free trade unions.

Then there is the unbelievable poverty in which so many of the Portuguese still live; and as this load grows heavier and more painful the traditional economic and political oppression becomes intolerable. Even television, despite the censor's control, has done much to emphasise what is an irreversible situation by showing people a prosperity they cannot hope to share. The living conditions of workers in Portugal are as depressing as they are humiliating, and partly explain a perilous increase in emigration, with the indictment that implies of

I

the time-worn make-up of society and the entrenched opinions of its least progressive members.

The 1969 elections did at least put the regime on the defensive. The leading lights of the authorised party, from the top man downwards, felt it best to dissociate themselves from the Salazarism of other days. Brazenly they disowned some of their apparently most cherished symbols. The *Estado Novo* became the *Estado Social*. The party was no longer the National Union, it was the *Acção Nacional Popular*. One no longer said PIDE, but 'General Security Department'. Nobody was deceived.

Similarly the National Union propagandists changed their spots for the elections and attempted to pass for what they called 'new men', or *novos homems*, eager to put a new policy into practice. Nearly all of them, as it happened, were men of the past, forgetting that in the eyes of the public at large they were branded as representatives of all that had been worst in Salazarism. Nasty, brutish and corrupt, it was they who set the tone of that election campaign rather than the colourless establishment men, the careerists and technocrats not quite sure where they stood.

Even supposing (though the point has never been proved) that any National Union leader were capable of framing a fresh policy, the dyed-in-the-wool traditionalists would never let him carry it out. This is why the Government in its campaign kept to two main themes. The first was the pre-eminence of Marcello Caetano, the new saviour and heaven-sent apostle of expansion : as though a legislative election was concerned entirely with a Prime Minister and the 130 deputies to be chosen had nothing to do with the case. The other was what, wilfully misreading the opposition, it chose to refer to and denounce as 'abandoning the Overseas Territories'. The whole official campaign was nothing but a smoke-screen behind which it was hoped to conceal the state the country was in.

As for the National Union, it refused any sort of dialogue with the opposition. Its own divisions were too deep, and its leaders too ineffectual, for it to be able to produce any constructive policy in answer to its critics.

And the *Estado Novo,* far from defending what the regime

had done for forty years and more, was blaming Salazar for failures it had previously denied but could conceal no longer. Its sole justification was that Patriotism Came First. That, and the familiar threats against 'traitors', a term taken to designate anyone who even mildly disagreed with Salazar's colonial policy. In this way it sought to engage on the Government's behalf the chauvinism and the emotional reactions of the simpler sections of the community.

Some of the democrats considered that, since it suited authority to fight the battle entirely among the shoals and quicksands of colonial policy, the opposition had fallen into a trap by parading its anti-colonialism. They thought that people had dropped away as a result, either because they were afraid, or knew too little about it all, or out of pure jingoism. But my own belief is that one good thing about this 1969 campaign was precisely its oversetting of the taboo against discussion of overseas affairs. The colonial question had been put before the country, and the consequences of that fact will be tremendous. Portugal does not like the colonial war; which is why the Government has never dared to hold a referendum on the subject, despite all the persuasive weapons at its command.

The opposition fulfilled its function in 1969 by openly attacking the colonial-mindedness of Caetano's administration and trying to find suitable solutions to the colonial problem by means of negotiation. Its forthright and outspoken attitude, in which all shades of democratic opinion were for once united, marked a turning-point in our country's political history. It helped to give the world another image of Portugal. More important still, it sowed the seed of ideas which will bear their fruit in the future.

Shortly before the close of the campaign the Government expelled a delegation from the Socialist International made up of members of the English, Italian, Swedish and Irish Socialist parties and led by the organisation's Secretary-General, Hans Janitschek. The official reason given was that its presence in Portugal constituted an intolerable intrusion in our national affairs. Semi-official comment in the press had it that the delegates came on the invitation of the CEUD candidates, to keep a watchful eye on the conduct of the election. Nobody invited them, as a matter of fact. The delegation was in Portugal of its own accord. These elections were being held at the time of the change-over from Salazar; the Government had guaranteed that this time they should be different, and free. What more natural than that leading movements in Europe—parties, trade unions and so forth—should wish to see if this were really so? With international solidarity as it is in the world today there was nothing odd or unusual in their interest.

But this was also the first time that the Portuguese Socialists, with the cry of 'Socialism and Liberty', were participating, as Socialists, in an election. They were therefore concerned with the presence, as observers only, of these recognised comrades-in-arms from other Socialist parties in Europe. Yet the Government turned this presence against the CEUD candidates and accused them, rather stupidly when one remembers how reactionary circles abroad supported the regime, of having enlisted foreign aid. In the concluding speech of the campaign Marcello Caetano brought the subject up once more and singled me out among our candidates in Lisbon who, he insinuated, were laying plots with foreigners against our own country.

To put the record right, the CEUD candidates sent an immediate telegram of protest: they had not asked for aid and had even forborne to praise the sympathy shown by Sweden for the African nationalist parties. But this true version did not reach the public until two days after the election, when the telegram was partially acknowledged in an official statement. By then, of course, it was too late and Caetano's words had probably taken their full political effect.

As we had expected, the leaden silence fell again when the results had been announced. Caetano could celebrate his triumphs in his own time and his own way, like Salazar before him. Persecution was back in two months and its first victims were the Socialists. Francisco Zenha and Jaime Gama, candidates in Lisbon for the CEUD, were arrested, and Paul Rêgo was put under surveillance. The injustice towards the Socialists surprised only those who had missed the whole point of the elections and of the issues involved. This comedy of the voting-booth marked the end of Caetano's liberalising programme. It had proved a disillusion. The opposition's final attempts at a dispassionate analysis of the poll were kept out of the newspapers. Our campaign offices were closed down and any signs of resistance met short shrift from the police. In comparison with its long and grievous years under the old dictator, the opposition was neither worse nor better off. It simply went on being shut out from national life. Paradoxically, Caetano's victory had reduced the likelihood of political progress. It showed him he was going to have to be a second Salazar, in heart if not in usage, and the more clearly he saw this the less inclined he was to liberalise. The hopes cherished by so many faded away. The political springtime heralded by the previous Prime Minister's departure withered on the bough.

Chapter Thirteen

A Time to Choose

'. . . We are following the road of reform, and no one is better qualified than we to do so,' announced Caetano when accepting the presidency of the *Acção Nacional Popular* in February 1970.[1] The unexpected sentiment, coming from a seasoned aide of the regime, should perhaps be read as an attempted justification of policy.

Such a declaration makes plain his attitude to what he calls Social Democracy. He has said that this cannot be the right solution for Portugal, nor are our workers likely to derive from it the benefits it brought to the capitalist countries at the end of the last century and in the first half of this.[2] Equally unconvincingly, he adds that Portugal has never really known what capitalism is, since 'the Corporative State has achieved, and can continue to give practical expression to, what the Socialist parties have aimed at in those countries where they existed.'[3] Here, then, we have Marcello Caetano, the disciple of change.

Clad in the rusty ideological armour of Corporativism, he called for urgent reform. Before he had been in power for five minutes he felt he must give his political stock an up-to-date look, the better to suggest to the people of Portugal that the system he represented could, in fact, be modernised. Fraga Iribarne, who used to be Minister of Information and Tourism in Spain, did exactly the same thing by way of preparation as Franco's heir, when he thought it wise, if only as a formality,

[1] See his *Mandato indeclinável*, published by Editorial Verbo, Lisbon, 1971; page 111.
[2] *Idem*, page 190.
[3] *Idem*, pages 109 and 110.

to announce himself a Social Democrat.[4] National circumstances differed, but the underlying motive was the same in both cases.

Caetano was well aware of the lamentable situation of Portugal; that the nation desired to live as a nation of Europe, with the economic, political and social advantages of Western Europe; and that the young, the most dynamic element, felt this more than most.

In the same speech he also mentioned 'intellectuals and technicians who, while abhorring revolution, sympathise nevertheless with Social-Democratic thinking'.[5] With such men in mind he tried to present his 'Social and non-Socialist State' (the title of a speech he made at Oporto on 21 May 1969), as an improvement on other regimes. If the country needed far-reaching reforms, then he, provided that he remained in power, was better placed than anyone else to undertake them. He would change the society of Portugal as required, smoothly and painlessly, from above. Yet once the time of hope and expectation had gone by, people began to wonder. Was Marcello Caetano, they asked, capable of devoting himself to a policy of reform, even if he truly wanted to? Had he the following, the means and the right men? Had he the wish to do it?

He has assembled all his public utterances of 1970 in his book, *Mandato indeclinável*, with its familiar main theme of 'renewal in continuity', of a reforming policy that will allow him to mobilise in the service of the regime those social currents whose purpose it is to make the country modern. But we have heard him on the subject for three years now, and reform has come no nearer.

Up to the present Caetano has not shown himself sufficiently independent of the circumstances that put him at the head of affairs. The situation in Portugal is complex, there is variance within the regime itself, and changing powers and pressures have forced him to vary direction considerably. Hence the unsettled nature of his policy.

[4] His avowal appeared in *Le Monde* on 10 March 1971.
[5] See *Mandato indeclinável*, page 108.

It should also be added that he does not yet appear to be entirely in control of his own supporters. Unlike Salazar, he has not made himself the recognised arbiter, standing above the clash of interests. Far otherwise, he seems willing to make sundry, and even perhaps contradictory, essays in an effort to strike the difficult balance; of being ready, for this purpose, to compromise as he thinks necessary. To pacify the Ultras he was obliged to go into some detail on his ideas about reform in his message to the National Assembly in December 1970 :

'The life of the nation demands continuity; there can be no productive renewal without it. But this is not a question of one choice or another. We do not have to say "yes" to continuity and "no" to renewal, but to affirm our desire for renewal within the framework of continuity; that is, to go on being what we are without growing rigid, or growing old, or falling behind.'[6]

The regime, then, is to stand fast, unchanged from what it has always been, at the same time avoiding petrification. But —liberty? Development? Standard of living, modernisation? Colonies, emigration? How are our national problems to be solved when nothing is offered us but Salazarism? The Catholic technocrats in the Cabinet, the new deputies of the old National Union, did not pledge their political future for 'reforms' like this. The country expected better things of Caetano when it turned to him from the dictator's death-bed.

In three years of office he exhausted the reforming potential with which he started off, so that today the nation feels the liberalising programme is over before it ever properly began. He disavowed any intention of being a dictator like Salazar and yet the same personal-power system still obtains in the sphere of politics and there are no more opportunities than before for the people to take part. Supreme and alone, Caetano decides for everyone, with a helpful suggestion now and then from the President of the Republic. There is no liberty, and

[6] Speech reported in the *Diário de Notícias*, 3 December 1970.

police brutality is in some ways more blatant, political justice more arbitrary, than under Salazar.[7] Where economics are concerned, things gradually get worse. The Government has not enough money to carry out effective administrative reforms and, while most of the population faces inescapable poverty and must emigrate to other parts of Europe, there is an unhealthy concentration of riches in the hands of a few.[8] Trade unions do not exist. Social

[7] In March 1970 the PIDE-DGS forbade the holding of a dinner in honour of Captain Carlos Vilhena, a veteran of over eighty, and arrested two of the organisers. One of them, Raul Miguel Marques, was viciously beaten. 'Just so you can tell them all we're still the same as ever,' said the PIDE superintendent, by way of farewell! In a book entitled *O Dilema da política portuguesa*, a Lisbon publication of 1971, Sotto-mayor Cardia gives a detailed account of the cruelties inflicted on him at police headquarters during the previous October. The same thing happened to Artur Cunha Leal in March 1971 when, in his professional capacity as a lawyer, he tried to prevent the arrest without warrant of one of his nephews. He, too, was beaten up and had to be taken to hospital in a very serious condition. Another case since Caetano came to power is that of Daniel Teixeira, a student who died in suspicious circumstances in the PIDE prison at Caxias. There are now more cadres of the political police and their savage incursions, notably among the students, amply demonstrate that the PIDE indeed remains what it always was, a state within the state. As in the time of Salazar there are still the special courts, the *plenários,* for dealing with 'political offences'. Despite every protest, the security measures are still applied to political offenders who stick to their beliefs. Nothing, in fact, has changed.

[8] See Caetano's speech, reported in the *Diário de Notícias* of 16 June 1971. 'Rarely has this country witnessed such a mammoth effort to improve present conditions and prepare the future.' But it is not efforts, theoretical in any case, that we are arguing about; it is results. And the nation has given its answer in the form of large-scale emigration, by the high road and the low: surely the most pointed expression of discontent that it could offer. In this same speech Caetano also mentions four huge projects for which he claims credit and which he advances as proof of progress made by his Government. In fact all four are due to private enterprise—the naval dockyards at Setubal are a CUF undertaking; the chemical and petroleum installation at Sines is the affair of CUF, SOPONATA and ESSO; the firm of Champalimaud has developed the iron and steel industry; and the motorways are built by a foreign concern yet to be named. All kinds of privileges are

insurance, labour conditions, education and justice are alike deplorable. The Social State, the *Estado Social* as dreamed of by the liberals in Caetano's camp, looks like a baleful black joke.

In colonial affairs, the regime carries on the policy it inherited, in spite of progress and what the world thinks, though perhaps with a shade less conviction. The young men who are the future of Portugal are sacrificed and her national resources are sacrificed along with them. The aimless policy seems to have no end in view save that of living from one day to the next. The country is entangled in a hopeless war which nobody approves of save the Union of South Africa and a few great powers who are affected in a marked degree by the international money market.

It is a devastating balance-sheet for the Prime Minister's first three years and there is a feeling among the intelligentsia that something must happen soon. He has held the country in a precarious equilibrium which cannot last much longer. Though they may not appear on the surface, the development of the colonial situation is causing differences that will prove fatal in the end. Portugal remains on the sidelines while Europe plans and builds her future, while England joins the Common Market and even Spain is stirring. Here and now, our most important choices must be made.[9]

granted to the foreign companies by the state, but the only people who stand to gain are the foreign investor and the big national combines that serve as cover for his investment. One may perhaps beg leave to doubt whether this sort of thing is the best of all preparations for our future, the more so since neither the priorities nor the conditions of these projects are admitted to public discussion.

[9] The Portuguese Government will not find it easy to enter the Common Market, in spite of its efforts to obtain the necessary support. The political aims of the European Community are, after all, intended as instruments of social and economic integration. One of the basic requirements is that governmental decision-making should be under democratic control, another that people, goods and ideas should circulate freely. It follows that a country lacking the institutions of democracy cannot belong to the Community, even as an associate member. The obstacles encountered by Greece, which is an associate member, and by Spain are some indication of what will happen over

The key problem, the impediment to all political and economic change in Portugal, is the colonial war, now in its twelfth year. For two main reasons the position in Africa depends very much upon the internal politics of the regime. First, because this is a war which could not have lasted so long in a democracy; and secondly, because the necessary prelude to its solution, except in the unlikely event of resounding victory for one side or the other, is a change of policy at home.

From 1961 onwards, Salazar's Government staked its future on keeping the colonies as sovereign possessions. No price was thought too high and everything was offered up—lives, and property, and the heritage of the next few generations. Portugal was thus confronted with a tragic situation from which it is extremely difficult to withdraw. Today the problem is not merely that of replacing an undemocratic system with one which will respect human rights and liberties and promote economic progress for the good of all. It is something much bigger, a problem of new foundations and national reconstruction.

Some time after the accession of Caetano—Prime Minister with the blessing of the right, as de Gaulle was President of France—we were given to understand that he, and he alone, could put into operation the policy of the left. He alone had the authority and strength, he only had the power, to open negotiations with the African nationalists and end the colonial war. But, we heard also, patience was called for. He must free himself from the pressure of the Ultras first, and there were certain hindrances besides, notably his obligations to the President. We should have to wait until this President finished his term of office and we had a new one, in 1972.

It must be emphasised that none of this was borne out by anything Caetano said or did, in speech or public act. At every opportunity he showed himself a faithful disciple of the

Portugal, whose position is far less promising, owing to the state of affairs in the colonies. At its eighth Congress, held at Brussels in June 1971, the Common Market Socialist Liaison Bureau declared itself opposed to the admission of Portugal in any form.

colonial doctrine of Salazar. But our national embarrassments as they grew worse helped to make his case seem reasonable, and the rumours of imminent change persisted just the same.

After a decade of crippling sacrifice the end of the war is as far away as ever. While the fighting spreads in Angola and Mozambique and the army needs more men and material, there is increasing criticism of our policy in international bodies, and not in the United Nations only. The recent NATO debates,[10] Portugal's departure, or indirect expulsion, from UNESCO[11] and that of the Pères Blancs, the missionary priests, from Mozambique,[12] are all indications that official pronouncements in Lisbon are out of tune with actual events. The Security Council meeting at Addis Ababa in February 1972 was another

[10] At the NATO meeting on 3 June 1971, in Lisbon, the Norwegian Foreign Minister, Chappellen, declared that 'Portuguese colonial policy undermines support for NATO in the countries concerned and is affecting that organisation's image in Africa and other parts of the world'. As Michel Tatu, special correspondent for *Le Monde*, reported two days later, this gave rise to a lively exchange with the Portuguese Foreign Minister. It must be added that these strictures on the Portuguese Government mentioned its 'constant violation of personal human rights', as well as the colonial policy.

[11] The Portuguese Foreign Minister, Rui Patricio, announced at a press conference on 28 May 1971 that the country was leaving UNESCO. 'Recent events in the Executive Council of this organisation,' he said, 'notably the approval of a resolution assigning funds to anti-Portuguese terrorists under the guise of an education programme in the so-called "liberated" areas, have forced us to take a stronger attitude.' His words confirm in a remarkable way my own theory that, in direct contradiction of what the Government has always tried to make its fellow-citizens believe, hostility to the colonial policy of Portugal is everywhere increasing.

[12] The Portuguese Government in fact announced the expulsion of the Mission without explanation, whereas the Dutch Superior of the Order, Father Van Asten, told reporters in Paris that 'forty of the Fathers have left Mozambique in protest against the way the Church kow-tows to the powers that be'. He also emphasised that the 'grave decision' had been taken 'after consultation with the heads of other congregations having missions in Mozambique' and that it was 'almost unanimously approved'. See *Le Monde*, 22 May 1971.

such pointer. Surely, at this stage, the normal thing would be to try to tidy up the mess.

Some of the Ministers, Opus Dei-type technocrats, are firmly convinced of this, especially those concerned with economic affairs. They may not say so in public, since the subject is taboo, but they admit it privately. Unless Portugal puts an end to her colonial wars she has no chance at all of moving into an era of progress and so lessening the tragic distance that separates her from the rest of Europe, or of breaking loose from her political and social immobility of the last few decades.

When Marcello Caetano took the reins he had, he said, 're-examined the problem coolly from beginning to end in the search for new solutions, other and better than those we have tried so far'.[13] And the best thing, he thought, was to march straight on, unfaltering, along the same road as before, since anything else would mean that he was shamelessly declining to fulfil the 'undeclinable mandate' which he claims the nation gave him.[14]

Despite the solemn statements, however, and all the precautions to ensure the continuation of Salazar's colonial policy, Caetano has gradually modified the time-honoured vocabulary with subtleties that are so many words to the wise. Terminology and trains of argument are not altered, in such a serious matter, without reason. General de Gaulle, for example, began by taking about *Algérie française*; then it was the *Paix des Braves*, or Independence with Interdependence; and when he got to the point of saying '*Algérie algérienne*' independence really happened. So Caetano began, while still protesting his entire fidelity to the old dictator's colonial procedures, to employ the word 'autonomy', that magic bit of double-talk which is in fact a pale semblance of 'self-determination'. 'Autonomy' was followed by 'progressive autonomy', by 'expanding autonomy', 'autonomous territories' and finally, when the Constitution was revised, he used the expression 'states' and qualified it with the word *honoríficos*. We have come far indeed from the Overseas Provinces.

[13] See his speech of 17 June 1969, in *Pelo Futuro de Portugal*.
[14] See his speech of 3 December 1970.

The speech he made to the District Committees of the ANP at the palace of Foz on 27 September 1970, when he had been two years in office, contains more of the new-look language than any other. The theme was 'Portugal belongs to all of us, and all of us are Portugal' and it contained a calm ideological demolition of what had been until then the official case for Salazarist colonial policy. Portugal's historic mission went by the board as the decisive justification for her presence in Africa : 'History is being made every day and the needs of the nation must be served, whether they accord with the past or not.' The argument that we are defending the West, so frequently produced for hesitant allies 'openly hostile to our position in the southern hemisphere, and behaving as though they were enemies', is another casualty. For 'we are not obliged to defend, alone, a cause that touches so many men and countries when they fail to recognise their own vital interests and neither realise nor are grateful for what we do for them.' Last of all he demolishes the revered Salazarist theory that 'the overseas possessions are essential because Portugal without them would lose her independence'. Caetano now admits this is not so. 'With much or little territory,' he says, 'Portugal will survive. For Portugal is not just a space, a given quantity of earth. She is a way of life. She is one way to be a nation !'[15]

Clearly all this is not accidental. To call in question the old justifications of the African policy of Salazar is a step forward, and the results may be important. In the first place, it means the end of many threats and prohibitions. The charge of high treason which the Ultras levelled so often against opponents of the official programme becomes, among others, meaningless. And if Marcello Caetano can re-examine the colonial problem in search of new solutions, then what is to prevent some of his fellow-countrymen from doing the same thing and finding solutions that may be different from his?

But the Prime Minister did not go on to take the next step logically to be expected of him. Instead, he produced new reasons for continuing the policy as before. For instance : 'We must defend the *Ultramar* for the sake of the thousands of

[15] All these extracts come from the same speech.

Portuguese, black and white, who trust in Portugal and wish to go on living there under her flag and to enjoy the blessings of peace.'[16] One may naturally inquire how he can make this statement without ever having consulted the populations concerned. Even admitting, for argument's sake, that the natives are as pro-Portuguese as he seems to think, nobody can be sure that they will not change their minds in the near future. Why, therefore, can the Government not negotiate a workable solution to the conflict? Caetano himself affirms that the Portuguese are in Africa to 'create open and tolerant societies without racial discrimination, the noblest and most brotherly example of co-existence to be found in the tropics, as fine as what has been and is being done in Brazil'.[17]

The allusion to Brazil implies, of course, that Angola and Mozambique could be like Brazil. But the war must be concluded before that can happen, and the thought of negotiations must therefore lie at the heart of this discourse. Caetano is not unaware that the Portuguese increasingly desire them.

Some time earlier the President of Zambia, Kenneth Kaunda, had made a significant gesture towards Portugal when, speaking at Addis Ababa in the name of African unity, he declared himself ready to seek, in friendship with her, a workable remedy of the colonial problem. President Senghor of Senegal similarly suggested a three-phase plan for peace, 'a cease-fire, negotiations with a view to self-determination, and independence within the framework of a Luso-African community of independent peoples in free and friendly co-operation.'[18] He claims that the nationalists have welcomed this plan, while Portugal has so far been deaf to his appeal.

The censorship has allowed the press in Portugal to publish these terms but not to comment on them. It even allowed

[16] There are, as we know, less than half a million white people in the Portuguese colonies altogether—less, that is, than half the number of workers who have emigrated from Portugal to France—and 1,300,000 blacks.

[17] See his *Conversa em família*, or Family Chat on the television, as reported in the *Diário de Notícias* for 16 June 1971.

[18] This proposal appeared in *Le Monde* on 15 June 1970.

publication of my statement to *Le Monde* that the Government should accept Kaunda's offer and attempt negotiation as the only way to end the war without delay and thus spare Portuguese lives.[19] This, in a country where every political item printed is carefully considered in the light of official interest, must have been a feeler put out to see how the colonialist faction would react.

Returning to Caetano's second-anniversary speech, he went on to say, 'With whom and about what are we supposed to open negotiations? Are we to bargain with people who are at each other's throats according as to whether they take orders from Soviet Russia or the Red Chinese? Give them the strength they do not have and land that does not belong to them, and put at their mercy women and children they will not respect?'

It is clear from the way he frames them how distorted his questions are. Guarantees are always settled as a preliminary to negotiation and the guarantee of personal security is naturally the most important of them. But if every outstretched hand is to be refused on principle and every contact rejected with indignant scorn, nobody can possibly know whether guarantees will be forthcoming or not, nor what effective concessions the nationalists are prepared to make.[20]

[19] What I said was, 'I believe the Portuguese Government should embrace this opportunity to end the colonial hostilities which, without hope of a solution by force of arms, have clouded our political and social skies for the last nine years. It is also the opportunity, in the old liberal tradition of our country, to recover the confidence of the African peoples. For this it is obviously essential to repudiate colonialism in all its forms and unequivocally to recognise the right of a people to choose for itself. In saying as much I am not voicing Socialist opinion only but that of all other groups of the opposition, Republican, Liberal and Catholic, who at the elections of October 1969 declared unanimously against the continuation of war in the colonies and for the immediate opening of political talks with a view to peace.' (*Le Monde*, 8 September 1970.)

[20] More recently, when the Security Council met at Addis Ababa, Amilcar Cabral, leader of the PAIGC, declined to ask for the expulsion of Portugal, preferring to appeal for negotiations. (See *Le Monde*, 4 February 1972). The response from Lisbon was, as usual, negative. Rui Patricio spoke of the Addis Ababa session as 'a degradation and

If the Government has never been brave enough to take up any definite stand over this difficulty, it has at least made wary efforts to discover some alternative line and to gauge the resistance it may have to overcome. But at every step of the way it has felt obliged to reassure the Ultras with solemn declarations about 'no change in overseas policy'. For the same reason it has increased the unprovoked persecution of avowedly anti-colonialist democrats.

In this connection I need only recall the virulent campaign it directed, or at any rate encouraged, against me after the conference I gave at the Overseas Press Club of New York in April 1970. All I did was repeat what had been said already, both inside Portugal and abroad, during and after the elections; but any pretext served, and there was an attempt to stir up public opinion with a witch-hunt and cries of 'Treason!' in the newspapers.[21] One would have thought I had been singing an anti-colonialist solo in New York, whereas the fact was that many people at home, some of them very near to the centre of power, were joining in the chorus. I thus became a sort of counter in the game or guarantee to the Ultras that the regime was faithful to the good old cause. Caetano himself appeared on television to land a few blows of his own and demonstrate that he was all the Ultras wished him to be. And when I think how more than one of his own team had for years held anti-colonial notions very like my own and were too frightened to speak out! When I think of the judges who were willing to lend their authority to a trial that was so obviously a political exercise!

Another victim was Mário de Oliveira, priest of the small town of Macieira da Lixa. He was imprisoned for several months, then tried at Oporto for having dared to disapprove

debasement of the United Nations'; and this despite the contrary opinion of Pope Paul VI, who praised it in the same paper one week later.

[21] And not in the newspapers alone. There were books as well, such as Ruben Sottomayor's *Carta aberta a Mário Soares (Open Letter to Mário Soares)*, published in Lisbon, 1970; or, another example, a brochure with the revealing title *Overseas Portugal versus Mário Soares*, by Luis Lupi, director of a semi-official news agency.

of the colonial war, notably in a letter written by him to a conscientious objector.[22] Less publicity was employed in his case, but the intimidation was the same and there was actually a further and more subtle purpose to it all : the Bishop of Oporto, a *bête noire* of the clerical reactionaries, gave evidence and the authorities were trying to implicate him personally.

But while the Government, pulled this way and that by different factions, was thus occupied, things overseas grew worse. The dead-end situation forced us into new liabilities, new military, economic and political undertakings, while some of our foreign commitments made it steadily harder to reach a real solution. As in any colonial war, the difficulties multiplied and worsened as time went by. The struggle was destroying every link there was between the African communities and the people of Portugal.

An offensive in Mozambique by General Kaúlza de Arriaga, supposedly one of Caetano's rivals in the power-game,[23] set off renewed fighting, rape and sabotage by the nationalists in response.[24] But definite victory went to neither side, nor has the country been kept informed of events since the invasion of Guinea-Conakry. Could this operation, as implied by a motion in the United Nations and in much of the foreign press, have been mounted in Portuguese territory to liberate Portuguese nationals held by the PAIGC?[25] The nationalist

[22] Father Mário Paés de Oliveira was arrested on 28 July 1970, and gaoled at Caxias. His trial opened at Oporto on 17 December and lasted until 17 February following, when, after seven months' imprisonment, he was acquitted. See *Subversão ou Evangelho? (Gospel or Subversion?)* by the lawyer and deputy José da Silva. This book is banned in Portugal.

[23] Kaúlza de Arriaga was Under-Secretary of State for Air at one time under Salazar and now commands the forces in Mozambique.

[24] Sabotage particularly of the coaster *Angoche*, which disappeared on 23 April 1971 between Nacala and Porto Amelia. With an inflammable cargo, she carried a crew of twenty-three and one passenger. She was sighted, empty and adrift, on the 27th. Fire had broken out and what actually happened is not known. Caetano announced two months afterwards, in June, that there had been an act of sabotage.

[25] The United Nations approved a resolution attributing to Portugal a decisive role in the plans to invade the Republic of Guinea.

movements, it is true, cannot claim any very startling triumphs, and the 'colonisers' are adept at taking advantage of the deep rifts between the various African countries. Such a policy may indeed produce immediate benefits, if only for those who want to make a fortune as fast as they can at the risk of having to leave it all behind at some later date; but anyone who thinks realistically about the country's future must see that it spells the ruin of every hope we have. The terrible thing is that the interests involved are so many and so complex that the obvious solution of peace and decolonisation may well be delayed. The tragedy will be so much the greater in the end.

There does seem to be some discreet modification of the official doctrine that Angola and Mozambique are provinces, in the same way that the Minho or the Algarve are provinces. Apparently the Government has in mind something like the Federal State that used to be one of Caetano's ideas, or even a community of independent states. If this is indeed so, then the constant references to Brazil are easier to understand, but it is exactly what the supporters of Salazarist integration dread the most. Since the Constitution was revised they have been talking, openly or otherwise, of treason; only this time the traitor is the Government.

In a recent article Adriano Moreira, who was Colonial Minister when the rebellion broke out in Angola, has questioned the authenticity and timeliness of certain changes in terminology, changes which he regards as dangerous and pregnant with future risk.[26] Fernando Pacheco de Amorim was more outspoken still, and uses the phrase 'policy of planned withdrawal' in his book, *Na hora da Verdade*, which is a thorough indictment of Caetano's colonial policy.[27] 'Autonomy,' he says, 'colonial self-government, is the step that, logically and historically, precedes complete political indepen-

[26] Article published in the magazine *Prisma* in April 1971, as part of a forum on 'The Constitutional Revision'.

[27] *Na hora da Verdade: colonialismo e neo-colonialismo na proposta de revisão constitutional (In the Hour of Reckoning: Colonialism and Neo-Colonialism in the Proposed Constitutional Revision)*, by Fernando Pacheco de Amorim. Published at Coimbra, 1971.

dence and total decolonisation.' It is his firm belief that a plot
is in being of which the country is unaware, a plot whose
imperceptible stages are leading her downhill to dismember-
ment and the gradual independence of her colonies.[28] Thus
it is Marcello Caetano who stands publicly accused of treason,
and by an odd turn of fate the charges are those he himself
brings against me and other opponents of the regime who
disapprove of the colonial war. But if his solution is the
creation of white-dominated states like Rhodesia, that of the
opposition is based on the principle of self-determination. To
recognise this principle is, we believe, the only way to promote,
in peace, multi-racial states with black majorities and ties of
friendship and co-operation with Portugal. It is an answer that
means the sacrifice of large interests and the end of centuries
of exploitation; but no other can enforce essential change in
rooted, metropolitan Portugal.

De Gaulle, despite the enormous differences between the
two countries, faced a very similar problem when he took over
in 1958, and he attacked it valiantly. His *Mémoires d'espoir*
tell how, when he assumed the government of France he was
resolved to free her from the constraints of Empire, and how
this was by no means a happy task. 'For a man of my age and
upbringing it was a cruel thing to become, in my own person,
the instrument of such a change.'

Caetano, certainly, is not de Gaulle. If he realises the
dilemma of his country he has not, in three years of power,

[28] *Idem*, page 141 et seq. Pacheco de Amorim cites especially a
speech Caetano made at Luanda on 11 June 1945, when he was Foreign
Minister. 'On one thing we must be rigorous, and that is racial
separation. Inter-breeding between blacks and whites, whether in
wedlock or out of it, brings serious social troubles for native and
European alike. It introduces the problem of the half-caste, a problem
whose biological aspects are not in my department but which is
certainly perturbing from the sociological point of view. Nevertheless,
if these inter-racial relations are to be avoided and condemned,
hostility towards the half-caste as such is unthinkable. He cannot help
his birth and it is unjust to visit the sins of the fathers on the innocent
victims.' On this it would be interesting to hear the comments of the
Brazilian sociologist Gilberto Freire, the advocate of 'luso-tropicalism'.

had courage or will to solve it. By prolonging the system of Salazar he has made his own regime no more than a political interlude.

There is no use in attempting to discuss the solution of our basic troubles while the colonial policy remains unchanged. Caetano can suggest botching and expedients, he will introduce nothing radically new. He will be unable to launch a wave of progress, to make sure that youth rallies to him with enthusiasm and the nation is behind him. So much was obvious when the pattern of the 1969 elections was unaltered, in spite of all his promises; obvious when he tried to limit the powers of the PIDE-DGS, and dropped the idea later, since an anti-democratic state has no choice but to continue as a police state. It was obvious, too, in that social legislation which seemed to be breathing a little fresh air into the corporative vertical trade unions and which in practice brought nothing but repression pure and simple, wih governmental demagogy revealed in all its nakedness.[29] Most clearly we saw it in the constitutional reform, where such alterations as were made served only to secure the continuity of the regime. This point may usefully be examined in more detail.

According to the liberal evangelists of Caetanism, the constitutional reform aimed,

(1) to make the regime in some degree legitimate by restoring the election by direct suffrage of the President of the Republic;

[29] The International Labour Organisation has more than once condemned the Portuguese trade union system; in May 1962, for instance, in May 1963, February 1964 and May 1968. Decrees signed by Caetano when first he came to power (Decrees No. 49,058 and No. 49,212), were relatively liberal in tone, but when workers tried to profit by them to choose non-Government candidates the regime responded with brutality, and leaders of their movement, such as Daniel Cabrita, were arrested and sentenced. See the booklet *A luta pelo sindicalismo livre em Portugal (The Struggle for Free Trade Unionism in Portugal)*, published by Portuguese Trade Union Movement under the auspices of the International Confederation of Free Trade Unions.

(2) to restore, in fact and not in theory only, certain political liberties, notably by a conditional lifting of press censorship and the granting of some personal sureties—reduction of the period of preventive detention, now standing at six months, and the right to have a lawyer present at PIDE-DGS interrogations, so that torture cannot be used;

(3) to modify the 'Overseas Provinces' statute in such a way as to tone down official policy and gain fresh support from the world in general.

Not one of these things has been done. The Government has yielded to the pressure of group after group and ended by leaving the Constitution more or less unchanged; the ambitious reforming plan of Caetano has faded away. Doubtless this is why the seven liberalising deputies walked out of the National Assembly when the suggested revisions had come up for debate in June 1971.[30] So markedly, in fact, has the Government regressed that the discourses of Caetano nowadays might be those of Salazar.[31]

Caetano has always sought to present a legal image of himself—the Professor of Law, forbearing by nature and inclined to liberalism, whose first care will ever be to uphold legality. But let us not forget that the law in Portugal merely expresses the will of a Government which does as it likes and rules by decrees that have the force of law.[32] And the Government in Portugal is a hierarchy in which the Prime Minister is above the Ministers, whom he may appoint and dismiss without

[30] The members of the present Assembly, though all returned as representatives of the sole authorised party, do include seven deputies with serious liberalising tendencies, who have accordingly grown more and more critical of the Government. A press bill introduced by two of them was thrown out undebated and it was in protest against the majority vote on this occasion that the seven quitted the Chamber together on 1 July 1971.

[31] See, for example, his speech at Braga on 29 May 1971, and the *Fireside Chat* of the following 15 June.

[32] Laws properly speaking are made by the National, or Legislative, Assembly, decree-laws by the Government.

appeal,[33] being answerable to none but the President of the Republic. The latter, elected since 1959 by a limited college drawn from the National Union and nominated directly or indirectly by the Government, is heavily dependent on the Prime Minister in his turn.[34]

When Caetano was installed, his partisans gave out that he meant to modify the Constitution and that the Presidency was to be decided by direct vote of the electors once again. His aim was to give some semblance of legality to institutions which lacked it, as they still do, and he, unlike Salazar, had good reason for wishing to be President himself: in 1972 it seemed the best protection from the faction-struggles going on within the regime.

But the constitutional amendments said nothing about direct election and, though Caetano has never really explained why, the reason was that the President took the scheme as a personal insult. He happened to have been elected on the new, indirect system introduced after the Delgado campaign, and return to the old method necessarily stripped events since then of their legality. Also, Caetano was not secure enough in 1972 to test the regime and his own power in the crucible of a presidential election. In short, he relinquished the idea of a lawful state in Portugal and made it a land fit for dictators to live in.

'But,' one might say, 'he was trying to relieve political tension and establish a benevolent dictatorship that could set the country on the road to controlled liberalisation'; and this was indeed the dream he cherished in his early months of Government. Or so, at all events, he led us to suppose. There were theorists, even, who held that the regime needs must develop because conditions in Portugal made development essential. The financial and industrial expansion of Portuguese capitalism, in their view, no longer called for the rigid props

[33] Salazar's way with dismissals was to send a visiting-card to the Minister in question, usually on the very day that the news was released in the papers. Caetano's method we have yet to learn.

[34] On both occasions when the President has been replaced it was Salazar who made the choice, of Craveiro Lopes and Américo Tomas.

of Fascism.[35] They spoke of Salazar as the dull financier of yesteryear, with Caetano representing the other face of capitalism—the kindly conservative, the tolerant man; the sort of man they had in Europe. Western Europe, under its new political leaders, was showing the path to follow. Spain herself, whose present development is ahead of that of Portugal, was facing the same problem and, with all her contradictory policies, making the effort to discard her retrograde institutions. This argument, however, ignores the terrible burden and constriction of the colonial war. But for the war, Caetano could be a different kind of politician; he could be like Lopez Rodó in Spain and make a good showing. As things are, prisoner of that endless conflict, lacking the ability to bring it to any termination, he is doomed to copy Salazar, in the spirit if not in the letter.

Nor are prospects much more encouraging for those public liberties which the liberal wing of the regime wished to see at any rate partly re-introduced as a step towards relieving the situation. The changes outlined in the constitutional reforms are minimal and meaningless. And for the first time a deputy has stood up in the National Assembly and addressed it on the absence of freedom. Clearly, boldly, in accents Portugal has seldom heard, Francisco Sá Carneiro said,

'It is twelve years since this House acknowledged, vainly, the urgent need for a law to put an end to the arbitrary treatment of the press . . . Limitation of the number of pages, the financial deposit and permit required of newspapers and publishers, printer's liability, official closure of printing-works by the police and state confiscation of equipment, distraints without appeal, these, by and large, are the chief legal instruments the Government employs. With them it raises an insurmountable wall and freedom of thought lies imprisoned within.

"All Portuguese subjects possess the right of assembly, so long as they do not assemble to discuss anything the administration sees as a social or political question. To do this they have

[35] This is the contention of João Martins Pereira in his book, *Pensar Portugal Hoje (Portuguese Thought Today)*, Lisbon, 1971.

whatever right the Government may accord, for permission to hold a meeting must, since 11 April 1933, be obtained beforehand.

'Anybody may form an association with anybody else, for any purpose he may please, provided that the rules are approved by the Government—which can forbid the association, dissolve the management and appoint a committee of its own to run it.[36]

'Religious liberty, except for Catholics, remains an empty promise. Compulsory official teaching-programmes and compulsory official text-books have drained the freedom out of education.

'But the gloomiest outlook of all . . . is reached when we contemplate basic human liberty and its safeguards. I mean actual, physical human liberty. Life-sentences may have been abolished, but still we have the security measures, and they can be indefinitely prolonged. . . . The safeguards of legal defence and cross-examination have been replaced by mere police enquiry which puts the onus of proof on the accused, leaves him for six months in the unrestricted keeping of the police, denies him the aid of a solicitor to which he is by law entitled, and places him wholly at the mercy of authority.

'Thus the freedom and rights of the individual are in practice null and void. . . . The constitutional guarantees in Portugal rest, *de facto*, in the hands of Government.'[37]

Deliberately, Sá Carneiro was speaking out against a constitutional amendment which did nothing at all about the liberties of the subject and which perpetuated the old injustices and violations as before.

The new press law is ambiguous and satisfies no one. On many points it aggravated, rather than resolved, existing limitations and authors and journalists protested at the diffi-

[36] Under decree-law No. 520/71 of 24 November 1971, which the National Assembly ratified despite the opposition of its 'liberal' contingent, even the official corporations now need preliminary permits from the Ministry of the Interior.

[37] Speech in the National Assembly, published in the *Jornal do Comércio* on 17 July 1971.

culties it raised.[38] Yet suggestions introduced by Sá Carneiro, Francisco Balsemão and other deputies were not even discussed in the National Assembly. In the end, pre-publication censorship was not abolished, it was merely run by different people; and even so the law was not applied, for the Government declared a 'state of subversion' forthwith.

In the domain of public liberty, just as in other departments, the reforms are nothing but a smoke-screen.

Foreign observers are disapproving and shocked to see our opposition living, as it does, on the margin of perceptible politics. Portugal in fact has no politics; there are the in-fighting and clashes in the corridors of power, and that is all. The masters of the regime take the big decisions, of which the public is told nothing and which it realises only when the consequences are felt in national life.

So we have gone on for the last forty-five years, and we are the poorer for it. Caetano, by refusing to admit the existence of an opposition, is working in a vacuum, as did Salazar, and the country is deprived of the most worth-while aid it could command. It is, for the establishment, an aberration to hold political opinions of one's own. Politicians therefore are either marionettes controlled by the dictatorship, or else they must have courage to risk, at any moment, prison, exile, or the life of secret subversion. Those who still wish to carry on the struggle are banished implacably from public life and reduced to silence; or they are left in a mockery of freedom with their private lives in ruin. It follows that most people with a taste for politics need no persuasion to stay silent and inactive rather than become yes-men.

None but official opinion may be expressed in Portugal. That is the rule. With none of the normal political machinery for checking or modifying its actions, the Government puts itself beyond the reach of criticism and is in its own view infallible by definition. This being so, we need more than

[38] In May 1971 various of the opposition sectors set up a committee for the Defence of Freedom of Speech, and this laid several demands before the Government.

relatively passive resistance if we are to combat the decadence of the country and create conditions fit for our people to live in. We must never renounce that right to take part which has always been denied us. Above all, we must know how to make common cause with the workers, and how to find effective ways of helping with the struggle and of changing the circumstances imposed on us by authority.

This is no easy problem in an ultra-police state like Portugal. The question of knowing what to do falls into two parts : first, how we are to do it, and second, how to shape an alternative policy to suit the country at the present time. How to act? And, of course, with whom? It will be a communal undertaking, at least to begin with, and it is important to know who one's friends are.

Plainly the opposition must from the outset be an opposition in the fullest sense. It must learn how to make itself felt at every moment of our national life, and that means incessant struggle against the obstacles raised by the Government, and practical action with each and every weapon it has. It must be alive, and learn to keep abreast of events, and this is not easy, either, in a land where news and communications are all under official control. Also, it must not give an inch. There can be no compromise between Fascism and the democratic opposition.

Difficult as it is to act in these conditions, and in a police state, I am one of those who believe that legal methods are productive; and few though such methods are, they do exist. With a little dash and imagination they could develop the will to resistance and the fighting spirit of the mass of the people, while giving the Government appreciably less room to manœuvre. Demands can be organised and written material circulated in spite of the censorship, with systematic criticism of governmental proceedings. Both inside and outside the framework of official trade-unionism the battle can go on to introduce democratic attitudes and expose the regime. We can take part in elections, even if they are falsified, for the sake of making our voices heard. We can denounce arbitrary methods, corruption and police brutality whenever and wherever they occur. I believe, in short, that we should make full use of the narrow margin of legality which not even totalitarianism can abolish altogether.

To be effective, however, such forms of action as these must be integrated into an over-all plan as part of our strategy in the battle for democracy; and here we come up against another problem, that of violence.

Face to face with an authority that has no legal basis but symbolises in itself the violation of law and order, it is hard to shut one's eyes to the fact that revolutionary violence may be the only thing that is really going to work. I detest violence in any form. The world is soaked in it and I think anything that anyone can do to end it is a positive step forward. Politically, I choose non-violence. But I am not, and I do not want to be, a hypocrite. The renewed outbreak of violence in Portugal in the last few months is perfectly logical, if not inevitable.[39] It is as though some machine has been put into action before anybody quite knows how far it will drag us. Yet the Government has refused discussion, shown no tolerance, usurped power. Who can overlook the terrible responsibility it bears in starting the whole process? And it is no use thinking that policemen alone are going to solve what is essentially a political problem. That method has been tried in Africa, with what results we have all seen.

Organised terrorism, incitement to revolt, does without a doubt exist in Portugal and the latent unrest may erupt at any moment. Though they may not realise it at the time, many of those who emigrate are in fact saying 'no' to life in an atmosphere of economic and political oppression. We of the opposition should listen to the youth of the country, the most open-minded and intelligent of them especially; we

---

[39] Several recent acts of sabotage have been attributed to the ARA, *the Acção Revoluciónaria Armada*, or Armed Revolutionary Action. But other organisations are equally ready to counsel, and try to use, violence. Such are the revolutionary brigades of the FPLN, the LUAR, the CLAC, or Committees of Anti-Colonialist Struggle, the Marxist-Leninist movement known as *O communista* and the ARCO, or Communist Revolutionary Action.

should try to see what they mean when they criticise our more traditionalist elements and our employment of legal means that have proved to be dead ends. Let us bear in mind that numbers of these young men have had to fight in Africa, where they have been mixed up in violence themselves. The consequences of this are unpredictable. They could well be tempted in their turn to take the shortest way and round on their oppressors, gun in hand.

The development of Catholic thought on the subject is not without interest. Confronted almost everywhere with the problem of violence, a great many Catholics distinguish between cases; they hesitate and are visibly perplexed, but they do not condemn outright. They try to comprehend it. Camillo Torres in Colombia may be a priest, but he is numbered all the same with the contemporary apostles of revolutionary violence, and the sight of oppression and injustice leads many another along the same path in South America, in Spain and Vietnam and Portugal. A recent television programme on the Church in Portugal gave French viewers a striking lesson on the facts of this growing radicalism.[40]

The opponents of violence are in a tragic dilemma in a society such as ours in Portugal. When its whole aim is to restore the nation's rights, how can they argue against it?

Beyond this vexed problem of ways and means we must also be clear about our aims. The connection, moreover, is obvious: once aims are precisely defined, understood and accepted unreservedly by the country at large, then the possible means of action are extended automatically, and with them the chances of success.

For some years now the Government has been referring, not to 'the opposition' but to 'oppositions', in the hope of persuading people that the various strata of dissent cannot possibly produce an agreed essential programme; that they set more store by their differences than they see the virtue of unity at the right time. The Government motto is, in fact, Divide and

---

[40] The programme, directed by Pierre Dumayet, was shown on French television in February 1971.

Rule, while it is vital for the opposition to close ranks if it is to make a solid construction of democracy.

To be honest, as we should, and tell the whole truth, we have to admit that there are indeed sectors of the opposition whose beliefs, like their ideas on strategy and tactics, differ widely. Nor is it always easy to unite the interests of the various social groups, or even of the various income-groups, among the antagonists of the regime. But these are dreadful days for Portugal and, without minimising such difficulties, we need to acknowledge that our national salvation depends, more than it ever did, on unity.

We must have unity. Not even the best-organised section of the opposition has the strength, after forty-five years of struggle and sacrifice, to bring about a change in the regime unaided. All our groups must strive to understand one another in order to present a combined alternative to Caetano and his system. And unity implies reciprocal concessions, the effort to arrive at points of agreement. We know of course that fundamental differences remain, but without abandoning principles we should make the most of those broad lines of belief we hold in common, and examine them in depth and detail. That is the road to agreement.

We must reinforce the bonds that link all anti-Fascists, whatever their politics, religion or ideology. This, I think, is very important, for the opposition is after all made up of those who suffer together under the same oppressor state. It is true that the manual workers have most to bear from the police and that political justice, as meted out by the Government, is still basically justice with class distinctions. But police brutality in any form is an affront to each and every democrat. Discord between individuals, groups and parties must, in politics, yield to solidarity and brotherhood.

I know they will not always do so easily. We live in a concentration-camp; bitterness and dissension are endemic. We are underlings, and so frustrated; and our frustrations can often cloud the real issues at stake and lead us to disparage our own nearest companions. No section of the opposition, it must be confessed, is innocent of this kind of thing.

It may seem reasonable to ask whether, after many unhappy experiences, we could still possibly unite. The pseudo-reforming policy of Caetano did, let us remember, offer a favourable glimpse of gradual change-over from Fascism to democracy; in certain respects the opposition did stand down and allow itself to be divided in the hope of legal recognition. But after three years of Caetano the truth is staring us in the face : if the opposition does nothing he will go on with Salazarism without Salazar.

Therefore the system must be changed; and in the light of this conclusion we must examine our consciences and realise that the opposition has to draw together. In other words, the solution must be on a national, not a partisan, scale, the outcome of accord between the political, economic and social groups who refuse to accept Caetano's rule. Marcello Caetano means the continuation of the regime, dictatorship for heaven knows how long, more strength to the dominant oligarchies, to big business at Government level, more and worse social injustice. He means the colonial war fought on until it drains the country dry. While he stays we shall have no relief. And so there are three great choices to be made, on Government, economics and colonial policy, and on them we must be united. Presented in what the overwhelming majority in Portugal believe to be the correct order of importance, our aims must be,

(1) to destroy Fascism and restore political democracy;
(2) to replace the bureaucratic and corporative system by a policy of social justice and of development planned in the workers' favour;
(3) to terminate hostilities in Africa at once by negotiation with the nationalist parties, and take the consequent first steps on the road to decolonisation. On these things the people of Portugal must take one side or the other; they mark the boundary-line between regime and opposition.

Some, of course, oppose Caetano because he is neither Fascist nor colonialist enough to please them. Such elements

are further to the right than he and yearn for vintage Salazarism as it was in the 1930s; but less is heard from them since
they nearly all discovered that he is in fact their man. Also
against him are those who wish to see public liberty but
nevertheless believe the present African policy should continue
and who, while disliking the corporative system, are all for
the reinforcement of capital and free enterprise. They include
the liberal Conservatives, a few dissidents, Monarchists who
have kept clear of the regime and even a handful of disillusioned, one-time Caetanists. But none of these represents
the opposition properly speaking.

In my opinion there are at the moment four groups who
could help to work out a practical alternative. These are the
Republicans, the Catholic democrats, the Socialists and the
Communists. Nor should we forget the militants of the far left,
Communist splinter-groups, Anarchists, disciples of Mao
Tse-tung, Trotsky and Che Guevara, whose finer distinctions
are not always easy to discern.

The four political creeds are by no means equal, in that
some have more support than others; and in future potential
they certainly vary a great deal. The level of organisation,
even the extent to which they hang together, differs in each
case. The Communists have their carefully ordered underground, with full-time devotees to man it, and they have
created a tradition of struggle in those parts of the country
where they are established. The Catholics, wavering between
the centre right and extreme left, have not fused into a single
party or movement, although Catholic Action gives them a
starting-point. The Republicans, divided between pure
Liberalism and Social Democracy, are scattered—the Democratic-Social Directive has almost ceased to function—though
they retain one or two minor strongholds. Most of the Socialists
have been gathered in to the recently founded ASP, the
Portuguese Socialist Action group.

There remain all those anti-Fascists who belong to no
particular party, subscribe to no particular ideology, but are
simply against the existing state of affairs and ready to support
any political endeavour of the opposition providing that it

works. A not inconsiderable floating vote, as it were, a mass of individuals whom the opposition could mobilise with ease, especially with a concerted policy.

Hostility to the regime is of course expressed in non-political spheres as well. Portuguese capitalism has concealed doubts and misgivings of its own, and contradictory influences and interests may clash from time to time within the same enterprise. It is possible to recognise one sector which, under the Government's wing, is committed to schemes of colonial exploitation and is consequently against development of any kind, while another, more modernist and dynamic, sees the loss of the colonies as inevitable and wants to get into Europe in order to survive.

Marcello Caetano, as we have observed, knows how this dilemma endangers the regime. He has tried to minimise it and play the double game of carrying on the war while starting negotiations to enter the Common Market. But war and economic development are facts that do not go together, nor has Portugal the slightest prospect of becoming a full member of the European Economic Community until she is a true democracy. Even as an associate she would find her entry difficult. This is why, for the first time, a representative section of Portuguese capitalism concerns itself with a possible change of Government and may be brought to look with favour on a democratic and anti-colonialist policy. It is a new element in the situation, linked with the growing and general middle-class protest against the suffocating embrace of foreign capital and against the crushing weight of the big trusts upon our own economy in particular. For the regime it produces a certain instability of which the opposition would do well to take advantage.

There also exists an authentic, as distinct from a political, trade union movement, which has never been known before. This attempts to make its way in spite of the official 'vertical' unions, and to give substance to the workers' demands.

Other factors, too, point in the same direction. We have the continual rise, in every department of economic and administrative life, of men who know and accept the tech-

K

niques of modern management and who possess a European
outlook incompatible with corporations and the Fascist way
of doing things. We have the progress of the Portuguese
Church, which has had to erase some marks of kinship with
the regime since the Catholic position was modified by the
Second Vatican Council. It would indeed be difficult for the
Church to go on upholding a totalitarian state, a social order
run for the rich and a colonial-minded, racist policy in Portugal, while she preaches quite dissimilar doctrines everywhere
else.

When the united opposition comes forward with its alternative policy, all these things must be taken into account.
What we shall have to produce is a blend of many solutions,
and every political group has a duty to stimulate democratic
discussion by all means and at all levels. This will awaken
the great mass of the people to political consciousness and
from their known wishes we shall learn what the blend is to
be. We must then distil a joint programme for an interim
Government, something lucid, undemagogic and feasible in
the present circumstances of Portugal. We have more to do
than resist the dictatorship, indicate the country's economic
backwardness and flagrant inequalities, and censure the colonial
war. We have to plan a future for Portugal and find realistic
answers to the many problems that beset her; and we must
do it in such a way as to attract the active support of her
people, for without them nothing worthwhile can be attempted.

We have fallen so low and grown so disheartened that the
main task lying before us—and nearly every task does lie
before us—is to make the nation eager and bold again. To
do so we must put first things first. Obviously political and
trade union liberties must be restored and personal human
rights respected scrupulously; and this we must achieve without disorder or over-diversified party activity. The executive
must be strong and stable enough to function properly, though
democratically controlled by an Assembly that represents the
whole nation, and by a free press.

If our colonies are to go and we are to draw much nearer

to Western Europe, then the entire life of Portugal needs to be reconstructed upon new foundations. Ancient privileges, unique now on the continent, must be swept away, inequalities as far as possible ironed out. The creative energy of the country must be released, and this, to a great degree, by ending the corporative system. Speculative investment must be curbed with the utmost severity. Finally, the sources of our national wealth must be used for the good of all.

In the economic sphere, generally speaking, democratic methods must be introduced and we must have nationalisation of certain basic enterprises. I am thinking here of the big banks and credit organisations, the industries involved in national defence, some specific industries with a part to play in getting the economy on its feet again, and the great public-service monopolies. We must ensure that the workers, and the citizens as a whole, command the nerve-centres of decision at national and at local level, and within the major public and private companies—workers' management, in fact. To speed our rate of economic development we need investment from abroad, but this should be regulated in the national interest. Industrial expansion must come first, but radical agrarian and fiscal reform will also be necessary, planned for the collective good. We should encourage large-scale tourism, but the country need not be sold to the highest bidder, which is what has been happening, nor need the Portuguese skivvy for foreigners. We should by every means encourage the people to take part in public life : affairs will be more productively run as a result, headway made against corruption and emigration decline. We must give high priority to the teaching-system at all levels; to adult education, objective and unbiased in matters of religion or politics; to poor relief, social insurance, housing and the equipment of collective enterprises; to the right to leisure and co-operative activity. We must create the proper conditions to attract home those whom politics or want have driven abroad, and to offer young men, especially those who have emigrated rather than fight in the colonies, the place that is theirs in the life of the nation. The country must belong to all its citizens, with no inglorious distinctions of income or ideology.

K*

In international affairs we must work loyally with the United Nations, re-establish diplomatic relations all over the world, in particular with the emergent states of Africa, and, without going back on old alliances when these serve the interest of peace, play an effective part in bringing about disarmament and a better understanding between peoples.

As things are in Portugal and in Europe today, the best watchword is perhaps More Haste, Less Speed. Before the Socialist transformation we shall have, I think, a phase of revolution, nation-wide and democratic, but whether peaceful or violent is not the question here. But we, like everyone else in Europe, must attain our Socialism by democratic paths.

Being a Socialist, I naturally regard Social Democracy as the only real cure for the ills of Portugal. The main thing, however, is to oppose Fascism, for Socialism can and must follow once we achieve demoracy. For this we must know who our allies, even our potential allies, are; we must beware of reinforcing the other side by driving away the fainthearted or the hesitant. We have also to remember that no political change can succeed in Portugal if it affects the world balance of power, since none of the great nations, it seems, either wants or would allow such a thing.

When Marcello Caetano launched his liberalising programme he was chiefly playing for more support for his Government, both at home and abroad, and did indeed manage to attract some measure of international approval. By exposing his pretensions for what they are and getting back to the country's basic dilemma of Fascism versus anti-Fascism, we are shifting the combat to the most alarming of battlegrounds for the regime : we isolate the oligarchy from the rest of the people and present it in a very awkward situation to the foreign onlooker.

I do not think the four political groups we spoke of would seriously disagree with any of this, although the extreme left is persuaded that conditions in Portugal are ripe for revolution. And, as they see it, a gradual revolution is too slow a revolution; all should be done in one great socialising jump. This indicates an important difference of opinion that vitally affects our overall pattern of alliances. It explains the bitterness with which elements of the left have attacked the Socialists, the Communists and some of the Catholics in recent years, lumping them together with the uncomplimentary label of 'reformers'. It explains, too, their disinterest in the real struggle against Fascism itself. Cuba and Chile furnish excellent examples from South America of the two ways of going about things.

I do not, personally, believe that what happened in Cuba could be repeated in countries like Spain and Portugal and, much as I admire Fidel Castro and the rest of the Cuban leaders, do not think it would be necessary or even desirable for us, were it possible. Making allowance for the differences between us, it is the Chilean pattern that seems to me feasible.*
But if we are to act on it we must convince the mass of the people first, and attain such political stability as will ensure public order and freedom, essentials without which no one can make plans for the future.

I do not claim that I, and I alone, am seeing straight. As I have said before, the policy to set against Caetano and his system has to be thrashed out by the leaders of all sections of the opposition, in concert. But the left, in my opinion, does not sufficiently allow for the facts of life in Portugal, which are not the same as those in other lands, Spain included. The men of the left live in a delightful utopia of their own. Ethically and aesthetically their attitudes are splendid, but of no practical use politically. Still, what they have done has revivified the struggle and forced us to sort out our beliefs. Let us give credit where credit is due.

I am convinced that the wave of protest which spread from the United States to break over Europe with the events of May 1968 in France, is an expression of very deep needs, especially the needs of younger people. In the East as well as the West they reject, with reason, the inequitable world their elders have prepared for them. The parties of the left, the

* This refers to the Allende regime—Publisher's note.

Socialists above all, should be ready to give them satisfactory answers. If they refuse this role, and fail to enlist the young in the battle, those parties must inevitably lose their *raison d'être*.

The fear of Communist participation makes many dissidents pause at the thought of a unified opposition programme. They point to Czechoslovakia in 1968 and fight the Cold War over again. Catholics and Republicans are for them easier and more natural allies. But the Communist Party has an extensive following among the working class in Portugal and without the Communist workers there can be no proper unanimity of the left.

Moreover, the Red Peril, used by the Government as a bogey all these years to justify the policy of deliberate repression, is a peril that simply does not exist in Europe today. The Communist parties of the West, revising old dogma and rejecting some forms of activity, are changing appreciably. The party in Portugal can hardly dissociate itself from comrades in Italy, Spain and even France, while the prospect of united action cannot fail to accelerate a process that will affect not the left wing only, but the country as a whole. For me, who believes so firmly in pluralism and the interchange of ideas between those of different political or religious faiths, Communists are citizens of Portugal, with the same rights and duties as have all their fellow-citizens. The regime has relegated them to a ghetto, and for the good of Portugal we must deliver them.

And now, to finish, I must explain my creed as a Socialist. It is an easy task and will reveal nothing out of the ordinary, but it completes the tale of what has brought me to the opinions I hold today.

I should first emphasise that none of the Socialist systems now in being seems to me wholly adequate. Communism, like all the people's democracies, has sacrificed the great essential, liberty, to the conception of the totalitarian state—a conception I abhor—while the para-Socialist experiments in those countries of Western Europe where Social Democrats have come to power, either alone or in coalition, have, in my view, lacked consequence and the strength of their own convictions, and so nearly always end up as the faithful agents of capitalism. Yet there have been achievements in both kinds which we must acknowledge as landmarks in human history, and such negative aspects as I have touched upon should not obscure the fundamental value of the experiments in question. Above all, they should not make us despair of Socialism.

Firmly I believe that man on his slow upward path will in time create a humanised society; a society where people do not exploit each other, whose collectivised means of production will benefit everyone and where the masses will have a democratic control over decision-making. I believe we can conquer poverty and the fear of tomorrow without losing our liberty in the process. This is why I support Socialism, Socialism with personal freedom, with the independence of the individual to manage his own affairs: to use a phrase abundant with promise, 'Socialism with a human face'.

As far as Portugal is concerned, I believe the country can solve her basic problems only if she destroys the Fascist dispensation and turns to Socialism. There is no other way to overcome the poverty of the people, the ignorance, hunger, sickness and lack of security that have drained her strength for years, save by planning the economy on Socialist lines, and by the sound and sensible use of national resources for the general good. If it is a formidable enterprise, the experience of other lands shows that it is not impossible. But it is not to be accomplished by the suppression of liberty and human rights. Rather, the Portuguese people must take their destiny into their own hands, make their plans and construct their future freely. They must do so on the farms and in the factories, in the trade unions and in provincial government. They must do it by controlling the workings of the state at all levels, by assuming the direction of local affairs and higher education.

The apologists of the *Estado Novo* maintain that conditions in Portugal do not admit of freedom yet. This, for them,

unarguable truth is supposed to justify the indefinite continuation of the dictatorship and they have acquired some
following, even among those who claim to be liberals. Yet it is
plain to see what forty-six years of dictatorship have made of
us—the most beggarly and wretched nation in Western
Europe, in an abyss of decline and penury. And since the same
causes must inevitably produce the same results, it is also plain
what is in store for us if we do not free ourselves.

The Portuguese are adult people, despite that long-suffered
dictatorship. Time and again they have proved as much
throughout their history. There is nothing the matter with
them, nothing to keep them from the rights and liberties
enjoyed by so many other nations. Order and public peace are
necessary if we are to have progress, but since when was
liberty incompatible with either? If order is to rest on trampled
human rights, then order is a tidy graveyard, nothing
more.

The decline of Portugal set in when intolerance triumphed
and human liberties were suppressed. Nothing can redeem
her but liberty and Socialism, immutably at one. This conviction, deeply felt and reinforced by time and much experience,
has been my guiding-light on a political path bestrewn with
disappointments. In thirty years of adult life I have never
known what freedom is. I have always lived, like the vast
majority of my countrymen, cooped up in a sort of pound
where at any minute the loss of the most elementary human
rights, prison, deportation or exile, can, and often have been,
the bitter penalty of thinking for oneself.

I cannot claim that my road has been easy, or even particularly brilliant. But it is good to be able to say one thing—that,
in spite of our sorry circumstances and every pressure of
authority, I have never come to terms with the accepted lies
of the establishment and I have never given in. Above all, I
have never abetted the dictatorship, even by keeping quiet.
This at least is something in a country like Portugal, and
morally it certainly means a great deal. Politically, however,
it amounts to less, for results are the only things that count
in politics and my generation, I must confess, can point to

very few. Everything has been against us and we have never had the opportunity to show what we could really do. Between us we have ensured that the fitful flame of resistance has not died, no more. And if some young man, trapped and suffocating in the life he has to live, gets up some day and tells us so, then we shall have to apologise to him, humbly.

The situation forces me to continue the struggle without wavering, as it forces all who are, and who intend to continue as, citizens of Portugal. Our country must be rescued from this debasing dictatorship, and her salvation is a task for her own people, no one else. We must be set free from the vicious circle of poverty, fear and oppression which has held us prisoner for so long. More is involved than direct moral duty or the use of one's intelligence. This is a patriotic duty that affects the deliverance of us all and we must fully realise the fact.

The would-be collaborators and the egoists, those who consult their personal, professional or family interests only, proclaim the cause is lost, and there is no more we can do. That way lie surrender and indifference. Against such argument our weapons must be continual integration in practical affairs, and the will to win. Only the man who stops trying can be said to lose a battle.

The savage intolerance of the regime and the fortunes of unfair fight have driven me into temporary exile, and often in these last few months I have felt the attraction of another kind of life. Easier, because it would be free; a life with culture in it and no eternal spectre of prison or persecution round the corner. Its appeal is strong, but always the voice of Portugal has proved stronger still. There are close on a million workers living as emigrants here in France to remind me perpetually in countless ways that nothing matters more, nothing is more urgent, than the struggle to liberate their country. My country.

In that country I have never found the concern and understanding with which I am welcomed in this refuge of exiles. France has given me the opportunity to think, and to finish this testimony. I have done a lot of other things as well, and when the interlude is over and the time is right, I shall go home. I have never lost my confidence in the future. Armed in that confidence, untroubled, I shall face my judges and, eventually, my executioners. I have a country. I serve an ideal. To both I owe that act of fidelity, as much as to myself.

Chronological Summary

1891   Republican rising at Oporto, 31 January: first attempt to establish the Republic in Portugal.

1895   Arrest of Chief Ngungunhana and battle of Chaimite in Mozambique.

1907   Beginning of dictatorship of João Franco.
Student strike at Coimbra.

1908   Abortive Republican rising at Lisbon, 28 January.
Assassination of King Carlos I and the Crown Prince Luis Filipe.
Resignation of João Franco and formation of Monarchist Government of conciliation under Admiral Ferreira do Amaral.
Accession of King Manuel II.

1910   Republican revolution, 3–5 October. The royal family goes into exile.
Proclamation of the Republic and setting up of a provisional Government under Teófilo Braga.
Expulsion of the Jesuits and closing of convents. Laws passed relating to the family and to divorce, the freedom of the press and the right to strike.

1911   General elections in June. The Constitution of the Republic approved by the Constituent Assembly (later Senate and Chamber of Deputies), and election of Manuel de Arriaga as first President of the Republic.
Law separating Church and State (Afonso Costa, Minister of Justice).
Educational reforms (António José de Almeida, Minister of the Interior), and creation of universities at Lisbon and Oporto.

1914   First budget surplus (Afonso Costa).

1915   Four months' dictatorship of Pimenta de Castro.

1916   German ships lying in the Tagus requisitioned.
Germany declares war on Portugal, 9 March.
The 'Sacred Union' Government (António José de Almeida

and Afonso Costa); Portugal enters the war on the side
of the Allies.

1917   Formation of Portuguese Expeditionary Corps (Norton de
Mattos, Minister of War).
'Miracle of Fatima', 13 May.
Successful military rising under Sidónio Paes, 5 December.
Beginning of the dictatorship. Resumption of diplomatic
relations with the Holy See.

1918   Persecution of the Republicans ('Leva da Morte' death-
march).
Battle of the Lys, 9 April; heavy casualties suffered by
Portuguese troops.
Assassination of Sidónio Paes, 8 December.

1919   Proclamation by Paiva Couceiro of the Monarchy in the
north. Rising at Monsanto of the Lisbon Monarchists.
Legal Republic re-established (Government headed by
José Relvas).
Creation of social security, sickness, incapacity and old
age pension funds, and institution of the General Con-
federation of Workers (Anarchist-inspired).
António José de Almeida elected President of the Republic.
Portuguese delegation to the Peace Conference led by
Afonso Costa.
The paper *A Batalha* (The Battle) founded as the organ
of the Portuguese workers' movement, and the weekly
A Bandeira Vermelha (The Red Flag) as that of the Maxi-
malist Federation. Much social unrest.

1920   Split between the *integristas* and King Manuel II, living
in exile in London.
System of High Commissionerships created for Angola and
Mozambique (decentralised administration).

1921   Creation of the Portuguese Communist Party.
The *balbúrdia sanguinolenta*, or Bloody Riot of 19 Octo-
ber—assassination of the Republican leaders António
Granjo, Machado de Castro and Carlos da Maia.
Appearance of the review *Seara Nova*, directed by Jaime
Cortesão, Raul Proença, Câmara Reys and, later, António
Sérgio and Azevedo Gomes.
Salazar, elected as a deputy of the Catholic Centre, leaves
the Assembly.

1922 Official visit to Brazil of President António José de Almeida for centenary celebrations of Brazilian independence.
First flight Lisbon–Rio de Janeiro made by Gago Coutinho and Sacadura Cabral.

1923 Manuel Teixeira Gomes elected President of the Republic.
Participation of *Seara Nova* group in Alvaro de Castro's Government.

1925 Military rising attempted, 18 April.
Afonso Costa, representing Portugal, presides over a session of the League of Nations.
Resignation of Teixeira Gomes and election of Bernardino Machado as President.
Left-wing Democratic Party founded by José Domingues dos Santos.

1926 Failure of opposition attempt to break the monopoly, granted to a handful of large firms, to make and sell cigarettes.
Military rising under General Gomes da Costa, 28 May; beginning of military dictatorship. Apointment of Salazar as Minister of Finance and his resignation some days later.
Republican Senate and Chamber of Deputies dissolved.
Decree establishing censorship.
Decree replacing elected Municipal Councils by administrative commissions.

1927 Military rising against the dictatorship, 2–7 February.
Dissolution of the General Confederation of Workers.

1928 A second military rising put down.
General Carmona proclaimed President of the Republic, 15 April.
General Vicente de Freitas becomes Prime Minister and Salazar joins his Government as Finance Minister, 27 April.
Mission agreement with the Holy See.
Faculty of Letters suppressed at Oporto university.

1929 Readmission of Catholic religious orders to Portugal.

1930 Passing of the Colonial Act in June (Salazar, interim Minister for Colonial Affairs).
Creation of the *União Nacional,* or National Union, as the sole authorised political party.

L

1931   Rising in Madeira.
      Renewed military rising in Lisbon, 26 August.

1932   Salazar becomes Prime Minister, 5 June.
      Publication in the *Diário de Notícias* of his interviews with António Ferro.

1933   Approval by referendum of the Constitution of the *Estado Novo*, or New State, 19 March.
      National Statute of Labour, 23 September : outline of corporative system.
      National Propaganda Bureau set up under António Ferro.

1934   Revolutionary general strike, 18 January.
      Election to the National Assembly, all members belonging to the National Union.
      First Congress of the National Union.
      Colonial Exhibition at Oporto arranged by Henrique Galvão.

1935   Unopposed election of General Carmona to the Presidency.
      Rising at the Penha de França barracks, Lisbon.

1936   Creation of the Portuguese Legion, 30 September; and of the *Mocidade Portuguesa* in October.
      Diplomatic relations suspended with the Spanish Republican Government in Madrid, October.
      Rising of Tagus seamen.
      Institution of the concentration-camp at Tarrafal.

1937   Anarchist assassination-attempt on Salazar, 4 July.
      Grave social and political unrest and creation of the Popular Front, uniting the clandestine parties and groups of the opposition.

1938   Portuguese Government recognises that of General Franco in Spain, 28 April.

1939   Iberian Pact between Portugal and Spain, 17 March.
      Declaration of Portuguese neutrality, 2 September.

1940   Meeting of Salazar and Franco to add a Protocol confirming alliances with third states to the Iberian Pact, 29 July.
      Exhibition, 'The Portuguese World', commemorating the recognition of Portugal as an independent kingdom in 1140 and her restoration to independence, after the union with Spain, under the House of Braganza in 1640.

Concordat with Rome and confirmation of the *Acordo Missionario*.

1941 Reorganisation of Portuguese Communist Party by Alvaro Cunhal.

Landing of Australian and Dutch troops on Timor. Protest by Portugal.

1942 Meeting of Salazar with Franco and Serrano Suñer at Seville, 17 February.

Japanese occupation of Timor.

1943 Creation of the MUNAF (National United Anti-Fascist Movement).

Azores base granted to Great Britain, 18 August.

1944 Portugal forbids the export of wolfram to Germany, 7 August; and breaks off diplomatic relations with Vichy, 23 August.

Severe social unrest. Large-scale strikes organised in the Ribatejo by the PCP

1945 Much anti-Fascist feeling demonstrated on the occasion of the Allied victory in May.

Salazar launches his 'organic democracy'.

Foundation of *Movimento de Unidade Democrático* (the Movement of Democratic Union, or MUD).

The opposition abstains from the legislative elections.

1946 Foundation of MUD Juvenil (MUDJ).

Mealhada Revolt, led by Fernando Queiroga.

Henrique Galvão's speech in National Assembly on slave labour in Angola.

1947 Rising of officers of the armed forces on 10 April and subsequent arrest of ten or so general officers of the army and navy. Sabotage of aircraft at the Sintra airfield by Herminio da Palma Inácio.

Resignation of university professors; student crisis at Lisbon.

Strike at naval dockyards.

1948 MUD officially suppressed and the Central Committee arrested.

Death of Professor Bento Caraça.

1949 Presidential elections, 13 February, General Norton de Mattos standing as sole candidate for the united opposition. Opposition abstains for lack of guarantees assuring valid elections.

Portugal signs the North Atlantic Treaty, 4 April.

Legislative elections in November. Schism among the opposition.

Movimento Nacional Democrático (the National Democratic Movement, or MND), founded under Ruy Luis Gomes.

1951   Death of General Carmona, April.

Presidential elections, the two opposition candidates being Ruy Luis Gomes (disqualified by the Cabinet) and Quintão Meyrelles (withdrew for lack of minimum guarantees). Unopposed return of the National Union candidate, General Craveiro Lopes (22 July).

Constitutional revision; the colonies henceforth rank as 'Overseas Provinces'.

Portuguese Colonial Empire dissolved.

Ministry of Corporations set up.

1953   First National Development Plan (*Plano de Fomento*), for 1953–1958.

1954   Satyagrahis movement in Goa. Repression. Difficulties with the Indian Union.

1955   Indian diplomatic mission in Lisbon closed, 25 July.

Portugal admitted to United Nations.

1957   Official visit to Portugal of HM Queen Elizabeth of England.

The opposition abstains from National Assembly elections in October.

1958   Presidential elections, 8 June, with two opposition candidates, Humberto Delgado and Arlindo Vicente, the latter of whom stands down. Election of National Union candidate, Américo Thomaz. Humberto Delgado queries the result.

Letter of the Bishop of Oporto, July.

1959   Prison-break of Henrique Galvão, 15 January.

Escape of Alvaro Cunhal and other Communist leaders from the fortress of Peniche.

Humberto Delgado takes refuge in the Brazilian Embassy.

Bishop of Oporto exiled.

1960 The Hague Court gives its decision on the Indian enclaves of Dadrá and Nager Aveli, 12 April.
Declaration by Portugal to the United Nations that the Overseas Territories are not colonies. UN declaration of anti-colonialism.
Portugal becomes a member of EFTA, 30 May.

1961 The liner *Santa Maria* pirated and renamed *Santa Liberdade* by Henrique Galvão, 22 January.
Programme for the Democratisation of the Republic published, 31 January.
Attack on prisons in Luanda by Angolan nationalists, 4 February, and outbreak of revolt in northern Angola, 15 March.
Abortive *coup d'état* of General Botelho Moniz, 13 April.
Abolition of *Estatuto de Indigenato*, September.
Opposition abstains from legislative elections for lack of minimum guarantees.
Occupation of Goa, Damão and Diu by the Indian Union, 18 December.
General Delgado returns secretly to Portugal. Revolt at Beja, 31 December.

1962 Student crisis in all three universities, Lisbon, Coimbra and Oporto.

1963 Guerilla warfare in Guinea begun by the PAIGC (African Independence Party of Guinea and Cape Verde), in September.

1964 War in Mozambique, August, the president of the FRELIMO (Mozambique Freedom Front) being Eduardo Mondlane.
Portuguese Society of Authors attacked and dissolved.
Creation of the ASP (Portuguese Socialist Action).

1965 Assassination of General Delgado, 13 February.
Opposition abstains from legislative elections, denouncing electoral fraud and, for the first time, the colonial war.

1966 The Security Council authorises blockade of the port of Beira in Mozambique as part of the programme of sanctions against Rhodesia.
Tagus bridge opened. Fortieth anniversary celebrations of the military rising of 28 May.

1967   Visit of Pope Paul VI to Fatima in May, for fiftieth anniversary of the visions.
Foundation of the LUAR (League of Union and Revolutionary Action). Herminio da Palma Inácio organises hold-up of the Bank of Portugal at Figueira da Foz.

1968   Illness of Salazar, 6 September. Appointment of Marcello Caetano as his successor, 27 September.

1969   Bishop of Oporto returns from exile, July.
Assassination of Mondlane at Dar-es-Salaam, by means of bomb concealed in a parcel.
Elections to the National Assembly, October. Participation of the democratic opposition, list of candidates being submitted by the CEUD, the CDE and the CED. Unanimous opposition protest as to validity of elections. Expulsion of delegation from the Socialist International. Escape of Palma Inácio from PIDE prison at Oporto.

1970   Pope Paul VI gives audience at the Vatican to nationalist leaders from the Portuguese colonies : Agostinho Neto, Amilcar Cabral and Marcelino dos Santos.
Death of Salazar, July.

1971   Schism in the FPLN (Patriotic Front for National Liberation); Portuguese Communist Party leaves.
Armed struggle begins against Fascism and colonialism; beginning of ARA (Armed Revolutionary Action) and Revolutionary Brigades. Programme of sabotage.
Constitutional revision, July. The deputy Sá Carneiro attacks Caetano's pseudo-liberalism in the National Assembly.

Index